5-STAR PRAISE FOR
The March Up

Winner of the 2004 William E. Colby Award
Winner of the 2004 General Wallace M. Greene Award

"An important and unflinching chronicle of contemporary warfare. Regardless of one's position on the war in Iraq—on any war—*The March Up* speaks with authority and legitimacy and cuts to the very bone to reveal the experience of the modern fighting infantryman."
—General Anthony C. Zinni, USMC (Ret.),
former CENTCOM commander

"It is one thing to know about Marines. It is another to know the sting of battle. To tell the true story of combat up close and personal, the authors must be there on the scene with the Marines in action.... That is exactly what the reader gets in *The March Up*.... An excellent look at Marine combat at its best in the 21st century."
—*Marine Corps Gazette*

"[A] gritty, insider's account that reveals ... the tensions, disputes, snafus, and successes that characterize a military campaign."
—*Booklist*

"A wonderful account of ... a brilliantly fought campaign."
—*Wall Street Journal*

"[A] crisp and immediate account of a professional fighting organization that is honest and without pretense ... *The March Up* is infinitely more revealing than the kaleidoscopic reports of embedded journalists."
—*Leatherneck Magazine*

THE MARCH UP

TAKING BAGHDAD WITH
THE 1ST MARINE DIVISION

Bing West
&
Major General Ray L. Smith,
USMC (Ret.)

BANTAM BOOKS

THE MARCH UP
A Bantam Book

PUBLISHING HISTORY
Bantam hardcover edition published September 2003
Bantam trade paperback edition / October 2004

Published by
Bantam Dell
A Division of Random House, Inc.
New York, New York

All rights reserved
Copyright © 2003 by F. J. West
Introduction © 2003 by John Keegan
Front cover photograph by Joe Raedle/Getty Images
Back cover photograph © Kuni Takahashi/Boston Herald/ReflexNews

Photo insert © F. J. West
Map © Jeffrey L. Ward
Book design by Glen Edelstein

Library of Congress Catalog Card Number: 2003062779

ISBN 0-553-38269-1

Manufactured in the United States of America
Published simultaneously in Canada

BVG 10 9 8 7 6 5 4 3 2 1

To
First Sergeant Edward M. Smith
a Marine's Marine
and
to all the other men and
women who died in
Operation Iraqi Freedom

Contents

Introduction	*xi*
Commanding General's Message to All Hands	*xvi*
Prologue	*1*
1. The Crown Jewel	7
2. Ambush Alley	31
3. A Land the Color of Dust	49
4. Screeching to a Halt	73
5. The Afak Drill	87
6. The Non-Pause Pause	99
7. The Making of Veterans	113
8. Across the Tigris	133
9. Run and Gun	153
10. Ring Around Baghdad	167
11. Assault into Baghdad	189
12. Seizing the Snoozle	209
13. A Tyrant Falls	231
Epilogue	*245*
The Mayors of Summer	*251*
Organization for Combat	*267*
Notes	*271*
Glossary	*287*
Acknowledgments	*299*
Index	*303*
About the Authors	*317*

Introduction

by John Keegan

THE UNITED STATES MARINE CORPS is one of the most formidable fighting organizations in the world. Its famous march, "From the halls of Montezuma to the shores of Tripoli," begins with a roll call of its early victories; to those its later history added Belleau Wood in France in 1918, the first major American engagement of the Great War, and a string of island assaults in the Pacific in the Second World War: Guadalcanal, Peleliu, Tarawa, Okinawa and Iwo Jima. By 1945 "Marine" had acquired a distinctive and exclusive meaning in the American military vocabulary. It stood for war-making by direct assault, off the ship, up the beach, straight into the enemy position. A war correspondent, describing the landing on Tarawa in November 1943, opened his dispatch with an eyewitness account: "A young Marine jumped over the sea wall and began throwing blocks of TNT into the mouth of a Japanese bunker." He could have been any Marine in any assault on any island. Marines fight to win.

The British counterpart served with the U.S. Marines in the First Gulf War of 1991. In the Second Gulf War of 2003 they had separate fronts. The British mission was to take Basrah, the second city of Iraq, while the Marines made the march to Baghdad, Iraq's capital, the subject of this book. Bing West, a former Marine officer, and Ray Smith, a retired Marine general, have a fascinating story to tell. They traveled at the forefront of the 1st Marine Division's advance, from the crossing of the Kuwait border on March 19 to the capture of Baghdad three weeks later. They witnessed the battle of Nasiriyah, where the Marines were caught in a confused and costly fight for an essential river crossing. They waited with the Marines while a way was found to cross the last water obstacle before Baghdad. They saw a dozen small local firefights on the road north. They were with the Marines as they entered the capital, found a way forward through the built-up area and took possession of the palaces of the Saddam regime. They saw their young Marine companions deploy into attack, form firing lines, advance by bounds against Iraqi strong points. They were with Marines who fell to enemy fire and bled to death from wounds.

This is a frontline book and its chief value comes from its provision of a picture of what life and death on the front line were like on the march up. There are recurrent themes. One is of the small Marine "family," the four or five men who fight, live and occasionally die together. Typically these families consist of a leader, his driver, his radio operator and his gunner, who travel together in a vehicle, survive the day's dangers and settle in the evening to eat an improvised meal of bad food in dirt and discomfort. They depend upon each other utterly, in a relationship which minimizes the importance of rank but is dominated by the demands of military efficiency. The leader is respected because he tries to assure the survival of the team. Any member of the team who threatens group survival becomes a liability.

Other groups the authors observe are those of the enemy. Their behavior puzzles West and Smith. Usually the enemy is invisible or disappears as soon as the shooting starts. Some, however, seem determined to die. Young, badly equipped Iraqis, who seem to lack any of the military skills the Marines possess, wait until the Americans are on top of them and then effectively commit suicide by staging acts of resistance that attract an overwhelming response. They emerge from piles of rubbish under the noses of the Marines, loose off ill-aimed shots and are pulverized by the Marines' firepower. They do not know how to prepare defensive positions, digging foxholes on the exposed sides of riverbanks. They drive their "technicals"—pickup trucks mounting machine guns—straight at American tanks. Some of those "fighters" are foreign—Syrian or Jordanian or Saudi—who have come to Iraq to fight jihad, holy war. Most of the Iraqi fighters are Saddam loyalists, members of the Baathist party, but without military training. Few of the professionals, soldiers of the Iraqi regular army or the Republican Guard, fight effectively.

A disturbing complication during the march up is the inexplicable insouciance of Iraqi civilians. The Americans expect the ordinary inhabitants of the countryside and small towns to keep out of the fight. Instead they constantly turn up in the middle of firefights, driving civilian vehicles straight into the zone of fire. Terrified of suicide bombers, the Marines shoot at cars which refuse to stop despite the firing of warning shots.

The authors' portrayal of the contorted and insensate nature of the war is one of its most striking features. Two, perhaps three wars were going on simultaneously. One was a conventional war between Iraq's regular forces and the invaders; it scarcely took fire, so reluctant were the Iraqi regulars to fight. The second war was between the Americans and the irregular defenders of the regime: some ideological Baathists, others foreign Muslim fundamentalists attracted to the fight by the chance to die for their personal vision of Islam. The third war was between frightened young American soldiers and the specter of a population of suicide bombers in which any car driver or civilian trucker seemed to threaten the Marines with death.

Yet, on the American side, there was only one conflict, the war to rid Iraq, the Middle East and the world of Saddam. That war, despite Saddam's mysterious disappearance, achieved its object. Iraq, since the conclusion of the march up to Baghdad, has been purged of Saddam's regime of killing and terror. As Tony Blair, the prime minister, has said, the world is a better place without Saddam. Credit for his removal belongs in large measure to the Marines who made the march up.

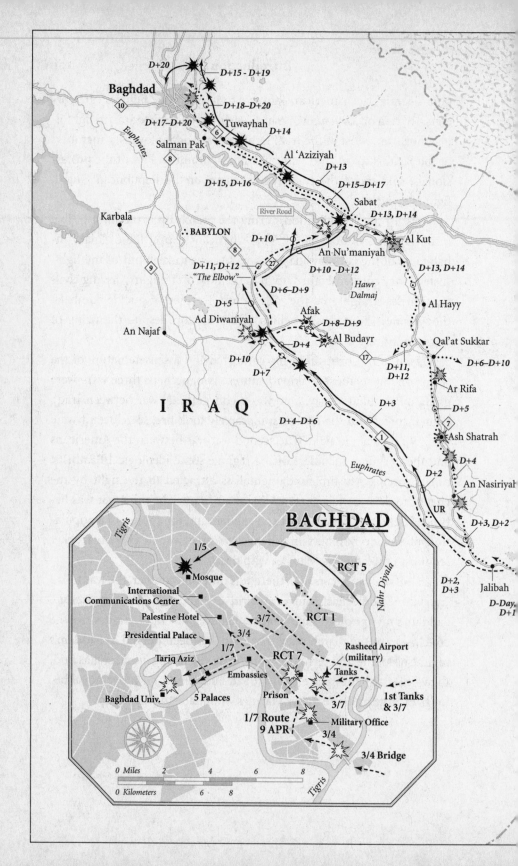

Baghdad

Euphrates

D+20
D+15 - D+19
D+18–D+20
D+17–D+20   Tuwayhah
Salman Pak   D+14
Al 'Aziziyah
D+15, D+16   D+13
D+15–D+17
River Road   Sabat
D+13, D+14
BABYLON   Al Kut
D+10   An Nu'maniyah
D+11, D+12   D+10 - D+12
"The Elbow"   D+13, D+14
D+6–D+9
Karbala   Hawr
D+5   Afak   Dalmaj   Al Hayy
Ad Diwaniyah   D+8–D+9
Al Budayr   Qal'at Sukkar
An Najaf   D+10   D+4   D+6–D+10
D+7   D+11,
17   D+12   Ar Rifa

I R A Q   D+3   D+5

D+4–D+6   Ash Shatrah
1
Euphrates   D+2   D+4

UR   An Nasiriyah
D+3, D+2

D+2,
D+3   Jalibah
D-Day,
D+1

BAGHDAD

Tigris

1/5

RCT 5
Mosque

International
Communications Center   3/7
Palestine Hotel   RCT 1   Nahr Diyala
Presidential Palace   3/4
1/7
Tariq Aziz   RCT 7   Rasheed Airport
(military)
Embassies   Tanks
Baghdad Univ.   5 Palaces   Prison   1st Tanks
& 3/7
1/7 Route   3/7
9 APR   Military Office
3/4

3/4 Bridge

0 Miles   2   4   6   8

0 Kilometers   6   8   Tigris

Movement of 1st Marine Divisions Regimental Combat Teams (RCTs) 20 March—10 April 2003

RCT-1

D-Day (21 March 2003), D+1 Across desert to Jalibah
D+2 Up to An Nasiriyah
D+3 Held up south of An Nasiriyah
D+4 Thru An Nasiriyah and big sandstorm
D+5 Up to Intersection between Route 7 and 17
D+6-12 Pause in movement
D+13, D+14 Feint at Al Kut
D+15–D+17 Close up to Baghdad
D+18–D+20 (10 April 2003) In east Baghdad

RCT-5

D-Day (20 March), D+1 Ar Rumaylah Oil Fields
D+2–D+5 Up Route 1 to Route 27
D+6–D+9 Pulled back to Route 1 /Route 17 cloverleaf
D+10–D+12 Up to and across Tigris River
D+13, D+14 An Nu'maniyah to East Baghdad
D+15–D+20 In and around Baghdad

RCT-7

D-Day (21 March), D+1 Defeat of Iraqi 51st Armored Div.; Seized the Crown Jewel
D+2, D+3 March west Cross Euphrates
D+4–D+6 Clear Route 1 behind RCT-5
D+7–D+10 Recon in force; Clear Route 17
D+11, D+12 Close on Tigris and cross
D+13, D+14 Attack Baghdad Div. at Al Kut
D+15, D+16 Turn west, close on Baghdad
D+17–D+20 In Baghdad

IRAN

Tigris

D+1

Ar Rumaylah

Al Basrah

D+1, D+2

8 Basrah

Az Zubayr

Crown Jewel

D-Day

D-Day, D+1

Safwan

KUWAIT

Persian Gulf

Kuwait

© 2003 Jeffrey L. Ward

0 Miles   20   40   60

0 Kilometers   60

1ˢᵗ Marine Division (REIN)

Commanding General's Message to All Hands

For decades, Saddam Hussein has tortured, imprisoned, raped and murdered the Iraqi people; invaded neighboring countries without provocation; and threatened the world with weapons of mass destruction. The time has come to end his reign of terror. On your young shoulders rest the hopes of mankind.

When I give you the word, together we will cross the Line of Departure, close with those forces that choose to fight, and destroy them. Our fight is not with the Iraqi people, nor is it with members of the Iraqi army who choose to surrender. While we will move swiftly and aggressively against those who resist, we will treat all others with decency, demonstrating chivalry and soldierly compassion for people who have endured a lifetime under Saddam's oppression.

Chemical attack, treachery, and use of the innocent as human shields can be expected, as can other unethical tactics. Take it all in stride. Be the hunter, not the hunted: never allow your unit to be caught with its guard down. Use good judgement and act in best interests of our Nation.

You are part of the world's most feared and trusted force. Engage your brain before you engage your weapon. Share your courage with each other as we enter the uncertain terrain north of the Line of Departure. Keep faith in your comrades on your left and right and Marine Air overhead. Fight with a happy heart and strong spirit.

For the mission's sake, our country's sake, and the sake of the men who carried the Division's colors in past battles-*who fought for life and never lost their nerve*-carry out your mission and *keep your honor clean*. Demonstrate to the world there is "No Better Friend, No Worse Enemy" than a U.S. Marine.

J.N. Mattis
Major General, U.S. Marines
Commanding

Prologue

AT THREE IN THE MORNING IT WAS FREEZING, pitch black, and smelly inside the Amtrac, an amphibious vehicle stuffed with troops dozing on two benches. The previous day the Marines had seized one town, and in four hours they would attack again.

A fist banged on the rear hatch. "Tate, get up. It's your turn on the up gun."

"Oh man, I just got off watch at two. I've had one hour's sleep."

"Tate, wake up. You made up the damn roster. Get out there."

I was lying on the cold metal floor, listening to them, trying not to smell the feet. A few weeks earlier the 1st Marine Division had welcomed Ray Smith and me as family, including us in every briefing and battle. Both Ray and I had previously served in the division in Vietnam, Ray as a company commander and I as a platoon commander. The troops frequently asked us—especially Ray—how their fights in Iraq compared with ours in Vietnam. They measured themselves against that hard war.

Now this war was ten days old, and the troops were desperate for sleep. It would be a small thing for me to pitch in.

"I'm awake," I said. "I'll take the watch."

There was a pause in the raggedy snoring as a dozen exhausted Marines savored the promise of a fresh set of eyes while they rested. For a moment no one said anything. Then out of the dark came a voice.

"This is Pfc. Tate, sir. I'm the trac crew chief. Thanks, but no. You put in your time. This is our turn. This is our war."

The March Up is inspired by the classic story of the *Anabasis*, written by the Greek warrior and author Xenophon, a disciple of Socrates. It chronicles the march up Mesopotamia—now Iraq—in 400 B.C. by ten thousand indomitable Greek fighters, called hoplites, who hacked their way through every army that challenged them. The king of Persia unleashed a force of a hundred thousand to crush the hoplites, but gave up for lack of enough warriors. When chariots charged them, Xenophon reminded his hoplites that, unlike horses, they did not require grass for food, and that their sturdy legs would get them home after the horses collapsed. When heavy snows fell, the hoplites trudged on in sandals. When blue-faced men rolled enormous boulders down upon them, the hoplites waited until they ran out of stones, then charged uphill. The *Anabasis* is an account of tough characters bound by an unflinching warrior code.

One key to the hoplites' success was their ability to advance shoulder to shoulder, challenging all enemies to fight to the death. While effective, this ferocity exacted a toll on the manpower of Greek armies. To avoid such casualties, the Romans, when they emerged as the world's dominant power, modified the Greek fighting style. Roman centurions were encouraged not to hack through their enemies but to outmaneuver them. The Romans fought in "maniples," literally "handfuls" of soldiers. Centurions shifted around immediately to exploit gaps in an enemy formation and maneuver replaced the headlong charge. For hundreds of years no tribe could stand up to the Romans, whose disciplined troops and centurions combined the straight-ahead courage of Xenophon's hoplites with agility on the battlefield.

In *The March Up* of modern times, the commanders of the 1st Marine Division, like the centurions of ancient Rome, relied upon disciplined troops and clever maneuver. The Marine Corps, like a Roman legion, is a military machine comprised of strictly disciplined men who attack with ferocity, whose nature it is to march off to do battle. In 1805, Lt. Presley O'Bannon crossed five hundred miles of desert to capture the harbor of Tripoli. In 1900, a battalion of Marines was part of the force that marched on Peking (as Beijing was then called). In 1945, Marines marched up the thirty-mile-long island of Okinawa, suffering more than three thousand killed in eighty days. In 1950, the 1st Marine Division marched forty miles back from the Chosin Reservoir in North Korea, fighting off eight Chinese divisions in freezing weather.

The 1st Marine Division was the first division to seize the offensive in World War II, landing in 1942 at Guadalcanal in the Solomon Islands, under the five stars of the Southern Cross. The symbol of the division, called the Blue Diamond, shows the five stars of that cross against the blue background of the evening sky. Under that symbol three generations of Marines have marched in answer to the nation's call: retaking Seoul in 1950; retaking Hue City in 1968; and retaking Kuwait City in 1991. The campaign to take the city of Baghdad in 2003 is the Marine Corps's longest march from the sea. *The March Up* is a chronicle of this expedition, as experienced and told by two former Marine infantrymen, Ray Smith and myself, Bing West.

Ray Smith came from the oil fields in Oklahoma and rose to become one of the most decorated warriors in the Marine Corps. During the 1968 Tet Offensive, Ray commanded a rifle company in the savage house-to-house battle for Hue City. He had walked in with 146 men; thirty-four days later, seven of them walked out with him. During the 1972 Easter Offensive he called in fire support against waves of North Vietnamese troops supported by tanks and artillery. In 1983 he commanded the battalion landing team on the island of Grenada, and later he went on to command a division. Ray has been shot, slashed, blown up, knocked dizzy by close misses, and nicked by the fin of a rocket-propelled grenade (RPG). He has a lovely wife, Colleen, and three sons. Now he builds custom homes, serves on charitable boards, and hunts deer. But in his heart he remains a centurion.

My family, the Wests, came from the Boston suburbs and spent summers on Cape Cod, where I loved to fish. Four generations of Wests have served in the Marine infantry. My great-uncle was a private first class in 1918, my uncle was a sergeant on Guadalcanal, and I was a Marine infantry captain in Vietnam. In my book, *The Village*, I described what it was like to patrol in the hamlets, wriggling through the muck of the rice paddies at night and throwing grenades at muzzle flashes. My son Owen served in Marine Force Reconnaissance in Operation Iraqi Freedom. As the Special Assistant to the Secretary of Defense when Saigon fell, I observed firsthand how Washington policymakers interacted with generals during war. In a later administration, as Assistant Secretary of Defense for International Security Affairs, I visited many crisis-torn countries where our military was involved. I am blessed with two sons, two daughters, and two grandchildren.

As for the men whom we were honored to accompany into battle in Iraq, the 1st Marine Division was diverse, a composite of Marines from three active-duty and one reserve division. Ray and I journeyed with these men in eighteen separate units over 1,200 kilometers and were with these units in combat on sixteen days. We have tried to draw on our combined battlefield experience to help the reader gain a sense of the combat and how dissimilar units such as tanks and infantry worked together to shape the outcome.

Many nonfiction books about war tend to stress heroism to the point of myth. Most people, when interviewed for a book after the fact, describe what they want others to read about themselves, not what was shameful, ugly, or just plain ordinary about their deeds. There are always gaps and disagreements. The kaleidoscope of battle is exhilarating, tragic, and confusing. Every man, from general to private, has his story of what he believed was true during a fast-moving campaign. Two men in the same battle often differ on what happened. Ray and I focus on what we saw and what we can address. Specific observations and quotes in this book are drawn from more than eight hundred photos, six diary notebooks compiled during the campaign, and over two hundred and fifty discussions (see Acknowledgments). Our intent is to convey the strategy, tactics, stress, errors, leadership, and perseverance that marked the journey of Private First Class Tate and his fellow Marines. Operation Iraqi Freedom *was* their turn—it was their war, and they acquitted themselves in keeping with the long and proud tradition of the Marine Corps.

In Iraqi Freedom, as in Desert Storm in 1991, the United States did not suffer heavy casualties. The critical policy concern was not the surety, but rather the speed of the ground movement to Baghdad. After the war began, a pause in the ground advance required the president to make clear to the military commanders the criticality of speed. The less speedy the campaign, the greater were Saddam's chances of retaining power. Saddam's hope was to endure bombing from the air until pressure from the international community resulted in a cease-fire. This hope was not far-fetched, given the inflamed anti-American sentiment around the world. In 1982 such international pressure had rescued the Palestinian Liberation Organization in Lebanon from destruction by the Israelis. On the other side of the coin, a swift movement to Baghdad would ensure Saddam's removal, enhance the aura of American power, and lessen casualties, both military and civilian.

The commander of the 1st Marine Division, Maj. Gen. James N. Mattis, understood this need from the beginning. On 17 December 2002 he brought together all his commanders for a review. "I know one thing," he told them. "The president, the National Command Authority, and the American people need speed. The sooner we get it over with, the better. Our overriding principle will be speed, speed, speed."

The speedy campaign that Mattis sought was a near thing, not easily accomplished. There were disagreements about timing and tactics, leadership mistakes, foul weather, and staggering logistical challenges. This is the story of a race against terrain and time as much as a battle against an enemy. Most important, it is a tale about today's hoplites— the inheritors of Xenophon's code of bravery and camaraderie—men who would be comfortable with short swords and convex shields, men with sturdy legs who would eat less grass than a horse.

1

The Crown Jewel
D-Day, D+1

With 1st Battalion, 7th Marine Regiment
Northern Kuwait, a few kilometers south of the Iraqi border
20–21 March 2003

WITH GAS MASKS ON, RAY SMITH AND I, along with all the Marines in 1st Battalion, 7th Regiment (1/7) were sitting in shallow fighting holes, hacked out of dirt as hard as concrete, feeling a bit frustrated. For the fourth time that morning the gunnery sergeant had stood on top of the command Amtrac [*Picture 1*] hollering "Lightning! Lightning!"— the code word that there had been a SCUD launch—and the Marines had hopped back into their holes, the bulging eyes of their masks resembling giant bugs from the black-and-white horror films of the 1950s. Cruise missiles had struck Baghdad around dawn, after the CIA had told President Bush it knew where Saddam was hiding. Now the Iraqis were shooting back with long-range missiles, and one had narrowly missed the headquarters of Lt. Gen. James Conway, the senior Marine in the Kuwait-Iraq theater.

We were in a pre-attack "assembly area," a dust bowl a few kilometers behind the Iraqi border, assigned to one of the Amtracs in the battalion. We were hitching rides because of the unusual route we had taken to get to the battlefield. Back in December, Ray and I decided to write a book about the upcoming war in Iraq, describing the changes in tactics between the fight in Hue City in 1968 and the projected fight in Baghdad City in 2003. Although initially reluctant to have a retired general and a former assistant secretary of defense on the battlefield, Headquarters Marine Corps kindly issued us orders to serve as unpaid consultants in support of a Marine Corps public affairs film crew, at our own expense. Once we were in Kuwait, the Marine Corps allowed us to go forward with two stipulations; first, that we were on our own, and second, that we keep a low profile because, as a senior Marine said, "We want to keep the focus on the young Marines, not us old guys—so don't get yourselves killed, because then you would be a story."

So here we were, traveling with an infantry battalion as it prepared to cross the Line of Departure into Iraq. Thousands of years of relentless winds had swept the sands from Kuwait and Iraq, leaving behind an ankle-deep cover of powdery dust which swirled like fog in the slightest breeze. In this featureless, bleak landscape, the two hundred vehicles of 1/7 were aligned in three neat, long lines, appearing as a mirage to any Bedouin tribesman wandering by on his camel.

The U.S. high command was convinced that chemical warheads would strike U.S. troops sooner or later. So the gas masks and the hot, tightly woven chemical-resistant bib overalls and jackets we all wore were reasonable precautions. Still, the war wasn't supposed to open this way, with the Marines waiting behind the lines, gas masks on, gas masks off, like pebbles washed back and forth by the waves.

Like everyone else in 1st Battalion that morning, members of the first squad of 3rd Platoon of Charlie Company sat and fretted, ducking when they were told to do so by their squad leader, Cpl. Shane Ferkovich. Ray and I had joined battalion 1/7 for its attack on D-Day in order to follow Ferkovich and his squad on their multibillion-dollar mission to seize the Az Zubayr oil pumping station.

A big, rangy youth from Montana, Ferkovich had bounced from high school to high school, preferring part-time work as a lumberjack. Motivated by the challenge, he had decided to join the Marine Corps, but was turned down because he hadn't finished high school. Ferkovich went back to school for another year, then was accepted. After boot camp he volunteered for 29 Palms, a remote base along the Nevada-California border where Marines train for mechanized warfare.

As we walked over to talk with the squad, the men exchanged glances. During the long days back at the 1st Marine Division's isolated staging base, we had introduced ourselves around the regiments and battalions. Many of the troops had heard of Ray, and they called him "Sir" or "General" to his face and "E-Tool" when talking over the radio or in the chow hall.

There was another cry of "Lightning!" and another quick donning of gas masks. When the all-clear sounded, Corporal Ferkovich asked Ray the question that seemed to be bothering them all.

"Sir," Ferkovich said, "that cruise missile strike this morning—do you think we got Saddam? We'll still go to war, won't we?"

The squad members didn't want their mission snatched away on the last day by a cruise missile. They had trained in the heat and mud, withstood mental and physical torments, endured months in an isolated camp sustained by the vision of carrying out a dangerous and valuable task. They had invested almost a year of their lives preparing for one day. They wanted Ray to reassure them.

In boot camp the squad had heard about Ray's exploits in Vietnam with an entrenching tool, or E-tool, a small, collapsible shovel. One instructor had told them that Ray's M-16 jammed during a night attack, and he had continued down the trench line swinging an E-tool, later remarking that a shovel doesn't jam. A different version had it that he had assaulted a North Vietnamese machine-gun position with an E-tool. Whatever the story, he was known in the Corps as "E-Tool."

Maybe the cruise missile had squashed Saddam, Ray said. But the campaign was to remove an entire regime, not just one man. A few missiles weren't going to change the squad's mission.

The eighteen-year-old infantryman goes to work each day preparing to kill other men, not an ordinary job. Shane Ferkovich could have gone to a community or four-year college, as half his classmates from high school did. Or he could have stayed in the logging camps, working outdoors in the land of the Big Sky, earning enough money for a good set of wheels and hanging out with two or three buddies. If he wanted to enlist, there were twenty or thirty military fields that would teach him a skill useful for later civilian employment, like satellite communications, the military police, or computer hardware.

Instead he chose the infantry. Each year only one out of four thousand physically qualified young men joins the ranks of the Marine infantry, yet Ferkovich's squad still reflected a cross-section of the nation. Of the twelve Marines, one was an immigrant applying for U.S. citizenship, one was African American, and four were Hispanic. Two came from self-described upper-middle-class homes; the rest were from working-class families. Ferkovich was an orphan, raised in foster homes. As diverse as they were, they had several traits in common. All had graduated from high school. All were volunteers. They had worked together as a team for over a year and were anxious to perform.

We asked them why they had chosen to join the Marines. They said that they wanted to do what was tough. Most mentioned they needed more discipline, and everyone knew what happens in Marine recruit depots: the drill instructors either shape you up or throw you out. Lance Corporal Answitz, twenty-four, had served in the Spetnatz, the Russian special forces, before emigrating to the United States. Spetnatz had pushed the recruits harder physically, he said, making them exercise in T-shirts in subzero weather, but the Corps was mentally tougher; those Marine drill instructors got inside your head.

A corporal mentioned a popular Super Bowl TV commercial, where a young guy climbs a mountain and fights a dragon with a sword. After slashing it in two, he turns into a Marine in dress blues. The others laughed, agreeing that was cool. Ray said that the commercial was about the transformation that takes place, as he put it, "when a lowly civilian earns the title Marine." The men laughed.

I asked if the squad members bought that, saying I thought the commercial was over the top. Did they really like it? These macho young men hesitated to answer. Finally Ferkovich spoke up. "Absolutely, I believe it," he said softly. The others then nodded or openly agreed in a variety of ways: "I'm different," and "Back home, everyone says I've changed," and "Yeah, I guess so." We pulled on the thread a little more. "How about being an infantryman? Why did you choose that?" A couple said they didn't choose, the Corps chose for them, but most indicated that they wanted to be infantrymen.

Once you decided to be a Marine, they agreed, you might as well be infantry—that's the real Marine Corps. Only 15 percent of all Marines belonged to the infantry. Not many of their high school classmates had joined the military, and practically none were in the infantry. So being a Marine rifleman meant belonging to a small, exclusive club.

There were two squads assigned to seize the oil pumping station and the other squad leader, Cpl. Alejandro Garcia, nineteen, joined his friend Ferkovich for the final review. Garcia, as tall as Ferkovich, had a looser approach to life. He was from L.A. and on weekends drove there from the base to go dancing, he said, while "Ferk stays in the barracks and studies tactics." The squad members nodded and laughed and Ferkovich, still serious, asked if we knew Colonel Boyd and about his theory.

Col. John Boyd, U.S. Air Force, was a fighter pilot who theorized that battalions and divisions could win battles the same way fighter pilots did: by turning inside the enemy's OODA loop. In order to shoot down another aircraft in a dogfight, Boyd wrote, you have to Observe what is going on, then Orient yourself in the battle, then Decide what to do, and lastly Act before your opponent has completed his OODA loop. According to Boyd, a fighter pilot didn't win by faster reflexes; he won because his reflexes were connected to a brain that thought faster than the opponent.

Marines like Ray were much taken with the theory. Getting inside Saddam's OODA loop, Ray told the squad, was the key to a quick victory. Make him fight your fight; don't get suckered into reacting and fighting his fight. For the squad, it should be the same. The mission of the squad was to seize the oil pumping station before Saddam's men blew it up. If things seemed off kilter once the squad was inside the station, don't wait for orders from anyone else. Secure the key elements—the manifolds, pump, and power house. Every year about $15 billion in oil exports went through that station. So don't hesitate—grab control and Colonel Boyd would be proud of them. Hell, Ray might be proud of them.

Ferkovich's squad sat in the dirt and went over the attack plan one more time while we listened. In all his firefights, Ray said that he had developed the habit of mentally running a video through his head, picturing what he expected to see. There was the least confusion when every rifleman had imagined—had thought through—exactly what he was going to do.

Ray and I felt at home sitting in the fighting holes with these tough, eager young men. It is a mystery why some are called to be grunts, to carry a rifle and an eighty-pound pack, to chew tobacco and swear and sweat and shoot and be refused a beer because of being underage. Although we didn't know it then, in the march up to Baghdad, the chances of becoming a casualty were one in 150 among Marines like this squad. In the U.S., the chances of a police officer becoming a casualty last year were one in 8,000. Being in the infantry was fifty times more dangerous than law enforcement. In March of 2003, it was the most dangerous job in America.

Some of this danger was due to neglect in the Pentagon budget. Secretary of Defense Donald Rumsfeld was constantly talking about "transforming" the military to be more high tech and agile, apparently unaware that a dramatic transformation had taken place since Vietnam. In preparing to attack Iraq, the Department of Defense possessed more combat aircraft than infantry squads and more combat pilots than infantry squad leaders. The "smart" bombs one aircraft dropped on one strike cost more than the equipment for an entire squad. In World War II, the physical risk to a pilot and to an infantryman were almost the same. Going into Iraq sixty years later, the rifleman was vastly more at risk. Technology had done little for him. Ray and I chatted with the squad and hefted their equipment. If we had the stamina, we could have picked up any pack and rifle and trudged off with them, forty years after Vietnam. No pilot from forty years ago would dare hop into the cockpit of a plane in 2003.

Less-than-cutting-edge equipment, though, did not faze Corporal

Ferkovich and his squad. As far as they were concerned, the Marine Corps revolved around them. They believed they were the top tier of the Corps. Infantry was the billet most sought by Marine officers, and many were turned down. There were not enough spaces for the number of volunteers. The prior Commandant of the Marine Corps, General J.L. Jones, had even signed his e-mails as "Rifleman."

Such prestige, however, did not translate into money. The average policeman in Indianapolis, for instance, earned $36,000 after two years on the force. Corporal Ferkovich was earning $20,000 after two years. But for Marines like Ferkovich, the opportunity to seize a multibillion-dollar pumping station was prestige enough, and he didn't want any cruise missile to land on Saddam's head and take away his squad's mission.

Now it was mission time, which meant proving time. We asked if everyone was set to cross the Line of Departure—to cross into Iraq itself. Nods and grins all around, except for the corpsman who said that he'd rather be back at the hospital. He had been sent to the squad three days ago and would stay because the squad might need him. But he hadn't signed up to be a rifleman and wouldn't mind if they called the whole war off.

"Well," Ray said, "one of us has some sense."

The U.S. Central Command in Florida, which had a forward headquarters in Qatar in the Persian Gulf, was responsible for planning and carrying out operations against Iraq. Desert Storm in 1991, or Gulf War I, as some called it, had left Saddam Hussein still in control of the country. Since then Central Command had been devising and revising plans for removing him. In August 2002, President Bush made it clear that Saddam must either disarm or be disarmed by force. Central Command's plan for applying force would send the U.S. Army into Iraq from the north through Turkey and the U.S. Marines from the south through Kuwait. Along with Saudi Arabia, Iraq had the potential to be the world's leading exporter of oil, primarily due to the rich Ar Rumaylah oil fields near the Kuwaiti border, in the Marine area of operations.

The major shock in Desert Storm had been Saddam's destruction of the Kuwaiti oil fields. By turning a few spigots, he had caused a black slick to spread over the waters of the Persian Gulf. By using a few explosives, he had turned over a hundred oil wells into torches, blackening the sky for weeks, costing the Kuwaitis billions in reconstruction, and sending thick streams of chemical particles into the jet stream, polluting the land and the oceans as far away as India.

With this experience to build on, the Saddam regime in 2003 posed a pollution threat on a scale the world had never experienced. The Rumaylah sprawled across 7,000 square kilometers of desert. Scattered through the fields were 454 producing wellheads and another 300 whose heads had been capped. So rich were the fields that, once tapped, oil gushed forth under its own pressure at over four hundred pounds per square inch. No pumps were needed to extract it from the ground or to send it on down the pipes from the wellheads.

With all that natural pressure on the lines, if the Iraqis stuffed explosives down well shaft pipings and then blew the wells (which was not done in Kuwait), they would impede recapping for months; in the interim hundreds of wellheads would gush tens of millions of barrels of black ooze onto the ground and into the nearby confluence of the Tigris and Euphrates Rivers. Inevitably much of it would reach the Gulf. Oil fires would burn for months, and the soot residue would be carried aloft and swept thousands of miles by winds at higher altitudes. Puncturing the aboveground pipelines would turn roads into sewers, blocking any onrushing American convoys. The waters of the Gulf would turn from turquoise to black. If the first days of the war went badly, the world would face its worst oil pollution catastrophe ever, and Operation Iraqi Freedom would not be off to an auspicious start.

Hence securing the southern oil fields became an essential D-Day mission of the Marines. Captured intact, they would provide Iraq with its main stream of revenue and relieve the American taxpayer of a substantial burden as well. But seizing the infrastructure would be a major task. In addition to the wellheads, the fields included several intermediary pumping stations and twelve gas-oil separator plants (GOSPs), which reduced pressure on the flow of oil. In August 2002 planners at the First Marine Expeditionary Force (I MEF) assigned units to seize each node. One particular node was so sensitive that, from the Central Command to the White House, it was referred to as the Crown Jewel.

The crude oil from more than 300 of the 454 active wells in the Rumaylah fields—over two million barrels a day—flowed southeast from the GOSPs to this single pumping station, located near the town of Az Zubayr. There a large manifold system was used to either divert the oil into holding tanks or send it into the pump itself, where three massive gas-driven turbines redirected the hot oil, flowing into twelve- and twenty-four-inch pipes running south 90 kilometers to the port of Faw.

In mid-March the Az Zubayr pumping station was generating over $40 million a day. If Saddam blew the turbines, the station would not resume operating for a year. One single pumping station was worth billions—money the U.S. taxpayer would not have to pay to rebuild Iraq if the Crown Jewel was taken intact.

Armed with weapons stronger than court injunctions, the U.S. Marine Corps became the de facto international Environmental Protection Agency. The Marine Corps in turn entrusted seizing the pumping station to the leadership of twenty-year-old Cpl. Shane Ferkovich from Missoula, Montana.

Ferkovich was the tip of a heavy and balanced spear. The Crown Jewel was the mission of all eleven hundred Marines in 1/7, commanded by Lt. Col. Chris Conlin. Back in the States, 1/7 was stationed at 29 Palms, where it trained in a vast slice of high desert, with slate soil, sandstorms, frigid winter winds, and scorching summer heat—a close replica of southern Iraq. The problem in planning the operation was that 29 Palms had nothing resembling a pumping station, and the Marines had no idea how to shut one down before it blew up or before the oil spilled over the holding tanks.

On that front, Conlin's troops received all the help they needed. The CIA liaison to I MEF said he would try to recruit some Iraqi agents from inside the pumping station. After the Marines took the station, the agents could point out which workers might cause trouble. The agents could also assist in shutting down the system without damaging it. The Joint Forces Command in Norfolk, Virginia, offered 1st Battalion a one-week course in oil-field operations and hazards. It also provided a PC software program called Falcon View, with three-dimensional digital imagery of the target area that enabled the Marines to simulate walking through the pumping station. The Marines enjoyed using the program in their squad bay, and eventually they believed they could have moved through the pumping station blindfolded. The National Imagery and Mapping Agency added a three-year-old detailed satellite map product, and the Marines pored over every inch of the glossy, visualizing their approach, their dismount from the Amtracs, the cuts in the fence, and the attack across the objective.

Lieutenant Colonel Conlin was concerned, however, that if a firefight broke out around the manifolds, his troops might blow themselves up and cause the destruction they were trying to prevent. If the machinery were damaged or turned off in the wrong sequence, gases could build up inside the pipe, and one bullet could spark a huge explosion. To address this concern, the Exxon Corporation quietly hosted one of the battalion's staff officers at a refinery near San Francisco. The officer returned several days later with a detailed understanding of the sensitive points in an oil pipeline system, knowledge of how to turn off the giant valves, and diagrams marking where not to shoot. The United Kingdom, America's major moral and military partner in Operation Iraqi Freedom, provided detailed plans of the actual pumps and manifolds at Az Zubayr. The turbines had been built by Rolls-Royce in the 1950s, when British Petroleum controlled the oil fields. While the fields had long since been nationalized, British Petroleum had several times over the years sent in engineers to maintain the turbines, which under Saddam were gradually falling into serious disrepair.

From British Petroleum and other companies, the Military Works Force, an arm of the British military, called to active duty seven experts on oil pumps similar to those at Az Zubayr. Together with twenty-one other British reservists, expert in oil-field demolitions, they would ride with Charlie Company and enter the pumping station as soon as

Ferkovich called for them. They would conduct the search for hidden devices and shut down the flow of oil.

At the base in 29 Palms, battalion 1/7 had built sand-table models of the station's physical layout, and by the time the battalion left in January for Kuwait, Ferkovich and his squad had seized the Az Zubayr pumping station many times. The squad's designated marksman knew where he had to position himself to fire without hitting squad members rushing forward or the critical pipes and valves in the background. Each fire team leader knew where to take up firing positions that would allow him to cover the next team's rush. They all knew what was expected of them and were confident that they could handle it.

On 20 March 2003 Ferkovich's squad members were sitting in the dust near the Iraqi border, enduring repeated "Lightning!" calls to put on their gas masks, and explaining their scheme of maneuver to Ray and me. *[Pictures 2-5]* They were so practiced in their answers to our questions that I laughingly asked how often they briefed senior visitors. "A bunch," they said. Two squads assigned to a multibillion-dollar target attracted attention—but the system was leaving it to them, not snatching it away and giving it to the CIA's Special Activities Division or the knife-edged Delta Force. In midafternoon of 20 March, when the battalion began wending its way to attack into Iraq, Ferkovich and his men were ready.

They were part of a huge military machine. Advancing slowly toward the Line of Departure that afternoon along a front of 120 kilometers were more than fifty Army and Marine units as large as or larger than Conlin's battalion. The Army, formed up in V Corps, was to the west; once inside Iraq, V Corps would attack to Baghdad on an axis about 60 to 100 kilometers west of the Marines. To the east of Conlin and closer to the Iranian border, I MEF was sending British and Marine units from shore and ship to seize Iraq's Faw Peninsula and advance north toward the city of Basrah, second in size only to Baghdad. Conlin and the rest of the 1st Marine Division were thus in the center of the attack line, with V Corps to their left and the Basrah-bound British-Marine force to their right.

The 1st Marine Division was organized into three regimental combat teams: RCT-1, RCT-5, and RCT-7. RCT-7 was assigned to take the Crown Jewel. Three battalions in RCT-7 would engage the Iraqi military and set up blocking positions, while a fourth battalion, 1/7, would sprint directly for the Jewel. Two of that battalion's three infantry companies would block from the outside, while the third, Charlie Company, secured the pumping station. The rest of the division would attack to seize the oil fields that were the key objectives for Central Command and the White House.

By late afternoon Ferkovich and the other Marines in the battalion's column of vehicles could hear the 155mm artillery firing, the distinct bangs of outgoing volleys. Safwan Hill was getting whacked, and the Marines agreed that they wouldn't want to be up there. The hill was only 90 meters high, but in the flat desert it looked as big as a mountain. Only a few kilometers inside Iraq, it loomed over the Line of Departure as an ideal Iraqi observation post. Maj. Gen. James N. Mattis, the 1st Marine Division commander, had no intention of launching thousands of vehicles while some Iraqi shouted into his radio, "You won't believe all the targets I see!"

Mattis didn't want to destroy the Iraqi observation post—he wanted to obliterate it, to wipe it from the face of the earth, as a terrifying example to encourage other Iraqi soldiers to run away. In one staff meeting he had pointed his finger at the tiny concentric circles on the map and said, "Before we kick off, I want this hill a foot shorter."

The troops loved hearing Mattis stories. A trim, bespectacled man with hawklike features, Mattis's life, not merely his career, had centered on command in the field. He had a remarkable record of infantry leadership: a rifle platoon; a rifle company; an infantry battalion like Conlin's; an infantry regiment; and a Navy-Marine Task Force of eight thousand men and women. Now he had command of the largest and most powerful division the Marine Corps had ever sent into battle.

The 1st Division had 22,200 Marines, plus Navy doctors, clergy, and medics, as well as liaisons from the CIA and Special Operations Command and a dozen Iraqi Americans who had volunteered their language services. Each day members of the division consumed 45,000 to 65,000 meals and 35,000 gallons of water, and filled its 8,000 vehicles with 200,000 gallons of fuel. Spread out over one highway in tactical formation, the division stretched over 280 kilometers. If it were in the United States, its lead tank would be in New York City before the rear guard left Boston.

As Ferkovich and battalion 1/7 proceeded slowly toward a forward position from which they could attack, Mattis and other senior commanders were discussing beginning the ground attack early. In the initial planning, Gen. Tommy Franks's air advisers had recommended that air strikes pound the Iraqis for several weeks before ground forces attacked. Retired Air Force generals such as Buster Glossen were often seen on television advocating that approach—after all, it had succeeded in Desert Storm. But this time the Army and Marine ground commanders recommended that Ground Day be simultaneous with Air Day to catch the Iraqis off guard and out of position, thus increasing the likelihood that the oil fields could be seized intact. General Franks had agreed, setting D-Day for both ground and air for dawn on 21 March.

Now, however, U.S. cruise missiles had hit Baghdad a day early, the Iraqis had fired back, British troops and Navy SEALs had seized a few small objectives to the Blue Diamond's east, and reports were trickling in that a few wellheads were burning. It was like watching a small grass fire burning next to a forest. If the division waited until the next morning, the oil fields might be ablaze. Central Command agreed the 1st Marine Division would begin the ground assault ahead of schedule.

At 8:30 P.M. on 20 March, RCT-5 became the first major ground unit to enter into Iraq, and by ten the next morning, Conlin's 1st Battalion had passed through the berms that separated Kuwait from Iraq. Ferkovich and his squad were on their way to the Crown Jewel. Battalion 3/7 and 1st Tank Battalion were clearing the road north for 1/7, leaving in their wake the scattered hulks of Iraqi vehicles. By noon 1/7 was rolling through the empty, shuttered town of Safwan, which was scarcely damaged by the fighting. To their west they could see

Safwan Hill, shrouded in dust and smoke from the pounding it had taken. The few civilians on the streets had their thumbs in the air and were smiling. The shops along the main street were shabby, and no building had a coat of paint. The place was composed of concrete, cement, and dust. Outside the destitute town military traffic clogged the wide two-lane road heading north, and no civilians were stirring, save for a thin woman in a black burka, begging by the side of the road, with two small children clutching her side. The land was dry hardscrabble, requiring a pick or an ax to prepare for planting. Scattered here and there were the mud huts of farmers, many flying black flags to show they were Shiite Muslims. No Iraqi flag was to be seen. A few ditches were filled with oil, some burning, with pitch-black billows of smoke pouring out.

By two in the afternoon of 21 March, the 1st Battalion was 60 kilometers north of Kuwait; the Crown Jewel was five kilometers up the road, to the northeast. Charlie Company's Amtracs picked up speed as they reached the "hinge" where they were to turn east onto Route 31 to the Crown Jewel. Ferkovich could see the 1/7 command group with Lieutenant Colonel Conlin pulled off the road with two command Amtracs, setting up tall antennae to establish communications with the regimental command and with the Direct Air Support Center (DASC). Two Cobra attack helicopters flew overhead, acting as the eyes for Charlie Company.

The Charlie Company Marines could hear and see firing from several directions. *[Picture 8]* A kilometer to the west another battalion was clearing a tree line. They were taking a few incoming mortar shells and returning fire with a .50-caliber that had hit a pipeline and started a sizable fire. A few stray rounds came over 1st Battalion's tracs and the command group, but the headquarters troops had the sense not to fire back and endanger other Marines. Two Marine snipers with their scopes were methodically sweeping the dry farm fields, praying for some sign of the enemy.

Across one of these fields, about 200 meters from Conlin's tracs, a tall old man with a white beard was slowly making his way toward a farmhouse. He was walking with a cane, deliberately lifting it, advancing a foot, then lifting it again. Three or four young men hovered around him and offered their arms, which he ignored. A woman ran out from the house, obviously urging him to hurry, but he refused to hasten his pace. The Americans with all their shooting were not going to upset his routine. He would show them. The woman put her hands to her ears, then to her cheeks, rocking her head back and forth. The young men clearly wanted to gain the safety of the house, but they wouldn't leave the stubborn old man behind. He had seen much in his life, it seemed, and not even a war would force him to compromise his dignity or change his routine. Something about him caught all of our attention—his attitude reassuring that normal life goes on, yet discordant in its irrationality. A stray bullet would not know it should honor the dignity of a stubborn old man.

As Ferkovich's Amtrac made the turn onto Route 31, he heard small-arms fire from the front of his company column. Screening to the front was Combined Anti-Armor Team Red (CAAT Red) in three Humvees, one armed with an automatic 40mm grenade launcher, one with the team leader and a .50-caliber machine gun, and one with a TOW, a large menacing tube that fired a rocket with the power and accuracy of a tank main gun. Shielded by no armor plating, CAAT Red relied on surprise and speed to survive.

CAAT Red was a kilometer west of the pumping station. On its left was a tree line, and to the right a pipeline with a farming village just beyond it. Two Iraqi tanks were smoldering by the side of the road. Suddenly, 200 meters in front of CAAT Red, a white SUV drove around a curve, saw the Humvees, hit the brakes, skidded around, and started to drive away. The CAAT commander, Lt. Josh Bates, hesitated a moment. [Picture 9] The driver could have been a frightened, innocent civilian, but only a Baath Party official or a military officer would drive a new SUV.

"Take it out!" Bates yelled. Lance Cpl. Scotty Price fired a burst from the Mk-19 40mm grenade launcher. A round struck the pipeline, and flames spurted forth. The SUV veered, slowed, resumed speed, and cut up a side road to the left. Price couldn't believe it. An explosive round bigger than his fist had hit the SUV, yet it had kept on running.

Bates ignored the SUV and turned right onto the access road to the pumping station. Knowing the shooting had alerted everyone at the station, he accelerated, not wanting to allow time for an ambush to be set up. There was no more firing, and Bates wheeled to a stop at a tiny roundabout. One road ran east into the station, the other north around it. Charlie Company closed behind him and turned left, according to plan. The Marines were standing up in the Amtracs. Over the high cement wall that enclosed the pumping station, they could see men and women in civilian clothes running frantically among several office buildings.

In seconds the Amtracs halted, each only a few feet from the one in front, their treads emitting a grating, high-pitched squeal, blocking out all human shouts. The back ramps went down, and the Marines piled out, taking hasty firing positions. Captain Lacroix, the Charlie Company commander, tried to orient them by his map and satellite photo, but nothing was lining up. The area was smaller than it had appeared to be on the three-year-old satellite photo, and the wall was thicker. The Amtracs were supposed to drive up next to the wall, but a tangle of pipes covered the ground. There was a complex of buildings, more than the satellite photo showed. The Marines climbed over the pipes and crouched at the wall, waiting for Lacroix to signal the engineers to blow a hole.

Lacroix was checking his list of "go or no-go" criteria for the assault. If certain conditions weren't met, he was to pull his company out. The critical indicator was flames spouting from the tops of the pressure-release pipes inside the station. That would mean that natural gas wasn't building up inside the hot oil pipes, waiting for a random spark to ignite an explosion that would incinerate his Marines. The Cobra pilots circling overhead told Lacroix all the other criteria were green—good to go. But peering through the dust haze, he could see the release pipes—and not a single flame burned from any of them.

There had been scattered shooting from the keyed-up Marines and CAAT Red had ignited one pipeline fire already. Once Ferkovich and

Garcia led their squads inside, one spark from even a small firefight could set off a huge explosion.

The Marines crouched along the wall, looking for Lacroix's signal, eight month's work on the line. This was the most important objective on the first day of the war, listed at the top of the computer screens at Central Command headquarters, at the Pentagon and even at the White House. Billions of dollars saved versus fourteen Marines burned to death. Lacroix reached for his whistle to abort the mission, sorting through his options. The pilots had radioed back to higher headquarters that all criteria were green. Lacroix wasn't about to leave his men exposed while he radioed for advice. This was his decision to make alone. He looked at his "go or no-go" list again. What else on that list was wrong here?

All those workers were out of place. As the gases built up around them, they would have known they were in the vortex of a giant bomb and run away. Yet he could hear dozens of workers shouting and rushing about.

The Crown Jewel had three 1500 horsepower turbine engines, pumping thousands of barrels of oil. The engines were the size of small houses. With all that machinery whirring away, he wouldn't be able to hear people talking on the other side of the wall.

"Shut down the tracs," he yelled.

When the Amtrac engines were turned off, he still couldn't hear the roar of the massive turbines and the pieces of the puzzle fell into place. The workers had remained because they had shut down the entire plant. Lacroix gave the thumbs up and sent his men in.

The engineers had already slapped an explosive C-4 charge against the wall. With a sharp *bang* a portion of the wall crumbled in dust and smoke. Ferkovich heard the explosion and moved his squad up, following 1st Platoon through the garage-door-size hole in the wall. The 1st Platoon fanned out, meeting no resistance. Ferkovich and Garcia quickly led their squads toward the road that bisected the pumping station, their objectives on the far side. Passing between two office buildings, they skirted a huge cesspool of open sewage that they didn't expect. Civilians were running in all directions, and Marines screamed at them to stop. A man dropped his bag, spilling out a pistol, and ran. A Marine shot him in the leg. At the burst of fire the other civilians stopped running.

Ferkovich and his squad ignored them. On the south side of the road across from the office buildings was a wire fence, and 100 meters inside was a set of eight huge tan pipes curved at the top in a right angle; at the top of each was an enormous spigot. It was the manifold, his first objective. The engineers blew the fence, and the squad sprinted to the manifold, flopping down, looking frantically around, expecting incoming fire from any direction. Some palm trees and two tan oil storage tanks stood to their right, and open ground lay on the other three sides. The area was clear.

Garcia waited a few seconds for Ferkovich's signal, then his squad ran by Ferkovich to the pumping station, a tall building with a tin roof and sides, open at both ends, housing in-ground turbines as large as a small house. *[Picture 6]* After a few minutes Garcia radioed that all was clear, and Ferkovich and his squad rushed by. A hundred meters east they reached the red-brick power plant. It too had expanded considerably since the satellite photo was taken. Ferkovich did a cursory search—a thorough search would take hours and dusk was falling—and called in the British explosive and oil experts to take over. The Crown Jewel was secure. Ferkovich was amazed. Over six months of preparation, hundreds of hours of study and rehearsals—and it was all over in thirty minutes. No enemy had shot at them. He hadn't expected it to go so fast. He and his Marines felt a little disappointed. They had anticipated armed resistance and had imagined how they would respond, cutting down the station's defenders.

The squad did not realize how close a thing it had been. Lieutenant Colonel Conlin had driven up, and the workers led him inside a building and pointed to a headless body, blood splattered across the room. Saddam's men had come that morning, demanding that the workers sabotage the pumps. They had cut the man's head off to make an example. The other workers had then thrown wrenches and rocks into the gears of the silent turbines. When the Saddam agents heard the Marines coming, the killers had driven away in an SUV.

Conlin ordered the body removed, while the Marines herded the Iraqis together into one building. With much gesturing and broken English phrases, they said they were all workers, with no soldiers among them. They asked for medical help for the man with a bullet wound in his leg. "No, no!" several Iraqis protested in broken English. "He's a good man, a guard. He ran because he was frightened."

The Marines rounded up and processed the workers as they had been trained, using plastic cords to tie their hands behind them. The troops knew these scared, smiling men posed no threat—most of them ten to twenty years older than the stern Marines guarding them. One old man with only one tooth was grinning and yelling, "Fuck Saddam! Hurray America!" Another man in threadbare clothes, who spoke good English, wanted to debate. "Saddam is not so bad," he said. "See, I have good pants and shoes. Why are you here?"

The CIA and the special forces in their gray jumpsuits drove up with several Iraqis, who were placed in a darkened room. The hoped-for revolt inside the pumping station and its takeover by Shiite rebels hadn't materialized, but the intelligence people had brought with them informers to point out those loyal to Saddam. The informers peered out from behind blankets that had been put up as a screen. Almost all the workers, they said, were "good men," and they pointed out only a few as "bad men." The Marines gestured at the man with the "good pants and shoes." The informers shook their heads. He was only a worker, they said, a show-off trying to impress them with a little English.

The British oil experts examined the turbines and said the damage from the junk thrown into the turbines was amateurish, repairable in a few days. The demolition experts walked through the tall grass, poking sticks into oil-slicked pools of wastewater and prodding at rusty barrels, wary of booby traps or chemicals. They found industrial waste but no explosives. The Marines and British alike were surprised by the sloppy, run-down look of the place. Outside the dilapidated administration building stood an oil canvas of Saddam in a ridiculous hat and capped white teeth, his smile as warm as a steel trap. *[Picture 7]*

The painting was the only fresh item in the pumping station. The scrawny patches of oil-stained grass hadn't been mown in months, pot-holes dotted the sidewalks and streets, and the cement around the doors and windowsills was pocked and cracked. The electric fixtures were bare wires, and the manifolds that pumped billions of dollars in oil were covered with rust. Inside the dingy office of the director, records kept in thick ledgers were scattered haphazardly. Patches of rusty water topped with oil scum lapped at the sides of the building. Saddam had been sucking dry the wealth of his country.

Satisfied that the disrepair had existed long before the Marines arrived, Lieutenant Colonel Conlin reported to the regimental command that the station at Az Zubayr had been taken intact. Although the tarnished Crown Jewel was badly in need of repair, millions of barrels of oil could still flow through its rusting infrastructure.

At dusk on 21 March Captain Lacroix sent Corporal Ferkovich's squad to stand guard at the eastern end of the compound. I remained with Lacroix near the manifolds, while Ray was with battalion operations at the C-7 command Amtrac. [Picture 12] Lacroix gave Ferkovich's squad high marks for their efficiency in moving through their objectives. He was less pleased with the overall coordination and irritated that the Cobras had not been better read in. He was surprised at the disrepair and squalor of the pumping station. While we were talking, a dog that looked half-hyena was lapping at the oil-slick cesspool water behind us. We watched him warily. He seemed more a threat than the Iraqis.

Ferkovich would probably have agreed—certainly the Iraqis he was encountering were not in a fighting mood. As he set in his squad, an Iraqi soldier waving a white flag walked slowly up to them. They tied his hands and moved him off. When they turned back, five more soldiers were walking forward with their hands in the air. The Iraqis had heard wild rumors that Marines slaughtered everyone, so as a test the soldiers had forced one in their group to surrender first, while the others watched.

A kilometer to the east, CAAT Red was spending the night on the highway, set to block any enemy armor that might turn up. Through his night-vision goggles, Ferkovich could see the infrared strobes winking atop the CAAT's three Humvees. He saw a few flashes of green, then a few bursts of red tracer fire. The sounds reached him a second later; CAAT Red was trading rounds with someone, he realized. Ferkovich made a mental note to check his own squad's fields of fire, lest his riflemen shoot too near CAAT Red's position. A few bad guys were shooting, and a few Marines were returning fire—to Ferkovich it was already normal stuff, happened all the time. For two years he had trained for this moment. Now that it had arrived, his training had taken over. This was who he was—a twenty-year-old combat squad leader.

Ferkovich later told me he had hoped for more of a real fight, as had his whole squad. They had trained so long that they wanted to be pushed, so they could push back and show what they had. Yet they had accomplished much more than they gave themselves credit for. The panicky civilians running around had not been shot; the pumping station had been seized and searched with no damage from nervous shooting; and Iraqi soldiers wanting to surrender had not been fired upon. Such restraint during an attack requires training, leadership, and maturity.

After a long night for everyone, Conlin was shaking Ray and me out of our sleeping bags. CAAT Red was in "heavy contact" with the enemy east of the pumping station. CAAT Red's radio couldn't reach the battalion, so a corporal in a mortar unit was relaying the message. Conlin didn't like the vague word *contact*—were his troops under heavy fire, or were they merely shooting at a fleeing enemy? He was on his way over to check it out and thought we might want to ride along. I calculated Conlin had had one hour's sleep in two days. We drove by Ferkovich's position, and a few minutes later Conlin was standing on the road with Lieutenant Bates, the CAAT Red commander. Bates said the "contact" reported by the corporal had been his Humvee driver shooting over the heads of some looters crawling into the Iraqi tanks.

"What tanks?" Conlin asked.

Bates led him across a field to a row of a dozen T-54 tanks and small armored vehicles called BMPs. Each one was in fine condition; they had loaded magazines and canvas dust covers over the barrels. *[Picture 10]* All were in revetments, positions dug with earth-movers that were just big enough for the tanks to get in for protection. But they were dug so deep that the tanks couldn't see to fire at anything. Three sorry-looking soldiers in green uniforms were sitting with arms tied behind them. All had had large wads of dinars in their pockets. No other soldiers were around, only a gang of men waiting to loot.

The tanks aligned in these prepared positions were less than two kilometers from where Ferkovich was at the Crown Jewel. Prior to the war frequent UAV sorties to video the area had detected no Iraqi tanks. The Iraqis could easily have used the tanks to destroy the pumping station before battalion 1/7 arrived; or they could have shelled Ferkovich and his squad as they moved through the station. Instead, they had abandoned the tanks.

Battalion 1/7 was finished with the Crown Jewel and had to move out quickly. It was a long way to Baghdad. They would refuel farther to the west, then begin the long march up.

As the Amtracs of 1st Battalion formed up on 22 March, Ferkovich and his squad rejoined Charlie Company. They were now "tail-end Charlie," at the rear of the battalion convoy, just another infantry squad heading for Baghdad.

Following the Amtracs of 1st Battalion was a procession of political and vehicular odd-fellows: white Nissan pickups driven by the special ops soldiers in gray aviator coveralls, CNN reporters in a new tan Humvee, and press camp-followers from half a dozen nations who were not embedded with any unit in a raggedy tail-end of beat-up SUVs. This was the first war in which the Marines, the special forces, the CIA/OGA (Other Government Agency), CNN, and media from France and other European countries all trekked across the desert as one caravan, respecting one another's space.

Conlin as a rule met alone with his officers, unless he chose to invite the press to sit in. CNN and the other embedded press were often so favored, which the nonaccredited press accepted as fair. The CIA and special ops drove in and out as they pleased, easily identifiable, never pestered. Not one photograph of an OGA or special ops person appeared in the press, and in stops along the road no reporter pushed overly aggressively for interviews. Despite the lack of any physical privacy, in terms of political decorum the war was more polite than Washington.

2

Ambush Alley

The Streets of An Nasiriyah

D+2 to D+4

With RCT-1 at Nasiriyah
22–24 March

As Ray and I clattered west in an Amtrac with Lt. Col. Conlin's battalion on 22 March, there was no word on whether Saddam had been hit by the cruise missiles. Other than that, the campaign was off to a good start. Air strikes and cruise missiles were pounding Iraqi government and military targets, while special operations forces had prevented the destruction of the oil fields in northern Iraq. The campaign's central objective was to seize Baghdad, thus "cutting the head off the snake." To do this, two enormous columns were advancing from Kuwait. The main effort was a sweeping left hook from the west by the Army's V Corps, advancing on Baghdad from an unexpected direction where the defenses were lighter. The second column was a supporting effort by I MEF, with the ground offensive centered around the 1st Marine Division.

I MEF was comprised of Task Force Tarawa from the 2nd Marine Division, the 1st Marine Division, the First U.K. Division, the 3rd Marine Air Wing and the First Force Service Support Group. Tarawa and the British were to secure the city of Basrah and southern portions of Iraq while the 1st Marine Division marched on Baghdad. The singular strategy of the division was to fight by maneuver, not by attrition or by brute firepower.

At the start of the war the Iraqis had one division defending the Rumaylah oil fields and Basrah. Five more divisions were posted along the north bank of the Tigris, the historical invasion route from Basrah to Baghdad. Nearer Baghdad, two elite Republican Guard divisions provided an inner defensive shield. The opening gambit of the 1st Marine Division was to seize the oil fields and feint toward Basrah, threatening to follow the traditional eastern route up the Tigris to Baghdad and thus fixing in place the defenders. The 1st Marine Division would then suddenly turn west, bypassing the five divisions north of Basrah and splitting the seam between the two Republican Guard divisions. The regiments would then destroy first the one and then the other, opening a clear highway to Baghdad and leaving the five Iraqi divisions along the Tigris out of the fight. To engage the 1st Marine Division, the enemy would have to leave their entrenchments and move away from the cities. Once in the open, they were easy targets for U.S. air, artillery, and tanks. As Major General Mattis told his regimental commanders, they would fight the terrain head on, not the enemy.

Thus while V Corps was moving up from the west, the 1st Marine Division was advancing against eight Iraqi divisions, intending to destroy three and outmaneuver five more. Initially the RCTs would advance up two separate routes to hedge against a setback on either one and reduce congestion. By the second week of the campaign, the three regiments would converge as a division on one highway, less than 160 kilometers from Baghdad. Mattis's guiding principle was speed. Wherever possible, cities and towns were to be bypassed. At no point would there be a pause. Make dust or eat it.

Traveling with the 1/7 command element and listening to the radios, Ray and I had a fair picture of what was unfolding. While RCT-1 was cutting west off-road across the desert, RCTs 5 and 7 had seized the oil fields and destroyed the 51st Division defending there. We were surprised, as were the commanders, by the small number of prisoners taken and the large number of abandoned vehicles. There were probably two waves of desertions by Iraqi crews, those who fled early because they feared air, and those who fled later when they heard the Abrams tanks approaching. The most significant thing about the opening of the war was what did not happen. The Iraqis had expected weeks of air attacks before American soldiers crossed the border, providing ample time to torch the oil fields. Instead, the fields were seized on the first day, preventing the world's worst oil environmental disaster.

On 23 March, all three RCTs were heading west to cross the Euphrates River near the city of An Nasiriyah. RCT-5, followed by RCT-7, would pass south of Nasiriyah and turn northwest up Route 1, a four-lane expressway under construction and mostly devoid of towns. At the same time, Task Force Tarawa would hold open Nasiriyah so that RCT-1 could pass through and proceed north up Route 7, a smaller road dotted with towns. Ray and I were trying to get to RCT-1, and Col. Steven Hummer, the commander of RCT-7, graciously let us hitch a ride on a Huey headed that way.

The Huey followed Route 8, going west. The sunny day provided a clear view. To the north, shallow lakes scattered over thousands of acres, lay parallel to the Euphrates River. South of the lakes the desert stretched into Kuwait, empty except for lines of U.S. military vehicles crawling across it. Stretching west to the horizon, columns of vehicles two to four abreast filled the highway. There were so many, it looked like all of California was driving into Nevada. Far to the east we could see a few columns of smoke rising from the Rumaylah oil fields—the wellheads that had been set ablaze before RCT-5 arrived. As we flew farther west, we could see some lines of vehicles still coming north across the open desert, and the highway below us was jammed with vehicles. The Huey swept over the vehicles and set down in a blinding cloud of dust 50 meters off the road. As we jumped out and grabbed our packs, Ray looked at the Marines on the highway, trying to cover themselves from the stinging dust off the rotor blades. "I bet that will make them welcome us," he commented.

As we walked the short distance to the command post, it became obvious that one more cloud of dust made little difference. The vehicles were caked in half a foot of dirt, congealed too hard to be broken with a closed fist. The faces, eyelids, nostrils, and ears of the Marines were full of dust; many were hacking and coughing up great wads of phlegm. Rinsing off with water was out of the question. You drank water; you didn't waste it on your body. For three days, RCT-1 had been traveling overland, cutting across rough, cut up, and unbelievably dusty terrain. For the past 48 hours, they had moved steadily, and even those not driving had been unable to sleep because of the roughness of the terrain. The choking dust was unrelenting, filling every vehicle and coating every surface on both men and machines.

The regiment was commanded by Col. Joe W. Dowdy, a thickset man with a shaved head whose intimidating musculature was softened by an Arkansas accent and a friendly way of speaking. Dowdy lived for the 1st Marines. He had grown up in its ranks, commanded the 1st Battalion, organized reunions and sent newsletters to the thousands who had served before him. As a lieutenant colonel, he had persuaded the Navy to host the regiment's veterans on board the *Iwo Jima*, a huge, gleaming new amphibious ship. Dowdy could recite minute details about the glorious history of the regiment and recall the middle names of illustrious past commanders, trying the patience of all except equally devoted historians.

Even his memory, though, was in low gear by noon of 23 March. When we met up with him on Route 8, about 20 kilometers southeast of An Nasiriyah, he looked exhausted. He was held up for a while, he explained, waiting to pass through the city. Task Force Tarawa had the mission of clearing the route for his regiment.

Commanded by Brig. Gen. Rich Natonski, Task Force Tarawa was composed of six thousand Marines from the 2nd Marine Expeditionary Force, based in the Carolinas, and was built around the 2nd Marine Regiment. Earlier a plan had been approved whereby Tarawa would open Nasiriyah for RCT-1 to pass through.

Nasiriyah was a dingy, neglected collection of one- and two-story cinder-block and mud houses sandwiched in square city blocks between the Euphrates River to the south and the Saddam Canal to the north. In essence an island four kilometers square, Nasiriyah had bridges on its north and south ends: two on Route 7 through the heart of the city, and two on Route 8—called Route Moe by Task Force Tarawa—that skirted the city's eastern border. On board ship en route to the theater, the Tarawa planners had pored over the maps and overhead photos and come up with a simple plan. The 1st Battalion, 2nd Marine Regiment (1/2), would move through the eastern border up Route Moe and seize the bridge at the northern end. Another battalion would then establish a picket line along Route Moe through the city. This would allow RCT-1 to pass through unmolested.

Under this plan, no Marines would be inside the city until after RCT-1 had driven through. The reason was to avoid becoming bogged down fighting in alleys and crowded city streets. Throughout the prewar planning cycle Tarawa Marines had referred to Route Moe as "Ambush Alley," making repeated references to the streets of Mogadishu, where in 1993 hundreds of Somalis had poured out to battle a trapped U.S. Army convoy. The analogy to Somalia had a powerful psychological effect upon the Marines.

In terms of history, however, Somalia and Nasiriyah presented different cases. In Somalia the local tribe in the ambush area had seen U.S. soldiers as the enemy. In Nasiriyah the vast majority of the population saw Saddam Hussein as the enemy. Immediately following Desert Storm in 1991, President George H. W. Bush had encouraged the Iraqi people to overthrow Saddam. The 400,000 Shiite residents of Nasiriyah had responded with a bloody uprising, killing the Baathist mayor and his son and setting up their own municipal government. Saddam's army had responded by killing thousands. The Baath Party reestablished a strong hold on the city, quashing the uprising and subduing the population. For the next decade Nasiriyah had suffered from neglect, despair, and repression. It had no drainage system now, large puddles of raw sewage covered many intersections, and the only paved road on the eastern side was Route Moe, the highway that RCT-1 planned to follow.

Agents assured I MEF that the city's garrison—troops from the 11th Iraqi Infantry Division—would quickly desert or surrender. But fedayeen were coming into town on buses and motorcycles. These youth troops were rabidly loyal to Saddam—the sons of Baath Party members and poor teenagers attracted by pay twice that of the ordinary soldier. Though they had little military training and no capability of organizing above a squad, the fedayeen were supposed to put backbone into the regular soldiers by threatening to shoot them if they fled. Task Force Tarawa assumed that the fedayeen, lacking military structure, would not be the first line of defense. They believed that the fedayeen would emerge as suicide bombers and snipers in the rear, after RCT-1 had passed through.

At three in the morning of 23 March the lead elements of Task Force Tarawa were encamped 15 kilometers south of Nasiriyah when they were told to roll. Although RCT-1 wasn't due to arrive until noon, an Army convoy had been hit south of the city. The 2nd Marines were to push up and help immediately.

At that time no Army unit was supposed to be on the outskirts of Nasiriyah in front of the 2nd Marines. The 3rd Infantry Division had secured a key intersection several kilometers south of Nasiriyah (leading to speculation that the Iraqi 11th Division would not fight) and then turned left and headed northwest; supply convoys were to follow that route. But many drivers didn't have maps and weren't accustomed to checking their location every few minutes, as is second nature for all frontline vehicles. All were wearing third-generation night-vision goggles, which enabled long lines of vehicles to roll without lights, each driver able to see the vehicle in front and to keep his place in line. The greenish hues of the goggles, though, can be mesmerizing, and at midnight, after twelve hours on the road, it was easy for a driver to follow the truck in front without checking the GPS receiver. The darkest day of the war for the American forces began after midnight on 23 March, when trucks of the 507th Maintenance Company missed their turn and drove straight toward the eastern bridge over the Euphrates.

The Iraqis had stationed defenders on the approaches to the bridges, an unexceptional military move. With no warning, the thin-skinned Army supply trucks ran into a hail of small-arms fire from up ahead and both sides of the road. The soldiers fired back, with little chance of hitting their unseen attackers. Trained infantry have an immediate action drill to dismount and band together to concentrate their return fire. But such reflexes couldn't be expected of maintenance soldiers, and the end played out in minutes. A few trucks managed to escape; the others were riddled; at least nine soldiers were killed. Some escaped into the darkness, and six others, low on ammunition and surrounded, put down their rifles and raised their hands. The Iraqis swarmed forward, hitting them with rifle barrels, pulling them from the trucks, jerking off their equipment. They pawed through the trucks, stripped them and set them on fire, and hustled the captives off. Within hours the Iraqi fighters had videotaped the dead and captured Americans. The videotape was shown on Baghdad television, an action that provoked deep anger among the American public. The wounds shown on television suggested that American soldiers had been captured and executed.

A few hours after daybreak battalion 1/2, tanks in the lead, reached the area. The terrain was a jumble of industrial one-story buildings, open fields, small irrigation ditches, and clusters of adobe houses. Some Iraqis firing machine guns were pummeled. Alpha Company of battalion 1/2 searched a cluster of adobe huts and thrashed through a thicket of palm trees, emerging tired and covered with mud. Five Army soldiers from the 507th were found alive and evacuated.

In late morning the tanks pulled back to refuel, while Charlie and Bravo Companies of 1/2 advanced by bounds. The companies were in the suburbs south of the Euphrates, not yet up to the eastern bridge into the city. When they reached the charred and smoldering Army trucks, rumors started that the Iraqis had surrendered, then opened fire with concealed machine guns. The battalion executive officer came up on the company frequencies and said that rumor wasn't true, but it stuck and became part of the story of Nasiriyah.

Just before noon the 1/2 battalion commander, apparently being pressed by 2nd Marines to move faster, told his companies they had to take the bridges. "It's time to run the gauntlet," he said. Alpha Company secured the wide eastern bridge. Bravo Company crossed and drove its Amtracs around the few blocks of cement houses on the east side of Nasiriyah, meeting no resistance except the mud that fouled the vehicles' treads. Bravo's column slogged slowly through sewage seepage and rain puddles until a number of its vehicles became hopelessly stuck. It was apparent that the approaching convoy of RCT-1 would not be able to improvise by pulling off Route Moe and swinging to the east around the city. RCT-1 would have to drive through the city on Route Moe, already nicknamed "Ambush Alley."

Even though Bravo Company was stuck, Charlie Company 1/2 crossed the eastern bridge in eleven tracs and proceeded north on Route Moe through the shabby town. The houses on both sides were set back 80 to 100 meters from the four-lane divided highway. Looked at through military eyes, each small house was a cement or adobe fort with few windows or other apertures from which to fire out at the street. Because each house was enclosed by a cement wall taller than a man, anyone firing from inside could be isolated and trapped. On the outside, though, were numerous alleys, intersections, and unpaved roads between the blocks, some 20 to 40 meters wide. A man could pop out into the open in an alley or intersection, take a shot with an RPG, then duck back behind a wall. Since the houses were set back from the main road, an attacker could maintain the initiative if the troops stayed mounted and on the road.

Charlie Company drove north for four kilometers along the highway. Marines with M-16s and 40mm grenade launchers scanned every house and every side street across an open expanse of dust, sewage, and greenish puddles. Four tracs were already over the northern Saddam Canal bridge when a rattle of small arms erupted, followed by a red streak and a sharp boom. The lead trac bucked and jerked to a halt, hit by a well-aimed RPG. Inside the Amtrac, shrapnel hit an AT-4 antitank rocket in a Marine's lap, killing him and wounding several others.

Charlie Company was now split, with four tracs north and seven south of the bridge. Capt. Dan Wittnam, the company commander, was north of the bridge with the 3rd Platoon, the 60mm mortar section and the fire support team. All Marines dismounted and began to return fire. Across the canal to the southwest groups of men in civilian clothes, some dressed in black, were scurrying among the houses, a few a football field away, others several hundred meters back. Two- and three-man teams were shooting RPGs tilted up at a 45-degree angle, using the rocket grenades like mortars. There were explosions on all sides of the Marines.

Lt. Ben Reid, commanding the fire support team, yelled at Lt. Fred Pokorney, the company's artillery forward observer, to call in 81mm mortars and artillery. After several unsuccessful tries, Pokorney yelled back that he couldn't raise them on the radio. All the fire support communication nets were down, but he believed he had gotten one through on the battalion net.

Reid's platoon sergeant, Staff Sgt. Phillip Jordan, directed the machine guns to fire close in on the southwest side of the canal. A large confident Marine, Jordan was highly respected by his weapons platoon, and the machine-gun crew hastened to obey him. Reid and Jordan had turned their attention to setting in the mortars when a large-caliber round arced into the position, killing Jordan, Lieutenant Pokorney, and Private First Class Buesing. Lieutenant Reid and three others were wounded.

His right arm dangling and full of shrapnel, Reid was trying to move an Amtrac back as an ambulance when he was hit again with shrapnel, this time in the face. Staggering and with his vision blurring, Reid knew he had to take care of the wounded before he passed out. He ordered Corporal Elliott, crew chief on the Amtrac, to drive the wounded back south across both bridges to the battalion aid station. "And get your up gun in action," Reid said, referring to the Amtrac's 40mm grenade launcher.

After the Amtrac left, a gunnery sergeant was treating Reid's wounds when they saw an American A-10 Warthog swoop by, circle around, and line up on their position for a strafing attack from north to south. Reid watched in disbelief as the "friendly" green tracers from the A-10 slammed into the vehicles herringboned alongside the road. Marines scurried for cover, dragging wounded out of the line of fire and looking for a red pyrotechnic to launch—the signal to identify friendly forces and to cease fire. The A-10 continued its run to the south and disappeared. The 3rd Platoon commander, Lt. Mike "Moose" Seely, a former staff sergeant who wore the Bronze Star and Purple Heart from Desert Storm, was screaming on the radio to the battalion to cease the damn A-

10 fire, but it had done its damage—shooting the buttocks off one previously wounded Marine—and departed before a red pyro could be located. The Charlie Company Marines weren't sure if the A-10 had just been passing by when it rolled in on them or was under the control of someone in the task force.

South of the canal two more tracs had formed up to escort Corporal Elliott's trac carrying the wounded. They'd barely started out when Elliott felt something slam into the rear of his trac. There was a huge explosion, and Elliott and his gunner were pitched forward. They leaped out and crawled away as the trac blew, its load of ammunition exploding in waves, splitting open the sides and top. All the Marines in back were killed. The trac immediately behind them was hit too. It was another catastrophic kill. Elliott and the other survivors were stunned. Marines from the next trac in line rushed up. Compression bandages and morphine injection needles were ripped open and applied. Marines rushed to aid the wounded and to begin an evacuation.

North of the bridge across the Saddam Canal, Captain Wittnam continued to organize the fight, unaware of the tragedy taking place farther south on the road. The Iraqis made no effort to close within accurate small-arms range. Instead, they popped out from around houses, fired RPGs at an angle, and ducked back to cover. Reid, along with other wounded, was loaded into an Amtrac, where corpsmen discovered a bullet that had entered his right shoulder and lodged above his fourth rib, in addition to the shrapnel in his face and right arm.

Around five in the afternoon, five hours after the battle began, Alpha Company drove up to the canal with tanks in the lead. The Iraqi firing slackened abruptly once the tanks arrived. CH-46s landed within the hour to evacuate the wounded and the dead and Charlie and Alpha Companies formed a perimeter.

Veterans and academics alike refer to the "fog of war"—this battle could be used as an illustration. With garbled communications and different groups of Marines fighting in different locations against different groups of enemy, information filtering up the chain of command and down to other units was fragmentary at best and misleading at worst. The man with the sharpest awareness of the situation on the ground was Captain Wittnam, and even he could accurately supply only part of the picture, and he was out of contact with the higher commands.

Ray and I were with Colonel Dowdy alongside the road 16 kilometers away while Wittnam was in the thick of the fight. Dowdy told us that 2nd Marines had a fight going on, but he couldn't raise them to find out exactly what was happening. *[Picture 11]* The radios of Task Force Tarawa were communicating on a different "load," or frequency hop code, than the 1st Marine Division. Dowdy was getting his information verbally from the Marines of 2/8, who were part of 2nd Marines, and were held up on the road next to Dowdy's column. Shortly after we joined Dowdy, the 2/8 Marines had climbed into their trucks and drove west. There was a fire-fight at Nasiriyah, they reported. Battalion 1/2 had taken the bridges, and they had been called forward. There was nothing to do but wait for the word to go.

Then over his iridium cell phone Dowdy received a call from the division main. After the call ended, he paced for a moment, sat down, and said to his commanders, "Division says that Tarawa is reporting mass casualties in Nas. They think they may have as many as 80 killed." Not thirty minutes before, 2/8 had moved forward, after telling Dowdy the bridge was secure. Now there were reports of horrendous casualties. This wasn't making sense.

To find out what was happening, Dowdy drove up to the command post of the 2nd Marines, which was not able to provide details about the fight or say when RCT-1 could move through the city. Dowdy drove back to his own regiment and discussed options with his staff. They considered asking the division command if RCT-1 could bypass Nasiriyah and follow RCT-5 and RCT-7 up Route 1. But that would place all three regiments on the same supply route, adding to congestion and risking a single stoppage point that would halt the whole division. In addition, RCT-1 was supposed to seize an airfield 100 kilometers up Route 7 so that the follow-on British brigade would have an aerial resupply spot. Dowdy ruled out the option and decided to "bust through Nasiriyah" at first light the next day, 24 March.

During the rest of the afternoon of 23 March, news of the ambush of the Army convoy and the heavy Marine losses inside Nasiriyah spread through the press and the ranks of the waiting Marines. The immediate effect was shock and disbelief. The chatrooms on the secret internets at higher staff headquarters lit up with rumors. A Marine battalion had been stopped dead in its tracks. A battalion! That just couldn't happen. A dozen rumors spread uncontrolled. The Iraqis were surrendering, then killing Americans; they were using children as shields; fedayeen ninjas on motorcycles were popping out of side streets to fire RPGs; women on street corners were acting as forward observers; children were dropping grenades into Amtracs from bedroom windows. No one knew truth from fiction.

The shock of the losses, the rampant rumors, and the fear of the unknown combined to make 23 March the blackest day of the campaign. As far as the troops were concerned, Route Moe in Nasiriyah was Ambush Alley, living up to the name given it months before.

Before full light on 24 March Colonel Dowdy had changed his mind about barreling on through the city. Nasiriyah was being called "the streets of Mogadishu," and Dowdy still had no reliable communications with the 2nd Marines. He drove forward to the 2nd Marines again, and word soon trickled back that seven hundred soft-skinned vehicles of RCT-1 would take an extra day and drive around Nasiriyah, while their 250 armored vehicles would push on through.

While we were held up, Ray and I talked to Avda Ilimghashghash, an American citizen who was traveling with RCT-1 as an interpreter, and had fled from Nasiriyah in 1992. He told us that he had been speaking with the local people as they passed by the convoy and had heard that the infamous Gen. Ali Hassan al-Majid, "Chemical Ali," had visited Nasiriyah two days before, urging the Baath Party "to keep control of the people." Avda believed the average Iraqi, remembering that Saddam slaughtered those who heeded America's call in 1991 to rebel, would do nothing to help in this war until sure that Saddam was really, really finished. For the Marines to delay in seizing Nasiriyah was in his view a mistake, because the fedayeen were not so powerful. It hurt the image of the Marines for the Iraqi people to see them delayed by such "children." The Marines would be seen as weak, and it would encourage more resistance.

In midafternoon on 24 March, RCT-1 left behind the soft-skinned vehicles like the Humvees and loaded the Marines on Amtracs to run through Nasiriyah. Ray and I left our assigned Humvees and climbed inside an Amtrac that was lightly loaded and was following Dowdy's command tractor as a security vehicle. The Marines had to make the trip buttoned up inside the Amtracs, unable to stand with weapons pointed outboard to defend themselves, which was the standard posture. Different reasons were given: closing the top hatches would minimize the effects of a chemical attack; Iraqis in houses were dropping grenades down the open Amtrac hatches.

About eighteen of us sat in the dark on ammunition boxes, and the Marines entertained themselves by verbally assaulting one another. I would ask a Marine where he was from, where he liked to go on liberty, that sort of thing. The others, safe in the dark, would leap in, explaining how poor his tastes were, how no self-respecting female would ever date him, how on such and such a night he had. . . . And so we passed two hours, clattering along, thinking we would soon hear rounds knocking on our door.

The Amtrac, or amphibious assault vehicle, can swim ashore or move on its treads across land carrying up to twenty-three Marines. It has a thin metal skin not built to ward off anti-armor shells or rockets and a turret with a .50-caliber machine gun and a 40mm grenade launcher, called the up gun. No fighting man ever has enough ammunition, and the Marines loaded extra metal boxes under the seats and onto the floor of every Amtrac. The up-gunner especially hoarded more and more ammo in the space beneath his turret. The floor of every Amtrac was therefore packed with explosives, and the best defense against an ambush from the side was for the Marines inside to pour out firepower so the attacker could not line up the sights of his RPG.

So when the word came down we were not going through Nasiriyah buttoned up, the Marines were pleased. The Amtracs halted on the southern outskirts of Nasiriyah, and the top hatches were opened. It was dusk, and in front of us an oil storage tank was burning, the column of black smoke lying low above their heads like a heavy mist. Artillery was firing regularly, and vehicles, large tents, and antennae were strung out on both sides of the road.

The 2nd Light Armored Reconnaissance Battalion (2nd LAR), leading RCT-1 with its LAVs and powerful 25mm chain guns, had dashed through Nasiriyah at dusk, taking and giving small-arms fire at the northern end but emerging with no casualties. As they went through, the 2nd Marines reported they were again in a firefight somewhere in the city. This was confusing—it made no sense that 2nd LAR and the 2nd Marines seemed to be describing two different actions. It was as if the road that 2nd LAR had gone through was different from the road that the 2nd Marines were on now. Concerned that something was still not right, and hearing from the 2nd Marines that the top commanders had come up, Dowdy stopped the rest of the convoy alongside the 2nd Marines CP, trying once again to figure out what was happening.

The Marines in RCT-1 were speculating as well. Two messages were passed from trac to trac. First message (authorized): *Some generals have come forward. We've halted while they coordinate.* Second message (unauthorized): *We've halted because the generals are worried.*

The second message was meant as a joke, but it had bite. To find out what was holding up RCT-1, Major General Mattis had sent forward his assistant division commander, Brig. Gen. John Kelly. The 1st Division hadn't been fully informed of the confused situation at Nasiriyah. It had seemed for twenty-four hours that the 2nd Marines were right on the verge of passing RCT-1 through. But it hadn't happened. Kelly and Dowdy drove forward to the causeway leading onto the eastern bridge over the Euphrates. AK-47 rounds were snapping overhead from across the river, so the two officers ducked low and took a knee to discuss the situation with Lieutenant General Conway, I MEF commander, who had also come forward. So too had Brigadier General Natonski, commanding Task Force Tarawa, as well as Colonel Bailey, commanding the 2nd Marines. All wanted to see for themselves what was going on.

What they saw was the fire from the 155mm artillery batteries pounding the city with volley after volley. Cobra gunships were raking the tree lines on the far bank. Two Marines had just been wounded on the southern embankment. The 2nd Marines had taken heavy casualties at the northern bridge and in the middle of the route through the city. Battalion 1/2 had vehicles stuck in the mud in the eastern part of the city. From the fragmentary reports he had received, Colonel Bailey said he might be hanging on by his fingertips. Bravo and Charlie Companies of 1/2 were holding the northern bridge over the Saddam Canal on the other side of the city. The 2nd LAR Battalion had just passed through the city. Dozens of troops from different elements of the 2nd Marines lay prone near the riverbank, looking for targets 200 meters away on the other bank. The "fog of war" prevailed among the command group at the southern end of the causeway leading into Nasiriyah. Only Cpt. Wittnam and Charlie Company had firsthand knowledge of the enemy. Communication with them was poor at best. None of the senior decision makers had spoken with him face to face.

Lieutenant General Conway's overall guidance was clear: Don't enter the town itself—control the route through, and move the RCT convoy through. There must be no more delays. Bailey and Dowdy hadn't worked out a plan. Bailey wanted tanks and LAVs from RCT-1, but the LAVs were gone—they had already driven through the town. Dowdy didn't see how assigning his fourteen tanks to the 2nd Marines changed things, when Task Force Tarawa could provide at least that many. Tarawa had elements on the northern and southern approaches to the city, but there were none inside the city guarding the route that RCT-1 had to take.

A generation of Marines had seen commissions appointed to investigate Marine losses in Beirut, Army losses in Mogadishu, and Air Force losses in Khobar Towers. The American public had become accustomed to war with few casualties. Dowdy faced the dilemma of having to get RCT-1 through Nasiriyah against an enemy of unknown size and capabilities—without suffering high casualties—while Tarawa was still fighting and had suffered high casualties, including some (it was not generally known) caused by friendly fire.

After the others had left, Dowdy discussed the situation with Kelly, who made it clear that Mattis wanted the RCT to move through that night. More artillery fire was not a solution. The layout of the square city blocks bisected by wide side streets lent itself to a line of pickets, dismounted Marines with night-vision goggles, and weapons at the ready for anyone darting out of an alley with an RPG.

After talking with Kelly, Dowdy drove back down the approach road to the garbage dump where all the Amtracs were parked on the shoulder. Ray and I were talking with a few of the battalion commanders when he drove up. When Ray was commanding a regiment, Dowdy had been one of his company commanders, and Ray held him in high regard. Dowdy took Ray off to the side and said he had decided to turn the route inside the city over to battalion 3/1. Task Force Tarawa was supposed to provide the protection and safeguard the passage of the convoy, but Tarawa had shared with him no immediate plan for doing that. The division needed Dowdy to move out now, regardless of Tarawa's timetable. Battalion 3/1 would move into the city and deploy its forty-two Amtracs along Route Moe, together with a company of attached tanks. The battalion commander, Lt. Col. Lew Craparotta, would choose where and how to set up the picket line.

Dowdy borrowed a Humvee and drove off alone to bring up his soft-skinned vehicles, while Lieutenant Colonel Craparotta planned his movement. *[Picture 13]* Three hours later Dowdy returned, and at midnight 3/1 moved into the town, deploying dismounted troops at strong points backed up by tanks. They encountered scattered resistance, which they quickly silenced. Finding bodies of fellow Marines still in burned-out hulks along the route convinced them that this was still a dangerous place. An hour later battalion 1/4 pushed through, while 3/1 stayed in its sentinel positions. The passage was completed without a Marine casualty. As the convoy drove along Route Moe, three batteries of artillery fired volleys of rocket-assisted projectiles, or RAP rounds, into the city. There were no forward observers inside the city blocks, and there were civilian casualties, but RCT-1 was Oscar Mike— on the move.

At about four in the morning on 25 March, however, all traffic through the city stopped amid confusion up and down the convoy, which from end to end could easily spread out over 50 kilometers. At the same time, 2nd LAR reported it was in a firefight ten kilometers north of the city. Radio transmissions reporting firefights or enemy contacts, usually fragmentary and often interrupted, plagued the command and control centers along the convoy. Most reports of enemy contact were too vague and added to anxiety without adding to information.

Before daylight on 25 March RCT-1 had come to a dead halt, with its artillery battalion sitting on the highway halfway through the city and soft-skinned ammunition trucks parked in the middle of Ambush Alley. A medevac was supposedly coming in on the road to evacuate a wounded 1/2 Marine. Poor communication between the 2nd Marines and RCT-1 was still plaguing Dowdy. He knew he needed to move and move fast, but he wasn't sure if one life, or even many lives, of 1/2 Marines were depending on that medevac.

Dozens of Iraqis were gathering on street corners. The Marines were in no mood to tolerate gawkers, not after the word was that Iraqis gathered to shoot Marines. The Marines shouted at them and leveled their rifles, determined that no civilian would approach them. Meanwhile, waiting to get through the city was an endless line of trucks carrying plywood, telephone lines, plows, folding bridges, bulldozers, jackhammers, hydraulic lifts, welding equipment, cranes, and on and on. All the paraphernalia for constructing a small city—for supporting six thousand Marines in a hostile land—was somewhere on that convoy. And none of it was moving.

Ray and I were stopped at an intersection where Colonel Dowdy was talking with Brigadier General Kelly. We were as frustrated with the hold-up as the two active-duty Marines were. Finally, the medevac arrived, and the column began to inch ahead.

As the vehicles drove through the northern end of town, the Marines saw three wrecked Amtracs on the median strip. One trac had been hit and disabled but was largely intact. The other two had been ripped apart, the force of the explosions having torn off the tops and peeled back the sides. The ground was littered with bloody battle dressings, pieces of uniforms, and torn-up individual fighting gear. Several dead Marines were still inside the Amtrac. Lt. Harry Thompson of Lima Company, 3/1, had placed a white cloth over the burned body of a fallen comrade. Each Marine in RCT-1 passing by viewed this gruesome scene, and remembered it.

At two in the afternoon of 25 March, fourteen hours after RCT-1 began to move, the final vehicle passed out of the city of Nasiriyah.

Confusion reigns in the initial battles of all wars. In World War II the campaign in North Africa took months to smooth out. In Vietnam the early battle in the Ia Drang valley was unscrambled and laid out only much later, in Harold G. Moore's *We Were Soldiers Once . . . and Young.* The 1993 ambush in Somalia, made famous in the book and movie *Black Hawk Down,* was confusing and surprising to the two-star general who was on the scene and watching much of it on video. The battle in Nasiriyah had exhibited the same lack of coherent information. The assembled generals could not make an informed decision. Soldiers and Marines could not act as veterans when they had no combat experience to draw upon. In Operation Iraqi Freedom all ranks, from general to private, would make mistakes and become veterans at the same time.

If the stumbling at the start of the battle was not unusual, the speed with which the bad news ricocheted around the world was. The embedded reporters wrote accurate and close-up stories about the change in Marine attitudes, about the shock of losing comrades, about the casualties that heavy weapons inflicted on the civilians. Meanwhile, encouraged by these developments, more fedayeen drove south to join the fight. Discouraged, the military experts in the television studios speculated that more U.S. forces were needed and that the campaign would last for months.

Due to the shock of the American prisoners and casualties at Nasiriyah, they all overlooked the speedy movement up Route 1 of RCT-5 and RCT-7.

3

A Land the Color of Dust

D+5 to D+7

As THE WIND STIRRED UP THE DUST and dirt, the RCT-1 column crawled out of the city limits of An Nasiriyah, twelve hours after beginning its torturous 12-kilometer passage through Ambush Alley. Ray was still riding in the trac with the forward command element, and I was with the security and convoy control group for the main command element. Now that RCT-1 was free of Nasiriyah, it faced a 200-kilometer drive up Route 7 to the city of Al Kut, where it would cross the Tigris for the final drive on Baghdad. Between Nasiriyah and Al Kut lay a half-dozen more towns, all potential ambush sites. For most of the trip the 1st Marines would be bound to a single two-lane hard-top road, hemmed in on both sides by the soft, shifting dirt of drained swamplands that would quickly entrap any heavy vehicle. In front of them were a dozen bridges, any one of which might be blown, so most of the division's heavy tanks were moving with the other two regiments.

Colonel Dowdy's lead element was the 2nd Light Armored Reconnaissance Battalion. The previous day 2nd LAR had sped through Nasiriyah, taking some fire at the northern end and blasting back with the 25mm chain guns on its LAVs. It had taken no casualties and had continued north of the city for over ten kilometers before stopping and "coiling" just off the highway. Just before midnight two white buses came down the highway from the north. The LAVs, with their night-vision optics, identified them as civilian buses and ignored them. A few hundred meters from 2nd LAR's position, the two buses pulled off the road and stopped. The bus doors opened, and men hastily stepped out and disappeared behind the berms lacing both sides of the road. Soon machine-gun and 60mm mortar fire erupted, impacting around the LAVs. The two busloads of Iraqis were firing and maneuvering toward the Marines.

Lt. Col. Eddie Ray, the 2nd LAR battalion commander, was a deco-rated veteran of Desert Storm, having earned the Navy Cross as an LAR company commander. In that conflict he had used the speed and ma-neuverability of the light armored vehicle to defeat Iraqi armor. Now he used the superior firepower and optics of the LAV to chew up the ad-vancing Iraqi infantry. He was surprised, even impressed, by the coordi-nated advance and the tenacity of the Iraqi fighters. Despite every rush being knocked down, the Iraqis persisted in regrouping, standing erect, and running toward the Marines.

On Guadalcanal in 1942 a Japanese regiment had waded splashing and screaming across the Tenaru River into the machine guns of the 1st Marine Division. At the Chosin Reservoir in 1950, 25,000 Chinese had died attacking the 1st Division in human waves. These were battles against fighting men whose bravery Marines of every generation since had admired, while questioning their tactical judgment. Lieutenant Colonel Ray had not expected to see Iraqis display similar foolhardiness or courage; they had not done so in Desert Storm. The engagement was over in less than two hours. All the Iraqi infantry lay dead, their civilian buses ablaze on the side of the road. The 2nd LAR had no casualties but was leery of enemy soldiers who kept running forward even when they saw the red bands of tracers sweeping toward them like a scythe. The 2nd LAR was determined not to be surprised by any "civilian" vehicles again.

* * *

Leaving the outskirts of Nasiriyah, RCT-1 was traveling two vehicles abreast. Other than 2nd LAR, so far only 3/1 had deployed against the enemy. The soft land and the maze of irrigation ditches prevented the battalions from striking out overland in their Amtracs, so the LAVs at the front of the convoy were the first to engage, while those back in line stopped and waited, cursing and imagining what was going on.

The wind was blowing strongly, and the Marines had their dust goggles on. Many had wrapped dirty scarves—medical slings for bruised or broken arms—around their mouths to cut down on the dust, not that the scarves had any practical effect. Most of the men had long since suffered through "the crud," that week-long period when the dust particles first infect the membranes of the lungs, choking off the vocal cords, causing constant coughing and the hacking up of enormous wads of yellow pus. After hacking and running a fever and feeling miserable for several days, the body adjusts to the dirt-filled air. The dust would still find a way through any scarf, but some Marines felt better with a swaddle around the lower face, Arab style, when the wind blew sharply.

Iraq is a land the color of dust. On the afternoon of 25 March the landscape was a dirty orange, lit by a feeble sun that couldn't penetrate the clouds of dirt that blew in eddies and whirled around the highway. The dull russet light seemed to flicker, and the Marines had to peer hard to identify what they were looking at. At times the men could see a row of neat houses with tall walls off the highway; then the wind would pick up and the dust would swirl in. The shatterproof glass windows on the Humvees were pulled up, and the Marines on watch in the Amtracs kept ducking their faces to avoid the dirt blasts driven in by the southerly wind. The dirt smothered and suffused the light in hues of ocher and mustard yellow. Not a living person could be seen in the surreal landscape.

In the middle of the four-lane highway was a wide median strip of gravel and dirt. Just north of a cement sign welcoming visitors to Nasiriyah, the cab of a reddish tractor-trailer truck was slewed across the median, its windshield punctured by dozens of small holes, most of them clustered on the driver's side. So neat and orderly were the holes that the truck could have been an advertising prop for an insurance company, displaying how its brand of safety glass would absorb any punishment. Before dying, the driver had opened the cab door, and now his head dangled near the ground, his feet entangled in the pedals. Several feet behind the truck a mini-car lay on its side. It was a Yugo type made of tin, too dilapidated to be seen on an American highway. Its windows weren't punctured; they were gone, as neatly as if they had been cut with a giant shears. The doors were ajar, and bullets had slammed the driver into the backseat, where he lay curled in a fetal position.

The convoy drove slowly by the wreckage, the Marines stealing sideways glances, their eyes darting away to check buildings for danger, then sliding back for a second look at fresh death. There was no firing, and no sounds except the clashing of gears in the Humvees and the high screeching of the Amtracs.

Col. Joe Dowdy, the commander of RCT-1, had taken advantage of the four-lane portion of the road to push his command group ahead, passing battalion 2/23 to join battalion 1/4 near the front of the column. The 2nd LAR was exhausted after being on the road alone in enemy territory for twenty-four hours and fighting several times. Dowdy had the battalion halt to refuel and rearm while 1/4 took the lead.

RCT-1, which had been put together only recently, consisted of six different battalions. They included artillery, tanks, armored vehicles for reconnaissance, and infantry from bases in southern California, North Carolina, and the Nevada-California border. Also in the convoy were a combat service support element and two bridge companies with large, unwieldy tractor-trailer trucks hauling pontoons and bridging. Some units were reserves who had trained in Arizona, New Mexico, and other western states. Because the battalion, not the regiment, was the training unit for overseas deployments, RCT-1 had never exercised all these battalions together.

The total column exceeded one thousand vehicles, including more than one hundred Amtracs, fifty LAVs, fourteen tanks, and 150 seven-ton trucks, plus dump trucks, armored combat excavators, and enormous flatbeds hauling bulldozers, generators, and water purification systems. There were at least five hundred Humvees of various types, including communications, supply, general utility, and weapons platforms (for .50-caliber machine guns, Mk-19 40mm grenade launchers, and TOW rockets). A self-contained city was on the move on a remote road across a drained swamp, with enemy lurking at every turn.

The essential challenge for RCT-1 was to join ten battalion-sized units together into a cohesive convoy and move them hundreds of kilometers into a battle zone, where they could disperse again as battalions and go into the fight. For the infantry battalions, this arrangement was especially trying. They had to ride as passengers while others made the decisions, and they were not accustomed to long, cramped journeys, interminable delays, and lines of vehicles without end.

Once they were on Route 7, the battalions were expected to stay together. Dowdy rode in his Humvee near the front. Behind the middle of the column his executive officer, Lt. Col. Pete Owen, rode in a C-7 command and control Amtrac. Owen knew that hundreds of vehicles spread out over 70 kilometers of road couldn't be controlled just by talking on the radio. Often the other party wouldn't answer, as the length of the convoy far exceeded the range of the radios they all used. Very quickly Owen became like the trail boss moving a herd of Texas cattle along the Chisholm Trail; he needed to grab a few unlucky but reliable cowboys and order them to ride behind the herd, rounding up the strays and keeping good order back there in the dust.

First Lt. Ty Moore was just about finished with his four years in the Marine Corps and had already accepted a job in civilian life with a software company when Colonel Dowdy persuaded him in February to deploy with RCT-1. Now he had his own Humvee, one .50-caliber machine gun, two radios, three corporals, a stack of maps, and the assignment to drive back and forth between the lead command group and whatever units were behind, carrying out whatever orders came down from an overworked Lieutenant Colonel Owen, all the time ensuring that the convoy was still together and accounted for.

First Lieutenant Moore found himself in a netherland lit by an orange glow, the wind howling, dust swirling outside and inside his Humvee. Smoldering wrecks and dead bodies slid in and out of view amid the buffeting winds—a scene from Dante's hell. The driver, Cpl. Garret Stone, warily eased by the row of Amtracs on his right side. Each Amtrac had a symbol and a unit identification number.

Moore would note the number and refer to the list on his clipboard. "Wrong order. Pull alongside to that Hummer," Moore would say, pointing at a vehicle.

Stone would cautiously accelerate until he was next to the other driver, as Moore signaled out his window. The Humvee would stop, and Cpl. J. Alex Alvirez would hop out, holding up his hand to halt the line of Amtracs. Moore would tell the other driver where his unit was supposed to be in the convoy. If he was ahead of his place in line, he was to wait. If he was behind, he was to move up when there was a break.

It seemed simple, except that there was firing at the front of the column, they were well over a day behind schedule, they couldn't see, and every half-hour one section or another of the convoy would stop for some unknown reason. Back and forth Moore drove, either demanding that a group of Amtracs close it up, or yelling at them to stop and wait their turn. Each time Moore got out, the gunner on the .50-caliber machine gun, Cpl. Chris Madia, climbed down, grabbed his M-16, and hastened out in front of his lieutenant.

"Look at him," Stone would say to Alvirez. "Madia is so gung-ho, always looking for someone to shoot at."

"I'll get my chance!" Madia would yell back. "Some hadji will ding you sitting there behind the wheel, and I'll drop him, and after that I won't have to listen to you anymore."

Gradually the banter petered out. The highway was too grim. With astounding speed the government in Baghdad had learned that the fedayeen had inflicted heavy casualties on the Americans at Nasiriyah. Iraqi reinforcements rushed south down Route 7, making the eight-hour drive in buses to blend in with the civilians. Despite American-supplied leaflets and other warnings not to drive, especially at night, large tour buses, minivans, SUVs, trucks, Mercedes, and twenty-year-old crumbling wrecks were sharing the road heading south. And rumbling north up Route 7 was the war party, led by the war wagons—the Abrams tanks, the LAVs, and the infantry battalions.

A few kilometers north of Nasiriyah, Route 7 narrowed into a two-lane highway, which forced the convoy to slow and converge into a single line. The land was flat, bleak, and scrawny, all livestock hidden away, the scattered mud hovels and cement buildings shuttered. Even the tough mangy dogs that fiercely guarded the impoverished farms were hiding. Moore had to swing out onto the dirt shoulders to scoot around the trucks and Amtracs. Empty trench lines and sandbagged bunkers lined the sides of the road. Here and there were the burnt-out hulls of Russian-made tanks and shattered trucks blown into dozens of charred black pieces.

Moore and his men passed an old white and orange Nissan with its windshield wiper swishing back and forth, the driver lying with his head at an impossible angle, someone slumped over in the passenger seat next to him. A few meters away was a car that seemed to have no damage; its driver was lying on his back several feet away, his arms folded neatly across his chest, the wind ruffling the robe around his bare feet.

"See the hole in his foot? No blood or nothing, just a big hole. That's weird, man. What did that?" Stone said. No one replied, and Stone concentrated on his driving.

They passed a large passenger bus with a dozen bodies strewn about, some crumpled inside, the others having fled several meters before being hammered down. There were a few women; the rest were men in civilian clothes. Along the road other bodies lay several meters from wrecked vehicles. The human body, traumatized and dying, flees from the spot where it has been mortally wounded.

Moore and his men glanced less and less at the shattered vehicles and the still bodies along the side of the road. Instead they concentrated on the line of Amtracs and Humvees, checking the map and the paper with the order of march, Moore talking on the radio, Alvirez in the open turret manning the .50-caliber, Madia in the backseat, M-16 at the ready, popping out whenever the lieutenant stopped to give orders to some errant driver.

By midafternoon the wind had risen to gale force, and the dirt billowed like dirty clouds. When the convoy stalled for twenty minutes, Moore drove forward to join the command group near the head of the convoy. A few 60mm mortars had hit near the road, and Colonel Dowdy had stopped his Humvee to talk with his commanders. The LAVs were farther back in the column, and the tanks had halted with Dowdy.

Seeing a chance to pull ahead, Capt. Jason Frei of 1st Battalion, 11th Marines (Artillery) swung his Humvee around Dowdy and kept going up the road. Lt. Col. Jim Seaton, commanding the artillery battalion, insisted that one firing battery and a counterbattery radar be in position to fire at all times, a procedure called fire capping. The counterbattery radars could detect an incoming artillery round and track it back to its source. The radar was digitally linked to firing batteries, and return fire could be delivered within a few minutes. To prevent possible Iraqi chemical shells from devastating the convoy, Seaton's battery commanders were constantly fighting their way forward in the column, finding firing positions and leapfrogging batteries.

Captain Frei and two trucks were moving alone on the stretch of road behind the advance screen and in front of Dowdy and the main body. Seeing a soft target, fedayeen fired an RPG from a close-in tree line. The rocket struck the right-hand door, failing to detonate but shattering Frei's hand. The trucks stopped, and the Marines piled out, fighting the fedayeen for fifteen minutes before—with reinforcements—driving them off far enough for the ambulance to come up for Frei.

At the same time, Lt. Col. Eddie Ray was trying to push his refueled 2nd LAR past Dowdy's group to put some firepower and longer-range optics at the front of the column. To the right, or east of the command group, was another town, as usual set back more than 100 meters from the highway. Opposite the town was a mixture of Humvees from the command group, LAVs, tanks, and trucks with troops from 2/23.

It would take a little time to untangle the convoy in the rapidly decreasing visibility. Before that happened, though, AK-47 rounds began to zip over the Humvees, seeming to come from two large cement houses enclosed by a sturdy cement wall, 200 meters away across a dirt field. A platoon from 2/23 began to maneuver from the south toward the houses. Other Marines from the command group element dismounted and lay in a skirmish line along the edge of the road, mixing in with squads from other units, facing out toward the two houses, which together formed an impressive-looking fortress. *[Picture 14]*

Marines on the up guns of a few Amtracs began to fire short bursts at the houses. A tank with a plow blade clanked up, its main gun pointing toward the houses. Another tank swung off the road and fired a burst from its .50-caliber at a building to the north. The hammering sound of the heavy machine gun and the keening of ricochets off cement walls incited the line of prone Marines. In seconds dozens of M-16s, 7.62mm machine guns, and 40mm grenade launchers were firing. An AT-4 rocket streaked across the field, and a house caught fire, the wind carrying away the smoke in a straight line. Rounds were snapping over the maneuvering platoon, over the tanks off the road, and over a squad crawling toward the houses.

When the bedlam broke out, I was with First Lieutenant Moore, a few vehicles down from the command group, talking with Sgt. Miles Johnson, who was in charge of the headquarters security platoon. Johnson was tough, with a quick temper, a no-nonsense infantry sergeant who had completed two deployments with infantry battalions and was now assigned to what he considered "rear echelon" duty. He hadn't volunteered for his job. After working a year to be selected, he had been on his way to 1st Force Reconnaissance Company, probably the most physically demanding unit in the Marine Corps. He had been looking forward to doing recon patrols deep behind enemy lines. Instead, at the last minute he had been sent to guard a headquarters staff that was now in danger of shooting fellow Marines.

Screaming at the top of his lungs, Johnson ran several feet out in front of the firing line where all could see him. "Cease fire! Cease fire, you idiots! Those are Marines out there!"

Johnson was so angry, he picked up a rock and threw it at the lead tank. He then snatched off his helmet and pulled it back, taking aim at a gunner on an Amtrac, who hastily threw up his arms to show he had ceased firing. In seconds all that could be heard was the wind. Most of the Marines who had been firing kept their heads down and looked at the dirt in front of them, hoping Johnson would not turn on them. Officers and sergeants followed Johnson's lead and began shouting orders. The tanks backed off, and the platoon out in the field finished closing on the houses, where the troops found no weapons and doused the fire.

Meanwhile, Cmdr. Ken Kelly, a reservist who was an emergency room doctor in civilian life, worked to save Frei's hand, but to no avail. The winds and dust made immediate evacuation by helicopter impossible. Brig. Gen. John Kelly, the assistant division commander, poked his head into the ambulance, startling the medical crew. Kelly had remained in the convoy since Nasiriyah but had kept his distance from the RCT-1 command group. He offered comfort to Captain Frei, who responded by asking after his men and joking about no longer being right-handed. Seeing he could do nothing further, Kelly then left to see what was holding up the column.

To the command group around Dowdy, the erratic firing had been an annoyance, properly handled by a sergeant. Their concern was that the AK-47 bursts and the RPG that had started it all had come from the town of Ash Shatrah to the east, while the 60mm mortars had been fired from the west, where Frei had been attacked. This had the makings of an ambush from both flanks. The weather had wiped out their day and night optics, making it a perfect time to attack the column, which was in disarray.

The wind made the dust so thick, it was impossible to open one's eyes without goggles. [Picture 15] The world consisted of a stinging, howling wind and dust in the ears, mouth, and nostrils and around the rim of the goggles. It was like trying to see underwater in a flashflood.

Two battalion commanders, the regimental executive officer, and the regimental operations officer stood in a semicircle around Dowdy, who was sitting in the passenger seat of the Humvee with his feet on the ground outside. Dowdy was hunched forward, head down against the windblown dirt that was scouring his face. He had pulled his goggles down and was working a tobacco chaw in his mouth, spitting into the dirt at his feet.

His senior commanders had to lean forward, almost touching his face, and shout to make sure Dowdy understood the message. It was unwise to stay put, they said, with the town on their flank. Intelligence reports suggested up to five hundred fedayeen were mixed in among the twenty thousand inhabitants of the town. An attack could be forming up as they spoke.

On the other hand, others argued, the incoming fire had died off. Maybe the dust whipping about and the keening of the wind exaggerated everything. Moving the convoy forward away from the town would take two hours, and it was growing dark and the storm was increasing. Turning around and going back to a more defensible space would be even more difficult. The commanders threw out different ideas, shouting to be heard. Some wanted to stay where they were; others wanted to move. Eventually, the commanders stopped yelling into the wind.

Dowdy wasn't listening. His head had dropped lower, and he wasn't spitting any more tobacco juice. He had momentarily dozed off, the constant strain having drained his body. Darkness was coming, the wind was increasing, the troops were firing at shadows, and the fedayeen might be gathering for an attack.

"I don't believe this," Lieutenant Colonel Ray said as he threw up his hands. "This is not happening."

Ray Smith was standing right there and simply touched Eddie Ray's arm and met his eyes. Lieutenant Colonel Ray quickly controlled his anger and returned to the discussion. To him, the situation wasn't tactically complicated. Throwing up a solid 360-degree defense was an ordinary task that didn't require a lengthy confab. Coordinating a night defense was normally a job for the operations officer. All it required was a little leadership and some sensible coordination. In less than twenty minutes the battalion commanders had agreed on their respective sectors of fire and left to tie in a 360-degree defense. After the others had left, Brigadier General Kelly drove up in the dusk and blowing dirt to talk things over with Colonel Dowdy.

Within an hour the units were unsnarled, and each battalion was placing its vehicles and troops for the night defense. First Lieutenant Moore went to help the doctor with the wounded civilians and to assign a guard roster for the several dozen prisoners taken during the day. I stayed with Sergeant Johnson, who organized the defense for the regimental headquarters. The otherworldly orange glow of the sandstorm had dimmed and flickered out. But the wind was now shrieking, and a man could lean forward at a 45-degree angle and not fall down. So thick was the dust in the air that the earth had become the sky, and each breath filled the mouth with dirt. It was so dark, it made no difference whether your eyes were closed or open, and no night-vision device could penetrate the dust. Even the satellite signals to the GPS receivers were intermittent.

Sergeant Johnson gathered his platoon in the lee of an Amtrac, paired them off, and checked ammo and gear. One Marine had left his rifle in the Amtrac. Johnson ranted and cursed the unfortunate Marine and his ancestry before turning his wrath on the Marine's squad leader. The two stumbled off, hands on each other's shoulders to keep from getting lost, and soon they came back, weapon retrieved. Johnson had found a long line of communications wire, and he tied one end to the Amtrac and walked in a semicircle along the western perimeter, setting in his men at fighting positions. Johnson yelled at his troops to use their compasses and count their steps whenever they moved. The Marines were muttering about fedayeen sneaking unseen and unheard into their positions.

"Butt-stroke them," Johnson said. "Use your E-tool. You're trained in hand-to-hand stuff. Or are you afraid of those fedayeen in their ninja pajamas?"

That did the trick. No member of the platoon would admit to fear in front of Johnson. They scooped out their fighting holes and sat in the stinging dirt, whispering back and forth about how they would hit the hadjis in the balls or break their jaws or snap their necks.

Around midnight above the wind came a low, coughing growl that then grew into a roar, followed by lightning. The thunderstorm lasted an hour, the rain lashing them, hardening into sleet pellets and finally into hail. Then the wind shifted from the south to the west and blew in as icy as winter. Throughout that night of wind, dust, rain, and biting cold, Johnson trooped the line, rotating his men to the cramped shelter of an Amtrac. Each took a turn out of the wind for half an hour, recovering body warmth and then following the communications wire back to their fighting holes.

The troops had seen the ambulance race up and down the convoy several times during the day, carrying Marines wounded in skirmishes. They had heard the bursts of firing from the front, and every unit had a story about stray AK-47 rounds cracking overhead or RPGs whizzing past. They had seen male bodies in green uniforms strewn by the side of the road and prisoners with blank, enduring faces, arms tied behind them. They had seen enough to know that somewhere out in the dust and wind real live men were hunkered in a trench or bunker, sweeping dirt and flies from their dinner of rice and tea, talking about how they would kill Marines.

Johnson and other sergeants hadn't organized their men against an imaginary enemy. Fedayeen were lurking in the towns all right, but no attack or probe of the lines fell upon RCT-1 on Route 7 during that night of storm and hail. Throughout the night I huddled beside an Amtrac, marveling at how I could hear Johnson's voice despite the wind, yelling at his Marines to stay alert.

The worst of the dust storm had passed us by first light on 26 March, although the day broke with sullen clouds and enough wind to keep the dirt whipping and swirling. I continued to ride with First Lieutenant Moore on his appointed rounds up and down the convoy, while Ray drove near the front of the convoy with the command group. While the convoy was forming up, Moore drove back to check on the battalion's first-aid station. Two CH-46s were inbound for the wounded—three Marines who had been hit in different fights the day before, four enemy prisoners near death, and thirteen civilians. The helicopter pilots asked no questions. By the book, only Marines and EPWs—enemy prisoners of war—were to be given anything beyond on-scene emergency care.

Civilians were supposed to be taken by other civilians to civilian hospitals. But Cmdr. Ken Kelly and other doctors throughout the theater persisted in putting seriously wounded civilians on the medevac helicopters whenever there was room. The system knew about it; it was one of those things no one wrote down.

When the helicopters came in, Kelly and Moore yelled that they needed help with the stretchers. Marines climbed out of their Amtracs and Humvees and carried them all—prisoners, civilians, and wounded Marines alike—to the helicopters. Marines who had been fearful and anxious in the dust storm and ready to shoot any approaching vehicle voluntarily helped the wounded the next day.

In addition to the wounded the regiment had about thirty prisoners, miserable and stoic in their flimsy clothes, arms bound behind them. *[Picture 17]* Four injured prisoners hadn't survived the raw, wet night. Corpsmen wearing latex gloves had moved the dead soldiers from the first-aid tent. A bulldozer was waiting to bury them along with a few dozen other Iraqi soldiers killed the day before. Marines had to move the row of bodies from the mud into the bulldozed pit, and they didn't have the necessary latex gloves. It was cold, and the rain and hail had turned the dirt into a goo that cloyed to the treads of the boots and made carrying a body slippery work. The men lifted each body gingerly, hoping nothing fell off that had to be retrieved by hand and thrown away with the rest of the body. Blankets covered the faces of the dead, but sometimes they fell off. There were no volunteers for that job.

The convoy then got under way, with 1st Recon Battalion, in Humvees and fast attack vehicles, moving off to the east to screen against possible armored attack. The dirt desert of the south, with tiny patches of vegetables nurtured by shallow irrigation ditches, had given way to farmlands with palm trees and green paddies. The convoy drove by kilometer after kilometer of empty bunkers topped with fresh sandbags, as though the entire country had conspired to fool Saddam by digging a Potemkin village of extensive defenses that no one had intended to use.

The terrain remained flat and open; even the swamps held scanty undergrowth. The towns offered the best cover for an Iraqi ambush, but RCT-1 now had an organized plan for a battalion to picket each town. Once abreast of a town, the Amtracs would peel off and halt in a line, facing the first row of buildings. Marines would dismount and spread out, ready to shoot anyone who popped out of a side street with an RPG. It was a sound plan. An RPG can shoot accurately at a vehicle from about 100 meters; a Marine can hit an Iraqi holding an RPG at 500 meters.

Lt. Col. John Mayer and his battalion, 1/4, took the first town, where several Amtracs peeled off and stopped without incident. Midway through the town they encountered a cement wall with Saddam's picture, fifty times life size, inlaid in tile. As the sixth Amtrac in the column passed the wall and began to turn in, Cpl. Joseph Smarro, standing guard in back, thought he saw an RPG flash by in front. The rocket was traveling so fast that for a second he thought he had imagined it. But Cpl. Dennis Crossen, standing guard next to him was already firing into the grass. Crossen said that he saw what looked like a ball of flame and a *whoom* of hot air. The rocket, fired from only a few meters away, missed and didn't explode.

The Amtrac stopped, the Marines looking every which way. Rifles snapped to shoulders when a boy, looking no older than fifteen, stepped out from behind the wall, waving a white flag. He looked into Crossen's eyes and seemed to smile—more like a nervous tremble. The range was perhaps ten meters. Four riflemen had lined up on the boy, who had to sense he had no chance. Still, he dropped the flag and reached down into the grass. Crossen thought the boy must have been looking at the RPG the whole time, knowing right where he and his buddies had hidden it. Perhaps there was more than one weapon. Perhaps two or three friends had made a pact and only this boy had stuck to it. Crossen watched as the boy began to pick up the RPG. He never got it to his shoulder.

Newspapers and military spokesmen repeatedly cited the deceit of Iraqis with white flags surrendering and then opening fire. How frequently that happened has not been documented. But against soldiers whose weapons are sighted in, as was the standard U.S. procedure whenever Iraqi soldiers approached with white flags, it was not a sensible tactic to employ.

After killing the boy, the Marines dismounted and spread out, their M-16s swiveling, waiting for the next attack. But nothing happened. For thirty minutes the rest of the convoy rolled by, and there was no more firing. Toward the end, farther into the town, the Marines did see a crowd dragging some people away, and heard screaming. They didn't venture inside the town, though. Once the convoy had passed, the front battalion climbed back into its Amtracs and took up the position of rear guard. Gradually, town by town, it would rotate back toward the head of the convoy.

With each battalion leapfrogging the others, the front or fighting end of the convoy rolled at a steady pace and made more than 40 kilometers for the day, passing through four large towns where the CIA had reports of hundreds of fedayeen. By the end of the day the Marines of RCT-1 thought they understood the pattern: if they saw civilians outdoors and waving all over a town, there probably were no fedayeen there; if they saw no one outdoors, fedayeen could be anywhere; and if they saw only one cluster of people outdoors and waving, fedayeen were probably among them, forcing the civilians to be their shield.

RCT-1 was just clear of the fourth town when First Lieutenant Moore, near the rear, ran into a delay. He had driven past a small white car that had been heavily shot up, lying halfway off the eastern side of the road; its rear end was sticking up in the air, and the driver was hanging halfway out the shattered windshield. The passengers in the backseat had tumbled forward into the driver's seat, a tangle of legs and arms. After hundreds of American vehicles had driven by, someone had gotten out to take a closer look and found a little girl alive. Now Moore was told over the radio to wait for the shock trauma platoon—specialists in keeping Marines stabilized until the medevac helicopters arrived.

The Marines had no set rules for when to fire on an approaching vehicle, or at what distance. Since Nasiriyah, rumors of Iraqi perfidy had flown up and down the column. News snippets from the BBC coming over the few radios of embedded reporters provided the link to officialdom. The troops heard that the generals at CENTCOM headquarters, the secretary of defense, and the president were accusing the Iraqis of suicide bombings. You couldn't trust a single Iraqi.

At four in the morning, an anxious and tired nineteen-year-old in a tank or LAV might have peered through his thermal sight at an approaching car half a mile away and pressed a red button. An orange arc would have streaked out and, quick as a wink, smashed the engine block; the car would have veered into a ditch, the gas tank would explode, and flames would engulf the passengers. In the morning the tank or LAV would have moved on, not checking for the explosives suspected of being in the car. Those who did the shooting didn't want to look.

Marines were taught to clean up after themselves. They carried a shovel with them when they defecated, and they buried the cardboard wrappings from their MREs. The system took care of enemy prisoners of war. But a civilian was the responsibility of the civilian system put in place by Saddam's regime, which wasn't functioning well in the midst of a war. The Marines had no platoon called Grave Diggers, no squeegee squad to splash water over shattered windshields and wash away blood, no fire team to collect body parts. No one had the mission of picking up after civilians.

Still, this time they did pick up. Some Marine climbed down from an Amtrac and got his hands bloody pushing and prodding the bodies in the crumbled car, and he cursed the fear and carelessness of some nineteen-year-old with a chain gun. Someone pried open the doors of the wreck or smashed out the final shards of the windshield, lifted out the little girl, and called for the ambulance.

Dr. Kelly, his ambulance, and several other vehicles pulled up and went to work, while First Lieutenant Moore sat in his Humvee and waited patiently. The others in the line weren't complaining. Marines— trained to smell cordite and hear rounds snapping over their heads as they closed with the enemy—wanted to be rid of the burden of civilian suffering. Civilians were to be protected and moved out of the way, because too many of them didn't have the sense they were born with. They drove down highways at night, knowing American armor was rolling. They shared the road with fedayeen driving in civilian buses and minivans. Civilians didn't belong on a battlefield.

Finally, after fifty minutes, two CH-46s landed on the road. Dr. Kelly, proud that a life had been saved, wanted to tell Moore how busy his platoon had been. Although he was not a surgeon, the doctor had operated on three civilians in the past few days. Moore, however, had a convoy of two hundred delayed vehicles to deal with, so the doctor collected up his staff and drove off.

Moore soon had the tail end of the convoy rolling. As dusk approached, they passed a burning car with two charred bodies by the side of the road and a man on his knees, his arms outstretched from his sides, the left side of his face black, his mouth open in agony or supplication.

"Someone should put that poor bastard out of his misery," Stone said.

No one answered him. Moore listened on the radio. The ambulance and the shock trauma platoon were coming up behind them once again. The corpsmen would take care of the dying man. Moore's Humvee drove on.

A kilometer ahead they came upon four LAVs, two on each side of the road. To the west, a few hundred meters out in a field, four women were fluttering around a man lying on his back, shooing the flies from his face. They were wringing their hands and running to and from their minivan, which had bullet holes in the windshield.

"We have to stay until the corpsmen arrive," a Marine on the LAV explained. He wasn't happy about it. It was obvious his crew had shot up the van and had been told to stay until the wounded received care.

First Lieutenant Moore told them to catch up to their unit. He would wait for the doctor, since it was his responsibility to account for the rear of the convoy. Moore signaled the Amtracs behind him to herringbone off the road. Dark was coming fast, the wind was starting to bite, and he couldn't make it to the regimental rendezvous point, only a few kilometers up the road. The regimental command told him it was safe to stay there, with one in four Marines on watch in night-vision goggles.

A bit later, Brigadier General Kelly drove by. After seeing the burned man on his knees next to the charred bodies, his driver had to pull over for a few minutes to recover. Kelly drove up to the regimental command post, where he took aside some senior commanders. There are civilians shot up on that road, he reproached them. It's daytime. You can see them coming for a half a mile.

"This is lousy," the brigadier general said.

A lieutenant colonel flared up, saying he had to take measures to protect his men.

"Don't go there with me," Kelly shot back, cutting off debate. He had been in the infantry for thirty years and knew the range of every weapon.

In no previous American war had troops feared suicide bombers in cars. The embedded press was not strongly critical of shooting at moving vehicles, because they were at risk too. Despite a hundred rumors, however, actual suicide bombers in Iraq had been few, one for perhaps every ten thousand cars approaching U.S. military vehicles. The balance between shooting the innocent and being blown up by not shooting had yet to be worked out. No one had sorted it out, not the president, not the American public, not the generals, not the troops.

Whenever an aircraft or a cruise missile was described as dropping a thousand pounds of explosives "precisely," Marines laughed. They knew better. They were the ones who agonized over firing five .50-caliber rounds weighing two pounds, because they saw the damage the rounds inflicted. They took note that the cruise missile attacks against Saddam so far meant that more than eight thousand pounds of high explosives had detonated, killing people other than Saddam and his henchmen. Knowing that others inflicted more civilian damage did not absolve them. They had a code. As Major General Mattis had told them, "Treat all others with decency, demonstrating chivalry and soldierly compassion."

While Brigadier General Kelly was at the regimental command post making sure that fire discipline improved, the doctor reached the wounded man in the minivan and the women attending to him. He radioed for an escort to take the injured man and the women to a village next to the regimental lines. A few hours before, the man had been head of his household, driving his mother, wife, and daughter to a safer place. Now he might die in the middle of nowhere, leaving three generations of women stranded among strangers.

First Lieutenant Moore and his men sat shivering in their vehicle, too chilled to sleep. A few hours later a Humvee with headlights on drove slowly by them, a body draped over the hood. Only one other civilian had been wounded back on the road: the man with the burned face kneeling by the charred corpses. Corporal Stone had gotten his wish—the man was now out of his misery, going to a bulldozed grave.

The sun showed itself with the dawn on 27 March, and for the first time in five days the Marines could see more than a few hundred dust-filled meters. Spirits lifted with the sunlight. Lt. Col. Ferrando's recon battalion struck out east to seize the Qual'at Sukkar airfield, while Lt. Col. John Mayer and battalion 1/4 attacked to secure a small town at the intersection of Routes 7 and 17. Route 17 ran west 100 kilometers to Route 1, which the division's other two regiments were following. Once Route 17 was cleared, supplies could be shuttled back and forth.

Lieutenant Colonel Mayer was known as a thinker, fresh off a tour at the Marine Corps Warfighting Lab. Most military laboratories researched high-tech systems; the Marines focused on small-unit tactics and techniques. Mayer had had enough of the tactic of running Amtracs along the outskirts of towns and performing picket duty. That allowed a convoy to pass by, but it required a large security force, wore the troops down, and had no lasting effect. The fedayeen remained secure inside the town, and the picket battalion had to return every time a convoy wanted to pass.

Mayer decided on a new approach. His Amtracs would drive up Route 7 as though they intended to bypass the town, then would suddenly turn off the highway, wheel up to the edge of town, and stop. The infantry would sweep through the town and out the other side. Pickets would remain outside the town; the Marines would go through on foot.

On the map, tiny black squares symbolized a typical town of maybe five or ten thousand people, two kilometers on a side. Based on a study of the map, the town appeared to have a row of commercial storefronts—squat, sturdy cement buildings that gave good cover to snipers.

Mayer told us there was room on an Amtrac, so Ray and I climbed on board. The Amtracs formed up on the highway and rolled north. The cloverleaf at the intersection was elevated, so as they drove up, they were looking down on the town. They saw that it wasn't a town at all. It had no cement commercial buildings, no advertisements for tires or used cars or refrigerators, no small restaurants or wood and canvas stalls, no people trading tomatoes and rice and smelly meat. It had nothing except a few two-story government buildings with closed gates and a mile of mud huts.

It looked like an East African village. The huts were square, solid, squat dwellings with crude cuts for doorways, without glass, metal, or wood. *[Picture 16]* They could have been constructed a thousand years before. The single anomaly was the thin strands of electric wires running to the flat roofs of many huts. A major power line ran a few hundred meters away, and a small transformer station stood at the intersection of the highways. Somehow the villagers had tapped into the line.

This was a typical Shiite village of the south, persecuted and ignored by Saddam's regime. As long as the villagers didn't revolt—and the massacres of 1991 had taught them not to do so—Saddam left them dirt poor. Literally, as poor as dirt.

As the Marines climbed out of their Amtracs at the edge of the town, an RPG flew out from among the huts, as if to signal the Marines not to come any closer. The up gun on one Amtrac responded by throwing a few 40mm rounds into the walled compound where the rocketeer had been sighted. Then the Amtracs and two tanks sat back and waited. In a few seconds, the tanks could have smashed that town as easily as breaking a pane of glass. The village was defenseless. It had been idiocy to fire an RPG. Lieutenant Colonel Mayer had only to nod his head, and no RPG would ever be fired at any convoy from that village, ever again.

Instead Mayer sent in a sniper and his spotter to climb the roof of one of the government buildings, which were considerably taller than the huts. When nothing further happened, two rifle companies—250 riflemen—spread out and advanced by bounds, one fire team covering another. But there was no firing. The sniper excitedly yelled down from the roof that a red car was heading west out of town. A tanker radioed Lieutenant Colonel Mayer saying he could take out the car.

Mayer weighed whether it was a resident fleeing in panic, his family stuffed into the backseat, or fedayeen with RPGs. Mayer had seen enough wrong calls on Route 7. "Let the car go," he radioed to the tank.

The Marines were now walking and running through the town. The houses were constructed of chicken wire, long wooden poles, and a dozen layers of mud, with a little plaster or cement stirred in. Open slits served as windows, and the floors were the same mud as the yards and streets. Faded green or black flags drooped outside a few of the huts. From top to bottom the entire town was mud from the recent rain— but in another day the town would bake under its normal coating of dust. Open pits served as bathrooms and garbage disposal areas. If the inhabitants had had any money, there was nothing they could purchase inside their own town. Wealth seemed to be measured by goats, chickens, and skinny cows.

The Marines tried kicking open a few doors—and almost broke their legs or shoulders. Stout doors seemed to make for good neighbors. Pounding on the doors with rifle butts eventually brought out several men in robes, who scurried to the mud house of the village chief, who emerged followed by several women. He was tall and thin, with a gray scraggly beard and black and white caftan. He walked slowly with a cane, forcing the Marines to adjust to his gait. Lieutenant Colonel Mayer had with him the human exploitation team (HET), two Marines who had studied Arabic, and two Iraqi Americans. The old man walked slowly through each block, mulling over the simplest of queries from the HET, solemnly answering in long sentences as some villagers gathered to watch.

Yes, there had been a few young men here. They were not from the village. They had left. A red car? There were many red cars. He didn't know of one in particular. Are there any other cars in town? No, the chief knew of no other cars in town.

The chief was going to reveal nothing. Others had tried before to remove Saddam Hussein and they had failed. He would wait and see. This was the Americans' fight. His Shiite village would stay out of it.

The CIA had believed that the Shiite communities along Route 7 would revolt, making the passage of RCT-1 much easier. That didn't happen. Predicting the actions of people who had been dominated for a quarter-century by a murderous tyrant was at best guesswork. Saddam had killed so many for so long that no rebellion occurred in the south. The few BBC broadcasts we heard—and the BBC was not exactly sympathetic with Operation Iraqi Freedom—suggested that a small number of Baath Party loyalists and fedayeen were shouting, slapping, threatening, and bullying many soldiers and militia into staying and fighting. Whether that was true or whether some in the military fought willingly, the end result was that RCT-1 fought a series of skirmishes along Route 7 both during and after the dust storm. It was not an easy passage.

4

Screeching to a Halt

D+7, D+8

With RCT-1 at intersection of Routes 7 and 17,
200 kilometers south of Baghdad
27 March

BY NOON ON 27 MARCH, RCT-1 had pulled itself together on Route 7 and had secured both its flanks. The division's recon battalion had pushed east ten kilometers and set up outposts at an abandoned airfield, which the British Air Assault Brigade intended to use as a resupply base. The sun was shining, the mud was drying, and Colonel Dowdy had had several hours of sleep. With the situation under control, Brigadier General Kelly climbed into a Huey for the 140-kilometer flight west to Route 1, where the division headquarters and the two other regiments were located. Ray and I went with him.

It was a fine day for flying, and the division's prospects looked equally fine. The indecision and tragic mistakes at Nasiriyah and the confused drive up Route 7 in the screaming dust storm were in the past. The division had reached the midway point in its march to Baghdad. Major General Mattis wasn't looking back; he was focused on the road before him, which he intended to seize promptly.

During the past week, while moving 250 kilometers north, the Blue Diamond's three regimental combat teams had engaged the enemy more than a dozen times, and the enemy's strategy had become clear. Had the Iraqi army fought cohesively, using its tanks as pillboxes sheltered behind thick earthen berms, the advance would have been slow. Although Iraqi soldiers had dug in their tanks with engines turned off to avoid detection by thermal imagery, they had not fought from them. U.S. aircraft were swooping down on any convoys found on the move. In the first week thousands of tanks and armored vehicles had been destroyed, most of them inactive and empty.

Saddam's best troops, the touted Republican Guard divisions, lay farther north, closer to Baghdad but not inside it. Fighting inside the rubble of a city, such as happened at Stalingrad in 1942, required an army and a population that were united against the invader. But Saddam feared that his army and the population would unite against him. He kept only a Praetorian Guard of five thousand superloyalists inside the city, while the Republican Guard divisions were stationed astride the major highways outside.

The key to the regime's survival was to extend the war. If Republican Guard divisions were to slow the American advance northward while fedayeen guerrillas attacked the convoys in the south, and if the Americans were to encircle Baghdad instead of attacking the city, then the United Nations might insist on a cease-fire as the war dragged on.

Indeed, the fedayeen in Nasiriyah had stopped RCT-1 for two days. But the division's main logistics route was Route 1, which bypassed Nasiriyah and for long stretches ran through desert, far from towns and fedayeen. Mattis held the fedayeen in scorn because they hid behind women and children, holding them in their houses while they fired. "They lack manhood," he said. "They're as worthless an example of men as we've ever fought." The regimental commanders viewed them as a nuisance. From the viewpoint of both the logistics and the mission of the division, the fedayeen were yesterday's newspaper.

Saddam Hussein still had a firm grip inside Baghdad, however, and his regime was communicating with its fighting forces. Whether that changed anything was another matter. Back in the United States, *Saturday Night Live* ran skits featuring the Iraqi minister of information. Watching comedy that centered on the ironies of human nature, the American public laughed and cheered for a portly man in an absurd beret who popped up on TV to proclaim victory, denying the bombing heard in the background. That some command and control still persisted between Baghdad and its forces in the field was embarrassing to advocates of the "shock and awe" bombing campaign waged nightly against the city, but it didn't hinder Mattis and his three regimental combat teams. Saddam could give all the orders he wanted—that wouldn't stop them.

Ray and I joined the assistant division commander, Brig. Gen. John Kelly, in the back of his Huey. We were flying due west along Route 17, which connects Route 7 with Route 1. Flying was much better than being jammed in a noisy Amtrac stuffed with ammunition and fellow Marines, alternately sitting bored on hard metal benches or standing up to peer into the dust that whipped over the top of the trac. Pilots had the life; flying was the way to go, especially on a day when the wind was down and the air was clear of dirt. The magic of flight brings to the fore the insouciance within the martial spirit, that nonsensical part of us that says we have total control over our lives, even when we have nothing but air beneath us. Pilots tend to be a cocky lot. It doesn't behoove them to think too deeply about what they are doing. Helicopter pilots don't have parachutes.

At the grand height of 150 feet, we passed over a few minibuses and small trucks on the wide, paved road below, and the drivers waved at the helicopter above them. The land ran flat to the horizon, a vast expanse of green fields irrigated by the Saddam Canal, which flowed straight south inside its concrete walls. The farms were widely scattered, giving the impression of tranquillity and a comfortable living for those who owned large tracts of the well-watered land. In the few villages along the eastern portion of Route 17, people stopped to look up and wave vigorously.

Once we were across the Saddam Canal and about 70 kilometers east of Route 1, the reception changed. Children on farms ran inside as our chopper approached, and few drivers on the road looked up or waved. We passed over a large town, Al Budayr, with two-story houses and lines of shops. There we heard a sound like a car backfiring several times, and the door gunner cocked his head. Again, a sharp *bang, bang, bang.*

"Ground fire, ground fire . . . there's one under you . . . nine o'clock, nine o'clock . . ." Kelly, Ray, and I were all yelling over the intercom, cutting one another off, telling the crew what they already knew.

In a courtyard below a young man in a light red shirt crouched behind a .50-caliber machine gun, so close I could see his features. He looked about fifteen. The helicopter tilted hard left, and the ground rushed by at a crazy angle; the door gunner fired, his .50-caliber sounding like a giant hammer. With impressive quickness, the Iraqi youth abandoned his gun station and darted around the corner of the house, the Huey gunner's rounds kicking dirt behind him. Several children were standing in the center of the courtyard gawking, and the door gunner ceased firing when the man disappeared. The Huey pulled out of its turn, throwing us back into our seats. Ray was looking out to the right, opposite where I had seen the .50-caliber.

"You got another one! Three o'clock, three o'clock!" Ray yelled.

Before the pilots could react, the Huey was by the gun emplacement and pulling away. We looked back at an unmanned twin-barreled 23mm antiaircraft gun set up in the street near an adjoining house. The children were standing stock-still, looking up—not waving, just looking up. The door gunner again checked his fire, and death passed them by.

"He had us," Ray said, referring to the youth who had dodged around the house. "He had us cold. All he had to do was lead us a little bit. It takes skill to miss something this big right in front of you. Thank God for piss-poor shooters."

"I thought you guys were used to that," Kelly said.

"Next time I'm walking," I said.

In his notebook Kelly wrote down the name, Al Budayr. Before convoys could run between Routes 1 and 7, that town, we all agreed, needed a bit of tidying up.

At 1st Marine Division Headquarters on Route 1
Ten kilometers south of the intersection with Route 17
Afternoon of 27 March

The division headquarters consisted of a few dozen tents staked in the dust 100 meters off Route 1. Kelly went off to a briefing, leaving his pack in the dirt inside a small tent. Everyone in the division, from major general to private, had slept in the dirt every night since they had arrived in theater eighty days before.

The command center consisted of four large tents whose openings overlapped to seal in light at night and air-conditioning. Outside, a set of generators on trailers chugged away with surprisingly little noise. One end of the main tent contained a large electronic map displaying the locations of those vehicles equipped with the Army's Blue Force Tracker, a system that uses satellite communications and the GPS network to track and report on the location of friendly units. Facing the screen, a dozen officers sat in a U-shape on folding metal chairs, receiving updates on unit positions and activities and coordinating and tracking indirect fire support. Rickety tables held their laptops, phones, and radios. The commander of the battle watch sat behind the group.

Much of what the staff learned came in via voice and could not be easily transferred to the digital display. So to the right of the electronic map there was a large board with dozens of small-scale military topographic maps taped together. The maps were overlaid with acetate, on which were drawn red and blue unit symbols. Despite all the electronic inputs, the paper map was the heart of the visual displays, because it could be updated quickly on the basis of locations provided via radio or cell phone. A small screen off to one corner carried a TV news feed from CNN or Fox, depending on the last person to switch channels.

Wing tents extended off from the central area on three sides, filled with banks of radios, laptops, and telephones. One wing housed the intelligence section, where screens displayed live feeds from whichever unmanned aerial vehicle was flying at the moment. Another wing was filled with planners and liaison officers from other units. A third wing housed the division's logisticians, with their own map, status boards, radios, and laptops.

In adjunct tents were the communicators, who also had occasional access to the unclassified net to send and receive personal e-mail, and the Direct Air Support Center. The DASC, unique to a Marine division, was manned by Marine and Navy aviators who understood on a minute-to-minute basis the operations of the ground units. They were receiving requests for air support by radio from other aviators stationed with each battalion, and they were in contact with the air control and allocation centers at higher headquarters.

The map board in the operations section showed that RCT-1 was now at the intersection of Routes 7 and 17. Near the western end of Route 17, where it joins Route 1, RCT-7 was in position to move. RCT-5 was already 40 kilometers farther north on Route 1 at Hantush and had seized what was called "the elbow," the intersection of Routes 1 and 27. All three regiments were ready for the next move and were aligned according to the division's plan, 220 kilometers north of the Kuwaiti border.

To move continuously so far forward had taken months of preparation and a radical paring down of the division's normal supplies. With full concurrence from Lieutenant General Conway before the war, Major General Mattis had stripped down the weight and baggage of the division. In 2001, as a brigadier general, Mattis had taken a reinforced battalion 800 kilometers from ships in the Indian Ocean to a dirt airstrip in Afghanistan—no small feat. The logistics officer from that extended operation was now supervising the division's logistics. Lt. Col. Chuck Broadmeadow, with an unflappable air and infectious smile, seemed junior for his responsibilities, but he had proven himself time and again.

Throughout January Broadmeadow had worked with Mattis on a list of specifics to pare down the weight and supplies of the division. Mattis put out an order called LOG LITE, for "lightened logistics." The items affected were large and small: limiting food to two MREs a day, placing a gypsy rack of thirty gallons of water or fuel on thousands of Humvees, placing fuel bladders on the tanks, seizing Iraqi commercial fuel depots, shutting down all engines at any break longer than ten minutes, and the like. Every Marine was warned that the campaign would be one continuous sprint. They shouldn't expect to stop. In his last letter to his troops, Mattis spelled it out: "We will move swiftly and aggressively."

So far the division had done that. Convoys were moving steadily up Route 1 from the south, and the division was about to add to its supplies by landing C-130 aircraft with five-thousand-gallon fuel bladders directly on Route 1, just north of the elbow. The Afghanistan operation had shown the versatility of the C-130 workhorse, and Mattis had confidence that air would deliver the final fuel component essential to keep the drive moving.

Utilizing both land and air for refueling was essential because the division had entered a critical stage of the campaign. The RCTs were now within what was called the Red Zone, the area so close to Baghdad that the intelligence community considered Saddam's use of chemicals, in a last, desperate effort to slow down or halt the advance, to be highly likely. The division did not want to stop inside the Red Zone and offer a sitting target.

Adding to the need for speed was the scheme of maneuver, now that the elbow had been taken. Above the elbow and the Hantush Highway airstrip (the highway itself was the landing strip), Route 1 became Route 8 and continued straight north into Baghdad. Because it was the shortest and widest route to the capital city, it was heavily defended. The Iraqi spy and intelligence net was surprisingly good, not least due to cell phones. To all Iraqis watching and reporting, RCT-5 appeared to be charging straight up Route 1 to Baghdad. That, however, was a ruse. Having seized the elbow, RCT-5 would take over the Iraqi airfield there and turn off Route 1 onto another hardtop road that ran east to the Tigris River. On the other side of the Tigris River was another highway leading into eastern Baghdad, and it had fewer defenders. Thus V Corps would enter Baghdad from the west, and I MEF from the east.

The Tigris crossing, however, was defended by the Baghdad Division of the Republican Guard, stationed at Al Kut. In order to deceive that division, the plan called for RCT-1 to continue up Route 7 as if determined to attack Al Kut from the south. Thus threatened, the Baghdad Division would remain fixed in place, while RCT-5 and RCT-7 crossed the Tigris farther to the north. If done quickly, two regiments would be across the Tigris and closing on Baghdad by a surprise route before the Iraqis could retarget their chemical systems. So by dusk on 27 March, while Kelly was being briefed at division headquarters, RCT-5 had pulled together its three battalions 60 kilometers to the north and was aligning them for the sprint east to the Tigris.

At precisely that moment, however, instead of attacking forward, RCT-5 had to move backward. The division was ordered to halt. The Coalition Forces Land Component Commander (CFLCC) had ordered a "pause"—a halt—in the ground attack of both V Corps and the MEF toward Baghdad. Given that order, RCT-5 could not remain at the elbow. If it did, the Iraqis might sense the deception that the division had planned and reinforce at the Tigris. To avoid giving away the division's strategy, RCT-5 turned its battalions around on Route 1 and drove back 38 kilometers, south down Route 1 to rejoin RCT-7 and the division's forward command post. For the troops of the 1st Marine Division on 27 March, Alice stepped through the looking glass.

By coincidence, Ray and I were at division headquarters when the news broke. Had we been out with the troops, we wouldn't have believed what was happening. To the RCTs, continued movement to Baghdad had just now seemed within their grasp. While the Army was attacking from the west, they were closing in from the east. As the MEF commander said, they were on schedule or ahead of schedule. The Marines in the RCTs, however, were isolated from external news reports. They received no TV pictures, scant radio broadcasts, and only a few old scraps of newspapers. But since Ray and I were at division headquarters we had a chance to read press reports about the fighting over the past week. The cumulative effect of these stories—not seen at the RCT level—painted a grim picture and conveyed the tone of a ground offensive that was struggling and that could not continue without a pause.

Practically all reporters carried satellite phones that connected to their laptops, and they were filing within hours after each fight. They mixed easily with the troops and had access to the commanders. Those reporters Ray and I occasionally observed at different units were straightforward and businesslike in demeanor. They were reporting accurately, with specific locations, dates, and events, on what they were actually seeing. And it was quite a story to read. By the end of the first week of the war, the frontline stories in hundreds of newspapers and on network and cable TV news shows indicated that U.S. forces were having trouble throughout southern Iraq, caused by a quasi-guerrilla campaign to wear them down, and that they were running out of supplies.

On Sunday, 23 March, the debacle at Nasiriyah had left six Americans captured, more than twenty dead, and scores wounded. The news stories focused solely on the supposed ferocity of the fedayeen, because it was not known then that some of the casualties were caused by friendly fire. What really grabbed people's attention was the captured Americans, especially the later stories about executions and the convoluted saga of Pfc. Jessica Lynch. On Monday, as the press reported, thirty-four Army Apache attack helicopters were shot up and repulsed while attacking the Medina Republican Guard Division. That was a major setback. At the same time Iraqi defenders at Najaf were forcing V Corps into a hard fight to subdue and bypass the city. On Tuesday the record-class dust storm had swept over the battlefield, slowing all movement and providing grist for a spate of dramatic news accounts. As we witnessed with RCT-1 in its halting and confusing movement through Nasiriyah and up Route 7, the combination of wind, dust, rain, cold, darkness, casualties, and incoming bullets had unsettled commanders facing their first battles. By Wednesday the 3rd Infantry Division, having expended much fuel and ammunition and having hungry soldiers, had paused for resupply. Lt. Gen. William S. Wallace, commanding V Corps, said that the planners had not anticipated the "bizarre" behavior of Iraqi fighters, while weather and overextended supply lines would likely lead to a longer war.

Not since the Tet Offensive in Vietnam, thirty-five years earlier, had the press reported such a sudden apparent reversal of fortunes befalling an American army in the field. Like a dust storm spiraling into a tornado, a confluence of setbacks had whirled within one week into a public maelstrom. The press sensed that the confidence of some top generals seemed shaken and that the timetable of war was on the verge of being radically altered. This sense of setback was abetted by what Vice President Dick Cheney called "the generals embedded in the TV studios," the large number of distinguished retired generals whose expert advice on television was that the armed forces should pause until more reinforcements could move forward from Kuwait. On 27 March, as the Blue Diamond was beginning its move to the Tigris, President Bush was visiting U.S. Central Command Headquarters in Florida. After a top secret briefing he told the press that "the path we are taking is not easy, and it may be long." The president later said that in the south "the fighters were a lot fiercer than we thought," with many reinforcements coming from the northern part of Iraq. Central Command had obviously briefed the president that the difficulties in southern Iraq had affected the timeline for advancing.

In the field in Iraq, different perspectives and different agendas were fueling contradictory views about whether a pause was needed. Since it is shipwrecks that make the news, the 1st Marine Division wasn't in the news. Indeed, the reporters embedded with the RCTs were careful not to report their remarkable progress up Route 1. They too were surprised by the pause. Each embedded reporter lived inside a battalion and saw the world through the eyes of that battalion.

At the higher levels the picture looked different. The four-star combatant commander in the Iraqi theater was General Franks. The key three-star general officers reporting to him were the land, air, and sea commanders. The land commander was the CFLCC, who determined the overall land strategy to be carried out by the Army's V Corps and by I MEF. I MEF included 25,000 British soldiers, who were the major "coalition" force.

After the dust storm, the loss of the helicopters, and the extended battle around Najaf, the CFLCC staff understood that V Corps needed to stop for fuel, ammunition, water, and food. That required time. In addition, two Army brigades were to be positioned in the south, to guard the rear against fedayeen attacks. That positioning too required time. Halting the ground attack to the north thus made sense for V Corps.

I MEF was a different story. Lieutenant General Conway had had no request from the 1st Marine Division to stop to resupply. Its regiments needed and expected no pause. Indeed, RCT-5 had been about to attack to the Tigris.

The CFLCC had designated V Corps as the Main Effort, making the Marines the Supporting Effort, receiving a lower priority for resources. To the Marines, that decision had not been a major matter. The Marines had adequate forces for the march on Baghdad—and Baghdad, not service pride, was the objective. Besides, on a personal level the Marines were rooting for the 3rd Infantry Division (which was the heart of V Corps), commanded by a tough, crusty general named Maj. Gen. Buford C. Blount III. The Marines admired and liked Blount. Before the war in a press briefing a reporter paraphrased him as saying that his division would be the first into Baghdad. That night in the 1st Marine Division's chow line, the troops joked that the Army was welcome to be first in, as long as the Marines were the first to leave.

But now that V Corps had to stop, the Main Effort could fall to I MEF, and the 1st Marine Division could continue the attack. Alternatively, I MEF could agree to a mutual halt. That way V Corps and I MEF would stay on parallel tracks, with V Corps remaining the Main Effort—thereby relieving everyone of the headache of rewriting and coordinating a mountain of plans. Although the 1st Marine Division would be stopped, Task Force Tarawa and the British could continue to clean up the towns in the south.

Technically, the I MEF commander could have resisted the pause. The 1st Marine Division did not need to halt for supplies, and it had momentum. But the needs of others had to be considered, and I MEF was the supporting attack. Lieutenant General Conway informed CFLCC that he would halt the 1st Marine Division. Late on the afternoon of 27 March, the MEF officially informed the 1st Marine Division that it was to pause. That same day at Central Command Headquarters President Bush obliquely referred to the pause by saying that the path to Baghdad might be long. That night at the headquarters of the Blue Diamond, no one knew how long the pause would be.

The next morning, Ray and I were still at division headquarters, trying to hitch a ride to a battalion. Earlier that morning Conway and Mattis had talked things over with the CFLCC. Mattis then called together his regimental commanders and emphasized that they would soon be back to the original attack plan. [Picture 19] The pause was supposed to be brief, lasting only seventy-two to ninety-six hours. It had been in effect in V Corps for the past day or so. That time frame suggested the Blue Diamond would be rolling again by, say, Sunday, 30 March.

While waiting to move forward, the division intended to tidy up its convoy routes—fedayeen groups had been reported moving south to set up in towns and to target supply convoys. So during the pause each RCT was to conduct reconnaissance in force operations on its flanks. Route 17 was to be cleared between Routes 1 and 7, giving supply convoys the option of bypassing the southern portion of Route 7 near Nasiriyah.

After the briefing at division Col. Steven Hummer, commander of RCT-7, offered Ray and me a ride back to his command tent. He had something he thought would help us.

Hummer was known as a careful planner, a reserved man who understood he was both battle leader and father figure. He was proud to have on his staff two Marines whom he had saved from less-than-honorable discharges. One was a private first class who had tested positive for drugs—a sure and fast way out of the Corps. Before discharging him, Hummer met with the parents and came away convinced it was they who deserved punishment. Hummer offered the private strict probationary terms instead of a discharge, and things had worked out. The private was now a Humvee driver, Hummer said, "working his ass off and happy, far from his dysfunctional parents."

Also on his staff was a lance corporal who had threatened suicide while the regiment was in California. His mother had asked for his discharge in order to place him in a hospital. After consulting the division's psychiatrist, Hummer refused and assigned him to a staff section under a demanding and determined gunnery sergeant. The mother wrote to her friend, a senator, and Hummer seemed headed for trouble. The Marine, however, firmly told the congressional investigators that he did not want a discharge. His buddies were shipping out for Iraq, and he was going with them. The gunnery sergeant said he had performed exceptionally since the campaign had begun.

Hummer led us over to a bunch of Humvees parked near the 7th Marines ops tent. Sitting there was a new yellow SUV, looking as out of place as a soccer player on a football field. On D-Day Hummer's regiment had captured an Iraqi general and his sturdy four-wheel-drive Nissan Pathfinder. The Marines had kept the SUV, but finding unleaded gas had become a distraction, and the SUV was not needed. Hummer said the word was that Ray and I were hitchhiking around the battlefield in Amtracs. We could take the SUV, he said, but we would have to hunt for our own gas. Ray said we'd get out and push it if we had to—it would beat bouncing around inside an Amtrac.

We called the SUV our Yellow Submarine since, like the Beatles, we lived in it twenty-four hours a day. Throughout the entire campaign it performed superbly, navigating 1,200 kilometers of desert and battle-scarred highways without a single breakdown.

With our transportation arranged, Hummer suggested we join the battalion he was sending the next day to clear Route 17. We agreed it would be nice to introduce a tank to the .50-caliber that had tried to shoot down the Huey we had flown in; Ray had stored the coordinates in his GPS receiver.

Hummer had a well-trained set of battalion commanders and prided himself on matching combat missions with their respective strong points. To take the Crown Jewel on D-Day—the key pumping station in the oil fields—he had selected Lieutenant Colonel Conlin and battalion 1/7. Now the mission of RCT-7 was to sweep Route 17 speedily and aggressively. That mission, Hummer decided, suited the style of Lt. Col. Brian P. "Base Plate" McCoy and battalion 3/4.

5

The Afak Drill

D+8, D+9

With battalion 3/4 in operations along Route 17
28–29 March

THE SON OF AN ARMY COLONEL, McCoy was a big man who loved being up front with his troops. He had a boyish zest for the field, not uncommon among the infantry. When he was a young mortar platoon commander, the company gunnery sergeant had called him "Base Plate." This was a play on his initials, B.P., referring to the large metal disk upon which a mortar is set for firing, because McCoy chose to carry it on long marches.

McCoy had not yet seen a firefight that he did not want to participate in. Whether the instinct sprang from his genes or from his personality was irrelevant to Colonel Hummer. What was relevant was McCoy's penchant for getting into the thick of a fight, which he had demonstrated on D-Day by trying to disable a tank with a grenade that bounced back, almost disabling him, and prompting his sergeant major to say, "Best not get killed by an unmanned tank, sir."

On the evening of 28 March, McCoy gathered his company commanders and asked us for any lessons from RCT-1 that would help in his sweep through Route 17. We explained how 3/1 had set a line of pickets inside Ambush Alley, that 2/23 had done the same after the dust storm farther on, and finally how 1/4 had dismounted and swept through a Shiite village rather than stand off and pound it with tank fire. We hadn't seen one instance of fedayeen interlocking fires and very little grazing fire. They typically shot high, and if you went after them, they tended to run.

McCoy then drew a few quick sketches on a white board to show how his companies were to attack in the morning. *[Picture 18]* The old-fashioned white board was prized by every battalion commander. The regimental staffs had a modest capability to use laptops and print out paper copies of frag orders—succinct "fragmentary orders" that modified larger orders already printed and issued. McCoy had a few laptops but not the means to print and xerox copies. His main tool was the map overlaid with acetate for crayon markings and the white board. For McCoy and the other battalion commanders, the world of high tech was something they watched in movies and chuckled about.

Similarly, intelligence about the enemy gathered by high-tech means such as satellites showing individual soldiers on a night raid had not yet reached down to the battalion level. Twenty kilometers back at Colonel Hummer's operations tent, Gunnery Sgt. Scott Stalker, the regimental intelligence chief, did have a monitor that showed video from a Pioneer UAV flying over Route 17. The experts at interpreting the images, however, were 100 kilometers in the rear with the Marine air wing. Thanks to satellite communications, Stalker had talked with them and had sent on to McCoy the coordinates of the locations of three technicals as well as several antiaircraft and artillery pieces. That was the extent of the hard intelligence that the battalion received about Route 17. In towns with thousands of people walking about, the overhead intelligence systems couldn't distinguish which were fedayeen. No radio intercepts indicated that any organized military units were waiting in set positions in any of the towns. Any additional intelligence the battalion would generate for itself.

Knowing that, McCoy kept his order for clearing Route 17 simple. Tanks would lead; CAAT teams in Humvees with machine guns and TOW rockets would screen the flanks; and two mounted companies would follow the tanks and dismount at each town, using a version of the picket technique first developed by 3/1 at Nasiriyah.

In the first week of fighting battalion 3/4 hadn't lost anyone. Now on 29 March, preparing in the dark to leave for Route 17, one of its Humvees slipped sideways and toppled into a large irrigation ditch, trapping the driver, Lance Cpl. William White. Men frantically attached a cable to a tank, but it was too late. Lance Corporal White had drowned.

A few days earlier the executive officer of battalion 3/5, Maj. Kevin G. Nave, and Gunnery Sgt. Russell Cederburg had pulled into their defensive lines, exhausted after leading forward hundreds of Marines over the previous several days. Both fell asleep on the ground, and their driver took the Humvee to refuel. In the dark another vehicle ran over them, killing Nave and crippling Cederburg. Just prior to the war an Army corporal had been uncoupling an Amtrac on the road near Major General Mattis's tent. The trac slipped, and she lost a leg. Word of each death rippled swiftly from battalion to battalion. Such tragedies were called accidents, but they were casualties of war, as fatal as if caused by a bullet. In the encampments every tracked vehicle required an escort, night or day, walking in front. Still, it was like sharing a camp with elephants: you tried to sleep where they weren't likely to walk. Every Marine lying on the ground in the dark kept an ear cocked for the screech and rumble of approaching treads.

McCoy asked for a moment of silence to honor Lance Corporal White. Then it was time to mount up.

By seven in the morning McCoy's battalion 3/4 was formed up in a long column. McCoy drove in a Humvee that did not have a machine gun mounted on top. Where he went, he didn't want to call attention to himself. Everyone dressed alike in Kevlar helmets, sapi vests—*sapi* meaning "small-arms protective inserts," armored plates that were supposed to stop a bullet—and the chemical-protective camouflage jackets and overalls called MOPP gear. McCoy had three bands of dull red tape wrapped around his left arm, his company commanders had two, and so on. At a glance, the Marines knew who their leaders were.

By eight, the column was approaching the first town, which was scarcely larger than a village. The troops wasted no time in dismounting from the Amtracs and banging on the doors of the houses nearest the road. In this village there was ready compliance—the residents eagerly volunteered that two carloads of Baath officials had driven away as soon as the first tank appeared.

The riflemen loaded back up, and the armed column rolled on. The next town was quite a bit larger, with row on row of cement houses and thick walls. Two Cobra gunships circling overhead radioed that three technicals were escaping south. The helicopters lost sight of them in a palm grove, and the column stopped while a CAAT unit searched.

Instead of just guarding the side of the road, Sgt. Maj. Dave Howell grabbed two Marines and entered a two-story school building near the road. Several minutes later he returned with three rifles and a French-made high-frequency military radio. In the abandoned observation post on the second floor, he said, rice and warm tea were still on the table.

A thickly muscled, no-nonsense man, Howell had served two tours in force recon and insisted that even the headquarters troops practice immediate action drills and keep the top plates of their Amtracs clear to return fire. This meant stripping off layers of gear that the headquarters troops and officers had squirreled away. Some troops, particularly Amtrac drivers, thought he was being too hard-nosed. But as his attention to detail and his tactical knowledge began to pay dividends, the troops began to watch and imitate him.

An hour later and 20 kilometers farther east the battalion rolled through Afak, a city of over 100,000, with canals crossing the highway at its western and eastern ends. Radio intercepts and agent reports indicated the fedayeen had reinforced the city. While the engineers up front tested to make sure the eastern bridge could support the seventy-ton tanks, the convoy stopped in the center of the city, which was a monochromatic dull brown. The streets, houses, and even the sky were a dirty tan that sopped up and obliterated any other color.

The troops, trusting no Iraqi after a week of rumors, RPGs, and stray

AK-47 shots, pushed back the curious crowds that quickly formed. The HET—human exploitation team—interpreters began asking questions over the blare of the loudspeakers mounted on their Humvee. In singsong tones the same Arabic phrases blared over and over: "*We have come to remove the evil regime of Saddam. That is our only purpose. We will remove the regime, then we are going to leave.*" The civilian men jostled one another, pointing up the highway, saying the fedayeen had fled as the tanks approached. This was a Coptic Christian community, they said, eager to be rid of Saddam. The Baath chief had left three days ago. After that the technicians at the power plant had not shown up for work, and without electric power, there was no clean or running water.

A sniper team trotted down a dirt street among the mustard-ocher cinder-block houses encased in sturdy cement walls and banged on the metal door of a two-story house. Two men in *dishdashas* and smiles opened the door, and the Marines ran to the roof, from where they scanned the streets and alleys. Seeing nothing suspicious, they walked down cement stairs without a banister, each step a cinder block seeming to be pasted to the next by only a little cement. They passed a sparse kitchen with a propane tank, a sink, and a fluorescent light with bare wires. The bathroom was a hole in the floor, without a shower or a washstand. The living room held a charcoal stove with a teapot, several cushions, two chairs, and a threadbare rug. On the unpainted walls were taped several pictures of Christ, cut from magazines. The walls and floor were cold to the touch. The house, like all around it, was built to retain coolness in the humid heat of the summer. Off the hallway was an alcove stuffed to the ceiling with neatly folded rugs. Were the inhabitants merchants? No, the rugs were for the twenty children and women who slept there. It was very cold at night. There was no television or telephone, and no radio or toys were in sight.

The engineers decided the bridge was safe to cross, but AK-47 fire was now coming from the north, inside the city. The convoy had been stalled for forty minutes, and some fedayeen had worked up the nerve to attack. McCoy ordered Kilo Company to envelop the block holding the snipers. The lead company, Bravo, held in place on the road, while Kilo, with its attached tank platoon, swung in from the west.

Each tank had its name painted on the gun barrel. The forward air controller (FAC) was in *Two Times,* a tank commanded by Sgt. David Sutherland. The FAC called in helicopters or fixed-wing air support for the tank company. To be up front when needed, usually the FAC rode in one of the tanks, temporarily assigned the duties of a tank crew member.

The Abrams tank had a crew of four: a driver, loader, gunner, and tank commander. The FAC, Captain Delpitro, was the loader, taking his orders from Sergeant Sutherland, who allowed that loading was a simple job, probably within the skill level of a pilot.

In Vietnam corporals on recon patrols had called in air support. Since then regulations had gradually tightened until only officers who were pilots were permitted to call them in. Most Marines in the ground combat arms considered this requirement to be overly restrictive—a dispute far above Delpitro's rank. As the FAC, he had two chances to engage—by directing air strikes on targets or by loading the tank guns.

Roaring in from the flank, the tanks startled a group of fedayeen who had been hiding behind buildings, looking to the south. They darted across the open streets, thinking the tanks were too far away to see them clearly, or that they could sprint across before the rounds could reach them. But whatever their frightened thoughts, the tanks picked them up in their optical sights and fired bursts from their coaxial machine guns. The tanks didn't have to close to apply accurate fire. The straight, wide dirt roads allowed them to fire from several hundred meters away, and their computers corrected for range, lead, temperature, wind, munitions temperature, and barometric pressure. The tanks knocked down the fedayeen one or two at a time as they ran across open spots. Delpitro's tank, *Two Times,* killed one soldier with a .50-caliber at 1,400 meters. In the next hour *Two Times* accounted for eight more.

The long-distance accuracy of the tanks miffed the Marine riflemen, who ran forward in their helmets and flak vests carrying ammo and water, sweating and covered with dust, hoping for just one clean shot, hearing the *bang bang* of the .50s. *[Picture 22]* Time and again they would arrive at an intersection and find a body or two. All they could do was collect the weapons and RPGs, to be disposed of under the tank treads. The bodies were ignored.

McCoy loved using this enveloping tactic. Major General Mattis continuously preached that Marines should set up a large base of fire and envelop with a smaller maneuver team of riflemen. But McCoy was convinced he had stumbled on a variant that worked even better: yes, put down an impressive base of fire, but then envelop with tanks as well as riflemen. The fedayeen were poor shots with the RPGs; they lacked cohesion among their ranks; they hid from armor, waiting for softer targets. And the Abrams tank was a brute that shrugged off RPGs and most other rockets—unless hit in the small opening of the engine compartment in the rear. But to get off a shot there, the fedayeen had to slip around the riflemen running to keep up with the tank on both flanks— riflemen who were praying that someone with an RPG would wait around long enough for them to get off a burst with their M-16s.

McCoy was so pleased with the results of the tank-heavy envelopment that he dubbed it the Afak Drill. From that one-sided engagement on he routinely called for a repeat of the drill whenever the terrain permitted. The riflemen dubbed the tactic the Oh Fuck Drill. They didn't mind sweating and checking the flanks, but they hated it when the tankers took all the shots.

By midafternoon the column had reached the outskirts of Al Budayr, the city where we had taken fire in a Huey two days earlier with Brigadier General Kelly. Regimental intelligence had identified Budayr as the site of the Baath Party provincial headquarters and had marked its exact coordinates on the road into town. [Picture 20] A CAAT team ahead of the main body had been observing the Baath building for fifteen minutes and said it was deserted. Regimental command radioed that the experts watching the video from a Pioneer UAV could see no armor or fixed defenses set up along the streets. McCoy, unimpressed by the fedayeen tactics in the prior towns, told Bravo Company tanks to turn south at the headquarters and roll into the middle of town.

No Marine unit had yet gone directly into the heart of a city. The book and the movie *Black Hawk Down* had had a profound effect on the Army and Marine Corps. Many officers automatically associated the phrase "city fighting" with images of twisting roads, burning tires, screaming mobs, men firing from rooftops, and American soldiers trapped in the streets, unable to turn their vehicles around.

Now, Marine Amtracs were driving down streets too narrow for them to turn around. McCoy was confident he had both surprise and firepower on his side—the fedayeen would be caught off balance and disorganized. The houses on both sides of the narrow street were shuttered, the gates on the walls closed and locked. The tanks, Amtracs, and Humvees passed through the first intersection, then the second. Not a shot was fired.

Al Budayr was a step up from the other cities that battalion 3/4 had seen along Route 17, with paved side streets and two-story buildings with balconies. Every house had electric and telephone lines. The few people outdoors took one look at the rumbling tanks and scampered indoors.

McCoy stopped in the city square, which was dominated by a huge poster of Saddam. An open-air market—rows of flimsy wooden stalls with canvas awnings—filled the eastern side of the square, while to the west was a line of two-story cement buildings. A few old wooden tables and several dirty white benches sat outside one shop with a locked grille front. A dozen older men were sitting and smoking, as if waiting for the shop to open for their afternoon tea or coffee. They didn't flee as the Amtracs stopped and as the Marines ran down the side streets. The interpreters walked up to them, and the men pointed toward a walled courtyard they said was the police station.

Tracs and tanks now had covering positions facing down each alleyway and cross street. More than a hundred Marines in squads and platoons were searching, spreading out from the square. Soon people ventured out and gathered opposite the courtyard wall. Men shouted and tugged at the interpreters, each telling a story to urge the Marines to attack the station. One man claimed his brother, who had run away from the army, was a prisoner in the jail. *[Picture 25]* Others said they too had relatives inside the police station.

McCoy didn't hesitate. "Let's take it down," he said.

A squad of Marines rushed toward the door in the courtyard, and Sergeant Major Howell yelled at them about booby traps. The engineers rushed up and slapped a C-4 explosive charge against the wall. The riflemen immediately pulled back to the safety of the side of the shop with the locked grille, where they crouched waiting for the detonation, curious to see if the engineers had used too much explosive. A knot of Iraqi men in their twenties and thirties stood behind the Marines and peeked over their shoulders.

The charge blew a four-foot hole in the wall, and the Marines went in through the dust. *[Picture 24]* There was no firing—the police had fled. About twenty prisoners were released, and as the Marines walked out through the far side of the courtyard, Iraqi men swarmed in the other side, either to greet the released prisoners or to loot.

Inside the courtyard were schoolrooms with dust on the desks and crayon drawings showing the flag of Kuwait below that of Iraq, symbolizing Kuwait as a province of Iraq. *[Picture 23]* The police offices were neat, Spartan, and functional, with glass cabinets holding stacks of looseleaf notebooks filled with Arabic writing. Black-and-white photos of men, and a few women, were pasted in many of the pages. Photocopies of a smiling, malevolent Saddam adorned the walls of every room. The crowd said about 150 Baath officials and special police had begun leaving three days ago, the last rushing out of town in the past hour. Everyone in town had heard the Marines were coming.

The Marines searching block by block eventually rounded up a dozen men in green uniforms, some very young, some crying, others trembling. They had heard very bad things about American Marines, the interpreters explained. They were only militia who did not want to fight. They did not know if the Baathists would return a few days after the Americans left.

A tank crew a few kilometers away guarding the eastern approach reported a strange episode to McCoy. From a range of 650 meters the tank crew had been watching a street with several shops open for business. Walking in the midst of the crowd of civilians were four men with AK-47s. The machine-gunner had aimed through the day optical scope and killed one of them with a single 7.62mm shot. The crowd had scattered for a few minutes, then re-formed, dragged the body off the street, and continued about their business. Some had even waved at the tank. Eventually the remaining three armed men emerged and stood gesturing at the ground where their comrade had been shot. The machinegunner shot and killed another one. Again the crowd scattered, then came back and dragged the body away and resumed their business, waving at the tank. The last two armed men did not reappear.

McCoy asked the American Iraqis what was going on. The interpreters shook their heads. Many Iraqis, they said, were simple people, with not much knowledge of the world; they thought Americans could come here and just shoot bad guys like the fedayeen. The interpreters meant that the townspeople were naïve about the nature of war and were so in awe of American technology that they believed the Marines could reach out and kill one person in their midst without harming any of the others. They wanted Saddam gone but felt powerless to get rid of him themselves. So when the Americans killed a fedayeen, they waved. The Marines had been careful and this time had taken good shots. The next time, however, the burst could easily be longer and not so carefully aimed. The people in that crowd hadn't understood that war is a sledgehammer, not a scalpel.

While the main group of Marines were concentrating on the police station, Sergeant Major Howell had searched the local school and, true to the fedayeen pattern, had found a cache of weapons and RPGs. Saddam had equipped the country well for street fighting, if anyone had wanted to fight for him. McCoy agreed that Howell could blow up the cache. In what was becoming an evening event in many battalions, the Marines piled together captured weapons and explosives for a big blast. The Amtracs pulled back, and Howell lit the fuse. Just then a band of joyous citizens came running forward, waving good-bye.

Howell gestured angrily at them, pantomiming an explosion, and the townspeople backed off just in time. The explosion was sharp and powerful and a large cloud of dust rose, but no rockets cooked off and went whizzing through the air in unpredictable directions.

At the outskirts of the town, Bravo Company had found a large fuel de-pot. As part of the LOG LITE regimen, each battalion carried a test kit to determine whether local Iraqi fuel was safe to use. The results here proved positive, and the vehicles lined up to refuel. The march had exceeded 70 kilometers, and each tank had burned two hundred gallons that day. The vehicles in the column took in several thousand gallons of fuel.

During the day battalion 3/4 had pushed through four towns with a combined population of over 200,000 people. According to numerous interviews with the local people, the Baath and fedayeen had indeed had a considerable presence, but they had fled. The Marines had fought only four minor engagements, resulting in fewer than thirty fedayeen killed and about as many taken prisoner, most of them militia. Contrary to what retired military commentators in the United States had predicted, the fedayeen attacks in the south had not portended stiffening resistance in the north. McCoy had struck aggressively with his Afak Drill along Route 17, and resistance had wilted, demonstrating that convoys could resupply the RCTs without diverting ever more frontline units to highway protection.

The townspeople had pointed out the police station but had offered no more information than that. Had fedayeen been hiding in nearby buildings as we talked with the crowd, the interpreters were certain the people would have informed on them—the people were not supporting Saddam's regime. But the situation was not as it had been in Eastern Europe, where the people toppled the Communist regime. As one interpreter explained to us, "We have a saying among the Shiites: if we see Saddam's body lying dead in the street, we must stay away for three days until the gas escapes from the body. Only then do we know the devil is gone." Too often in the past Saddam had survived and come back to torture and murder those who opposed him. He was like the devil; he couldn't be killed.

The vast majority of the people of Iraq welcomed the arrival of the American forces. It was up to those forces, however, to finish the job by seizing Baghdad.

6

The Non-Pause Pause

D+10

With battalion 3/4 on Route 17
30 March

As usual, the day began at 4:30 a.m. with the "stand-to" alert, everyone awake and in a fighting position in case of an attack at first light, when a tired unit is apt to be asleep. An hour later we had morning coffee with a chipper Lieutenant Colonel McCoy on a crisp, sunny dawn. A resupply convoy for Colonel Dowdy's RCT-1 had passed by during the night, escorted by vehicles from battalion 3/4. Not a shot had been fired. Whatever fedayeen elements remained on Route 17, they were not coming out even during the night to fire an RPG at one of the hundreds of soft-skinned vehicles that passed by. They were hiding from the Marines instead of challenging them.

McCoy had had his normal four hours of sleep, and the deepening fatigue showed on his face—but it did not dampen his spirits. He believed that the pause, which had begun near Najaf on 25 March, and for the Blue Diamond on 27 March, had run its course. When he flew back to regiment for a commanders' conference, he expected to receive a frag order to continue the march on Baghdad. Refueled and resupplied, RCT-1 was parked and waiting along Route 7. On Route 1, meanwhile,

RCT-5 and RCT-7 were in position. All three regiments had taken on fuel, were rested and good to go.

Three hours later McCoy hopped out of the Huey. He wasn't smiling. In careful, neutral terms he told his company commanders that the anticipated end of the pause had not occurred—the division was told it could not advance. His orders were to bring his supply vehicles, which he had left with the regimental combat train, up to his current position. The battalion was instructed to patrol in the vicinity of Al Budayr until further notice.

The other battalions of RCT-7 would be doing the same thing in Afak and the other towns along Route 17. Meanwhile, patrols around Al Budayr would keep the battalion busy and not expend too much fuel. But since the Baath officials and fedayeen had fled the area, it would not be an exciting combat mission. The information that trickled down to us was that the staff of the Coalition Forces Land Component Command (CFLCC) had indicated that the pause might last up to twenty-one days—into the second week of April. An embedded reporter with battalion 3/4 told us and the 3/4 command staff that he had heard on the BBC that the pause would be eighteen days.

In Desert Storm in 1991 Gen. Norman Schwarzkopf believed he knew enough about land combat both to be in charge of the overall war and to act as the CFLCC, giving direction to the Corps commanders, Army and Marine. In Operation Iraqi Freedom in 2003 Gen. Tommy Franks appointed a separate CFLCC commander, Lt. Gen. David McKiernan overseeing the operations of the Army's V Corps, commanded by Lt. Gen. William Wallace, and I MEF, commanded by Lieutenant General Conway. V Corps had been established in Kuwait in mid-February as a last-minute adjustment after Turkey balked at allowing the U.S. Army to move through and attack Iraq from the north.

V Corps, as the Main Effort to the west, was executing a left hook at Baghdad, moving across hard desert, where the population was concentrated in a few cities. The 1st Marine Division, as the Supporting Effort, was advancing on one main highway (Route 1) and one secondary (Route 7), amid spongy fields and numerous irrigation ditches that Iraqi engineers had dug after draining the marshlands between the Euphrates and Tigris Rivers. The 1st Marine Division was relying on speed and maneuver to get to Baghdad, leaving many enemy divisions in its rear.

Now the division was stuck in one place, and the troops in battalion 3/4 were not happy with the news that the pause would continue. Eating dust all day and searching for a second time the same towns with scant hope of enemy contact did not appeal to them. They had become infected with rolling down the road. They all knew the key turnoff points and constantly asked how many kilometers to Baghdad.

When the embedded journalist listening on his shortwave radio picked up the BBC report of an eighteen-day pause, wild rumors began circulating in the battalion. Some said the Marines were going to move out regardless of what anyone said. Others said high-frequency radio intercepts had picked up non-Arab voices from the towns farther north, so the division was getting set for a heavy fight, maybe against North Koreans. Or perhaps Saddam was dead and a mass surrender was being negotiated. The perennial joke was dragged out: Jennifer Lopez had dropped dead, the rest of the world had stopped, the war halted to mourn J-Lo's passing.

While the troops were speculating and waiting, Ray and I hitched a ride back to RCT-7 to retrieve our yellow SUV. We didn't want to be stranded for weeks out on Route 17 with no means of moving around. The executive officer of 3/4 was organizing the supply train and had a spot for us in the queue of vehicles when we arrived back on Route 1. He said it would be several hours before he moved out, so we spent the time talking with various staff officers, trying to understand what was going on. From the regiment up, laptops were connected to the Sipernet, a classified internet with multiple chatrooms. One effect of this communication link was that, while commanders were talking via video links, the staffs were exchanging views and providing alerts about what they believed their commanders had decided. Some at the CFLCC level were claiming the pause wasn't really a pause because special ops were going on to the north and air was pounding away at the Iraqi divisions. Distinguishing between the air campaign and the division's halted ground campaign struck some at the RCT as a rhetorical dodge.

The division's partner and alter ego was the 3rd Marine Air Wing, with sixteen thousand sailors and Marines, almost as large in personnel as the 1st Marine Division. The air wing had flying daily 130 fixed-wing attack aircraft—F-18s and vertical-takeoff AV-8Bs—and sixty Cobra attack helicopters. All were equipped with heat-detecting infrared radar and anti-armor weapons. To reduce the ammunition supply burden by ground routes, the division was relying on the air wing as its first line of artillery. To argue that a pause in the ground offensive toward Baghdad was not a pause in the overall operational offensive sounded convoluted to the division. Aircraft were not going to occupy Baghdad.

While we waited, we learned some history about ongoing differences of opinion. Before the war the CFLCC and V Corps had seen wisdom in a lengthy pause for resupply when the troops were about halfway to Baghdad. McKiernan and Wallace, personal friends who had gone to Army schools together, had moved up the ranks in the same system and, as Wallace observed, were "both products of the same institution." I MEF had disagreed with the proposal to pause. There was a service tinge to the differing perspectives based on how they packaged their logistical support. The Marines were accustomed to barebones expeditions, and Mattis through LOG LITE had further stripped down the division.

After the CFLCC ordered the pause, the concern of both I MEF and the Blue Diamond was its open-ended nature. Logisticians, like economists, never have enough data to reach a conclusion. The pause, if determined by logistical requirements, would stretch on. Similarly, searching each town looking for fedayeen would play into Saddam's strategy of stretching out the duration of the combat. Faced with a longer pause I MEF and the division were searching for compelling arguments that it was time to roll.

The CFLCC staff, I MEF, and the division agreed there was a Red Zone encircling Baghdad where the Iraqis were likely to employ chemical weapons as a desperation measure. The division had been inside that zone for four days without moving its main units. There had been incoming artillery each day, indicating that the Iraqis knew where the units were. The RCTs were a sitting target in the desert, where they had access to no water for decontamination if hit with chemicals. On 29 March the division requested permission to advance to the Tigris in order to be in a position to wash the chemicals off the vehicles, even as the operational pause continued.

The request made clear that the division was capable of immediate forward movement and wanted to move. If ordered not to move, its vulnerability to chemical attack increased with every day, with no source of water to mitigate the resulting casualties. In 1993, after the Blackhawk helicopters had been shot down and eighteen soldiers were killed in Somalia, an investigation revealed that Secretary of Defense Les Aspin had refused an earlier request for tanks to be sent to Somalia as a backup force. Aspin lost his job. No one wants to take responsibility for leaving troops exposed when a logical alternative is put forward. The division had put forward a powerful reason to allow it to move.

Word of this back-and-forth among the higher-ups did not trickle down through the regiment to the battalions right away. All Ray and I knew on 30 March was that 3/4 was being pulled back and forth. In the morning the battalion was to rejoin the regiment; at midday it was to bring its supply train to Route 17 for an indefinite stay; in the evening it was again to rejoin the regiment. All we knew at the battalion level was that I MEF was in serious discussions with the CFLCC and that a change in the pause was anticipated.

Inevitably, an operational pause with an ambiguous and shifting end date attracted the attention of the White House. It was only a question of when that would happen. The process for giving orders to the military was not complicated. While General Franks might be at his U.S. headquarters in Tampa or at his field headquarters in Qatar or elsewhere, that made no difference. Through televideo, he attended every White House meeting to which he was invited.

There had always been two overlapping power centers; Washingon and the field. During Desert Storm in 1991 Gen. Colin Powell, then chairman of the Joint Chiefs, had been both a Washington and a battle-field player because General Schwarzkopf was too volatile to be left un-attended. He was given to temper tantrums—even generals were reluctant to deliver bad news to him. In 2003 General Meyers as chair-man had no such need to closely oversee General Franks, who was ad-mired for his common sense and his down-to-earth, approachable manner. Numerous leaks to the press indicated that before the war Secretary Rumsfeld, leaving no doubt about what he wanted, had sat with Franks as an equal in shaping the battlefield plan and the resources. But once the shooting began, Rumsfeld focused on shaping policy in the Washington power arena, while Franks ran the war. Like Eisenhower, Franks had the capacity to accommodate the inputs of others in order to achieve the overall military objective.

Civilian political appointees, including the Secretary of Defense, were informed about developments on the battlefield by a strict, formal system. They did not have access, through the computers in their offices, to reports from the battlefield to Central Command; nor could they pick up a phone and talk to just any general. Officials in Washington received their key information about the battlefield from General Franks and from General Meyers. The J-3 Operations Division of the Joint Staff, which worked for General Meyers, kept in touch with the theater on a twenty-four-hour basis. So Meyers and Franks stayed on the same page in terms of information flowing in to them and out to their civilian bosses.

Traditionally, military officers have deflected civilian political appointees who try to involve themselves in operational matters. While "jointness" was sacred in the Pentagon—it refers to the military services working together—it did not include civilians. Within the civilian Office of the Secretary of Defense—Rumsfeld's staff—there were many military officers with de facto policy responsibilities. Within the Joint Staff serving the chairman of the Joint Chiefs, there were fewer civilians, relegated to more technical jobs. On policy matters the information flow between military and civilian was a two-way street, but on operational matters, it was more a one-way street.

The nadir in civilian-operational information had come at the end of the Vietnam War. In one case a Navy enlisted man on Dr. Henry Kissinger's staff was accused of delivering sensitive documents to the office of the Chairman of the Joint Chiefs, Adm. Thomas Moorer. When confronted with this accusation, far from being apologetic, the admiral fired back that civilians were meddling in military operations and strongly suggested he personally distrusted many of them. In another case, when an American freighter called the *Mayaguez* was seized by Cambodia, President Gerald Ford personally instructed American pilots how they were to attack, and when he believed his tactical instruction had not been carried out literally, he became incensed.

Since then civilian-military relations had improved. But institutionally the military preferred to keep civilian officials, including those in the Pentagon, at arm's length on matters operational. The military information system was designed to work accordingly. Civilians were told what they needed to know to make sound policy, but not about disagreements among subordinate commands. Regarding operational matters, the military was like a watchmaker who tells the buyer: *I'll deliver to you a sound watch that runs on time. Don't tell me how to make it—that's my job.* So Washington civilian officials understood there was a pause; the length and reasons for the pause were more ambiguous.

The officials in Washington were reading nothing ambiguous about the war, however, in the headlines of the national press, which served as the informal window onto the battlefield. For a week, from the point of view of the administration, the major stories had been harsh and disturbing. On 23 March scores of soldiers and Marines had been killed or wounded, taken prisoner, or gone missing in Nasiriyah. On 24 March an Apache attack helicopter was shot down and the two pilots captured, while thirty-three others were ambushed and riddled with bullets. Gen. Barry R. McCaffrey, who had commanded an Army division in Desert Storm, went on television to criticize Rumsfeld, quickly followed by several other distinguished retired Army generals who asserted that more divisions were needed. For years, Rumsfeld had been arguing that the Army needed to lighten its equipment. Now the retired generals struck back, saying the Iraqi campaign was in jeopardy because the Army lacked sufficient heavy forces to move forward while having to protect an ever-lengthening supply line.

With hundreds of press reporters filing stories, the cumulative effect was a swiftly growing perception that the war could last for months. On 25 March, the 3rd Infantry Division fought a major engagement, an effort reported as "having distracted significant parts" of the division, now "alarmingly low on water, and in danger of running short of food." Asked if the war was likely to last much longer than some planners had forecast, Lieutenant General Wallace was quoted as saying that "it's beginning to look that way." Changed circumstances, he said, in terms of logistics and enemy resistance, would lead to modifications in the U.S. approach. Lieutenant General Conway was quoted as saying I MEF was "on time or even ahead of schedule," but his view was not prominently mentioned. Instead, the *Washington Post* cited "top Army officers" as saying the war might last well into the summer. The national newspapers were reporting that the campaign had been seriously set back.

In the course of a few days the CFLCC's operational decision to pause had become a major policy matter in Washington. Many Muslims, Arabs, and even many Europeans had opposed the violent removal of Saddam's regime from the outset and were strident in their objections. Any sign of weakness or hesitation by the American military would be met with glee and would undercut international respect for the United States, with long-term political, economic, and foreign policy consequences. The spectacle of the American military bogged down in the desert would endure long after the seizure of Baghdad.

President Bush had confronted the same type of situation in his opening war on terrorists. The bombing in Afghanistan had begun over a month after the attacks on the World Trade Center and the Pentagon on 11 September 2001. At first, the U.S. bombing did not appear to be affecting the Taliban regime in Afghanistan, and the press reported misgivings within the U.S. military. On 26 October 2001, President Bush called a meeting of his "war cabinet" and went around the room, asking each principal either to reaffirm his belief in the strategy or to express his concerns openly. The message was clear: If you wanted to stay on the Bush team, you didn't waver. General Franks had been in that meeting.

On Saturday, 29 March 2003, President Bush met at Camp David with his advisers, including General Franks via televideo. At issue was whether the principals still agreed with the strategy of sustaining a ground offensive to seize Baghdad. In the field, the CFLCC had some commanders who wanted to pause, but Conway and Mattis had asked to move forward.

After the Camp David meeting an administration official said that the president had urged that the push to Baghdad continue while Army reinforcements flowed in. The meeting concluded on a sharp note. The *Washington Post* reported that the meeting reminded dissenters what the commander-in-chief wanted. Needless to say, no active-duty general officer chose to be in the ranks of the dissenters.

"There is no pause," an administration official said.

When he first ordered the operational pause, the CFLCC erred not only in shifting the main effort to securing the supply lines in the south but also in not setting a firm end point to the pause. Instead, the CFLCC staff entertained options of extending the pause over a longer term. The president put a stop to that. The Camp David meeting reversed the CFLCC's priorities: U.S. forces were to push on to Baghdad rather than secure their supply lines and consolidate their positions in the south. The 24 March repulse of the assault by the Apache attack helicopters was a significant victory for the Iraqi regular army and forced an adjustment of the battle plan of V Corps. But even if the Iraqis could repeat their success against massing attack helicopters, that would not affect the fixed-wing aircraft, artillery, and Abrams tanks that were the mainstays of Blue Diamond's firepower. In contrast to the threat to the attack helicopters, the guerrilla attacks on the supply convoys were an impediment but not a show-stopper for the properly prepared.

LOG LITE had ensured that the 1st Marine Division was prepared to continue the attack. That General Franks had planned a campaign with two main forces—and so had hedged against a setback to either one—showed why the White House had confidence in his military sense.

By the evening of the twenty-ninth the pause had been ended by the Camp David meeting, but the news took some time to reach the lead battalions. On the thirtieth, after several hours of listening to rumors from radio and chatrooms, Ray and I climbed into our SUV and followed the supply vehicles of 3/4 to join up with Lieutenant Colonel McCoy. We had gone only a few kilometers when the convoy halted. Go back to your original position, the vehicle drivers were told. McCoy and the rifle companies are coming back in.

As abruptly and mysteriously as it had begun, the pause-that-was-not-a-pause had ended. The division was back on the attack. We stood by the vehicles while the troops joked about the push-pull of the different orders throughout the day; first they were going one way, then they were going "no-ways," now the battalion was coming back to where it had been days before. We had been at the end of the convoy; now Ray and I found ourselves in the lead vehicle, advancing to the rear perhaps, but still at the head of the line. It was dark now, but with our trusty commercial GPS we drove back to the exact spot we had left earlier in the day. The convoy overshot our position by a few hundred feet and Ray kidded the battalion executive officer about the superiority of our commercial GPS.

McCoy lost no time passing the word that things were looking up. Colonel Hummer, who usually had a calm, deliberate manner, was excited. McCoy sensed that the regimental commander had another interesting mission for 3/4.

The troops were happy that the RCT was rolling again. Ultimately, they wanted to sleep, take a shower, get out of the dust, and get out of the Amtracs. They joked that the road to "Southern Cal," home of the division, lay through Baghdad. Ray and I shared that sentiment. No one in the battalion I talked to wanted to sit around in the dust any longer. It was time to get on up the road.

With battalion 3/4 at the intersection of Routes 1 and 17
31 March

On 31 March, RCT-5 attacked north up Route 1 to secure Hantush highway airstrip, where the regiment had been on 27 March when the pause was officially declared. The RCT had then pulled back, lest the Iraqis discover that the regiment intended to head east from Hantush rather than continue north up Route 1. Now RCT-5 was going back up the same 38 kilometers of road, and sure enough, the Iraqis had set in a series of defenses. Overcoming them would require maneuver and tank fire and, in some instances, the deployment of infantry. Retaking Hantush, defended on the northwest by an armored company, would be an all-day affair for RCT-5.

Once the last of RCT-5 had left the intersection of Routes 1 and 17, we drove up to the cloverleaf with battalion 3/4. Each RCT had about a thousand vehicles in its convoy train, and with the delays due to the fighting at the head of the column, it was dark before the battalion had topped off with fuel and coiled for the night of 31 March.

No battalion ever seemed to have time to set up before dark. Each of the eighteen battalions of the Blue Diamond, spread over a thousand square kilometers, followed the same nightly ritual. Earlier in the week the nights, with no moon and with a sky filled with dirt, had been as black as a tomb. Now a sliver of moon and a sky of stars provided more than enough light. Back in Kuwait, Major General Mattis had forbidden all lights outside, but the Marines could perform any task in the dark. Each Amtrac and each platoon knew its appointed place in the circles of vehicles, machine-gun pits, and sentry posts. While the squad leaders assigned the watch shifts and the troops dug fighting holes, the officers and staff NCOs gathered to plan the next day's operation.

A tent was attached to the rear of Lieutenant Colonel McCoy's command Amtrac, a rare bit of extra space. The company commanders stood or sat on the cleaner end of wooden ammo boxes with labels like "S-4's Pooper." Hummer had assigned 3/4 quite a task. A few kilometers west of the cloverleaf was the city of Ad Diwaniyah, a formidable complex of concrete houses, apartment buildings, and factories, with a maze of paved streets and a population of several hundred thousand. The city was reputed to be the command headquarters and stronghold of the fedayeen; groups were routinely bused from there south to Nasiriyah and other towns.

On 23 March during the dust storm the Iraqis had ventured from Diwaniyah to engage RCT-5 along Route 1. Battalion 3/5 outflanked them, leaving no escape route and cutting them down. During the four days when RCT-5 had been held up in the vicinity of the cloverleaf, both 3/5 and 2/5 had had more fights and skirmishes with Iraqi forces in the vicinity. Intelligence indicated there was probably a commando brigade in the city, as well as a fedayeen stronghold. In addition a huge ammunition storage facility had been discovered between Route 1 and the city on the thirtieth. It wasn't clear whether the Iraqis would stay in the city or attempt to come out and further disrupt the division's supply line coming past it. Either way, the division was not going to leave its flank open.

The plan was that while RCT-5 headed north, battalion 3/4 was to attack west in a "reconnaissance in force," to determine how much of a fight the fedayeen were prepared to put up. It was the kind of mission McCoy and his company commanders loved, because it gave them the freedom of action to develop the battle as they saw fit. In turn, that was what Colonel Hummer expected of his battalion commanders.

McCoy and his commanders checked the overhead photos of Diwaniyah taken by the Pioneer UAV and were impressed by the city's size. To the east, open fields directly abutted the first line of apartment buildings, providing good fields of fire for the tanks. The fedayeen camp was a palm grove to the southeast, just inside the city. The commanders agreed they should probe along the city's eastern edge, oriented toward the fedayeen camp. On the white board McCoy sketched the elements of the Afak Drill—a strong base of fire and a strong envelopment by tanks supported by infantry, with hardback Humvees with .50-calibers on the flanks.

The commanders left to brief their troops. Once the briefings were finished and the weapons cleaned, the men sat down to dinner. Every Marine had a family—three, four, or five friends—crouched in a hole, ripping open the plastic wrapping of MREs, bartering M&Ms for shortcake, hoarding peanut butter and crackers to nibble while on watch, hoping the main meal wouldn't be the Captain Charlie's Country Chicken, which wasn't chicken but a congealed patty of soy products. They would slip the bag containing pasta or meat into a bag with chemicals that heated up when a few teaspoons of water were added. While waiting for the meal to warm, they'd chat about the day's work, what weird kills they'd seen, the RPG that had bounced off a tank, what had caused the .50-caliber to jam, that stupid radio operator who couldn't keep call signs straight, who had the bayonet off that AK-47—the usual small talk around a family dinner table. They didn't speak of fear, and they rarely spoke of home.

Jobs—staying alive—determined a Marine's family on the march up, not rank or ethnic background. Those you lived with were those you fought with and who would keep you alive. Major General Mattis traveled with his sergeant, and his aide. At dinnertime the three of them hung out together. It was the same at regiment, battalion, company, and platoon levels. McCoy ate with Lance Corporal Baynes, a superb shot with the 240 Golf machine gun; Corporal Monge, who drove and handled the radio; and Lance Corporal Shealy, who desperately tried to get in front of McCoy in the fights because "otherwise the colonel takes all the shots." Gunner Halleck, Sergeant Major Howell, and Corporal Evnin were the rest of McCoy's family.

Before collapsing into sleep, these small families chatted for a few minutes, conversation interrupted by aircraft passing overhead. On call if needed, the aircraft were either pounding Baghdad or hunting kilometers north of the columns. Sometimes in the distance artillery would fire, usually only six or twelve rounds at a time, given Major General Mattis's order to conserve artillery missions.

The tank crews had the best night life—a one-burner stove for heating coffee for only four men and room inside for three to sleep out of the dirt, wind, rain, and cold. The Amtrac crews could get out of the weather too, but their seats didn't recline like those on the tanks. A few riflemen could lie down or sit up and doze in the back of a trac, where no one ever took off his boots; by the seventh day, all Marines had learned why God put feet far away from noses.

Most infantrymen, though, dug and slept in holes along the line near their vehicles. No one strayed far from his vehicle, and when not on watch, the warmth of a sleeping bag was precious. Told that whiskers on the face would prevent a gas mask from sealing and believing that sooner or later "slime"—chemicals—would happen, the troops shaved regularly. Electric shavers were shared each evening. It was odd to see clean-shaven faces always caked with dirt. Lying in the dust, breathing it, scraping it off the food, cleaning it out of the weapons and ears six times a day became second nature to every soldier and Marine on the march in Iraq.

7

The Making of Veterans

D+11

With battalion 3/4 in the attack on Ad Diwaniyah
1 April

LT. COL. MCCOY UNDERSTOOD that Colonel Hummer intended his battalion 3/4 to intimidate the fedayeen in the city of Diwaniyah so they would not be bold enough to launch serious interdiction strikes along Route 1. Intelligence reports indicated that there was, or at least had been, a company of tanks dug in under a palm grove in the southeastern corner of the city. The headquarters of the commando brigade in the city might be there as well. Whatever was in that palm grove, McCoy intended to destroy it. He hoped to lure the fedayeen out of the heart of the city and deal with them, too. He directed that the Afak Drill be used: eight tanks from Bravo Company 1st Tank Battalion and a platoon from Kilo were to drive straight for the grove and establish the base of fire. Then Kilo, with two platoons of infantry and one platoon of tanks, would envelop from the south. The tanks would be the anvil, and Kilo the hammer.

The lights from Diwaniyah shone brightly in the distance, indicating that the municipal workforce under the local Baathists was still on the job. Other evidence also testified that regime loyalists were in Diwaniyah. The previous night two rockets had hit 1,000 meters from us, but McCoy hadn't changed our position, believing we were safest where the inaccurate Iraqis were aiming. The rockets had come from just north of Diwaniyah; the 11th Marines' radars picked them up and had counterfire rounds in the air in seconds. The Iraqi Americans in the human exploitation team, after chatting with passing Iraqis, reported that the fedayeen had been riding around the streets on new motorcycles and had organized a citywide militia that held daily drills. They had cut out a man's tongue the previous day and left him to bleed to death, claiming he was an informer.

"Let's knock on the city door," McCoy said. "See if anyone wants to come out and play."

A week before, in Nasiriyah, two regiments commanding eight battalions had struggled. Now a battalion commander with two companies was picking a fight. After four cities and towns, battalion 3/4—along with the rest of the Blue Diamond—thought it was learning how to play the game.

The battalion drove west from the cloverleaf at six A.M. on the first of April. Four Humvees with TOW rockets led, followed by Bravo Company tanks, then Kilo in twelve Amtracs. The road was wide, straight, and clear, with not a civilian car in sight and no one stirring in the cinder-block houses on either side. A bit farther on we came to an overpass with a commanding view of an expanse of fields and a few palm groves. In the background loomed the outline of an imposing city, row after row of thickly packed apartments and two-story houses, all with high cement walls.

As it approached an intersection about 1,500 meters east of the city, Bravo began to receive fire from a palm grove to the north. The enemy was firing RPGs and small arms at long range, as usual not very effectively. Capt. Brian Lewis, the company commander of Bravo, began to close on the grove with his tanks, while Kilo Company moved up on his left. The two companies moved forward by bounds, while CAAT Red swung farther south, looking for a route to flank the enemy positions.

The two companies advanced for another 1,000 meters, covering each other's movements by fire, until Bravo got its tanks up onto the on ramp and the overpass of the cloverleaf. This high ground provided the tanks with superb fields of fire, looking down into the enemy positions in the palm groves and along the edge of the city. Recognizing the dominance of the position, McCoy held Bravo there as overlook while Kilo turned left and headed south toward the location where the Iraqi tanks had been reported. RPGs were coming in at Kilo; gunners hiding behind berms were lobbing shots that had scant chance of hitting a moving target. The soil was marshland soft, so the Marine vehicles stayed on the single strand of hardtop, a dozen .50-caliber and 7.62mm machine guns chattering. Earthen berms dug up by bulldozers ran parallel to the road on both sides, some within rock-throwing distance and others farther out. Spurts and puffs of dust indicated the positions of the attackers and attracted swarms of tracers that smothered all resistance.

Kilo ran on for several hundred meters, then neared a traffic circle lined with tall buildings. Sniper fire was coming from an imposing factory several hundred meters to the right, or west, and a tank was returning fire with a .50-caliber. Although a firefight was taking place right in front of them, women in black burkas continued to walk by as if ignoring a minor distraction, and small, dingy cars careened around the traffic circle, as though the drivers were determined to go to work and the fedayeen and the Americans should stop shooting and go away. For several minutes Ray and I watched this astounding refusal to acknowledge reality. Gradually the traffic petered out as some awareness of the need for self-preservation took hold.

One large city bus, with lettering on its side, drove east at the traffic circle and, several minutes later, drove back west at a high rate of speed. McCoy and Sergeant Major Howell watched it with suspicion but gave no order to light it up. The desultory shots from the west were increasing, and a tank responded by putting a 120mm shell into the factory, which shrugged off the impact. Next to the factory was a line of two-story houses, some with high cinder-block fences surrounding them. In single file about eight men in black ninja outfits and black scarves wrapped around their heads were darting from house to house. They were half-crouching as they ran, weapons low in their hands. Their speed was impressive, and from a distance they looked like eels slithering smoothly along, or like ninjas in an '80s action film who had bumbled onto the wrong movie set.

Staff Sergeant Moreno was swiveling his 7.62mm sniper rifle around the top of Howell's truck, furious that he hadn't been alerted to the ninjas seconds earlier, knowing he was in a race with the optics on two or three tanks. He could see the figures in black but didn't have time to adjust a proper lead. One tank's .50-caliber fired a short burst; then the other tank joined in. The ninjas ducked behind another house and did not reappear.

Sergeant Major Howell heard a commotion to his front, followed by a burst of firing. The Marines guarding the flanks of a tank had seen heads pop up from a ditch. A man tried to run but was cut down. Another was crawling out on his stomach, waving a stick with a white flag. Ignoring the Marines shouting at him in English to halt, he wriggled his way through the dust and gravel toward the hardtop, as if that would give him sanctuary. Howell knew what was coming next. The man had seconds to live.

"Ah hell, you Marines shut up. I don't know who's dumber, you or that dipstick!" Howell yelled. "I'm going to bring him in. Anyone who fires draws a double watch for the rest of this goddamn campaign."

Not a shot was fired as the sergeant major aimed in, got up, and walked forward to where a pudgy middle-aged Iraqi man in a green military uniform knelt, arms in the air, a terrified, soulful look in his eyes. [Picture 29] Howell called for an Iraqi American from the HET, who quickly learned the man was from the city militia. The fedayeen were shooting anyone who didn't fight. The fedayeen had just run away, so he had fastened his white flag to surrender. Howell said for the man to gather up his clothes, march himself over to the side of the road, and wait for a truck with the other prisoners, guarded by a lance corporal. [Picture 30] The Marines poked around his hiding place—a culvert only 50 meters in front of the lead tank. It held a dozen RPGs and various explosives that, in the right hands, would have spelled trouble for that tank.

But the fedayeen were not prepared to be martyrs. Young and on their own, they chose not to die. The close presence of the Marines had badly frightened them, and they stayed hidden in the culvert until the Marines were distracted by the sniper in the factory. Then they sprinted for the safety of the houses next to the factory and made their escape.

McCoy decided to wait and let the next group of fedayeen come to him, with the tanks and Amtracs of Kilo Company neatly herringboned on either side of the hardtop 100 meters short of the traffic circle. On the far side of the circle was the city proper. Two platoons had gone on foot to search the nearby apartment buildings, which had the architectural flair of Moscow circa 1950—square slabs of unpainted concrete decorated by rows of square windows without trimming. Raw sewage seeped from broken underground pipes. A few residents huddled farther down the dirt street, risking death to look. They obligingly told the HET Iraqi Americans that arms were in a school building, which they pointed out. Finding a large weapons cache, the Kilo platoon commander radioed for permission to blow it in place. McCoy hesitated a minute, then agreed.

Ray had grown restive about being out on the long, straight street and suggested that it was a long walk to Baghdad, unless I wanted to be stuck back in an Amtrac. I took his point, and we climbed back into our Yellow Submarine Nissan and parked it on the lee side of a concrete apartment building that looked as if it had been built to withstand wrecking balls and cruise missiles. Seeing what Ray had done, Sergeant Major Howell told his driver to move his open-back small truck up behind a tank. The Amtrac gunners ignored us and sat in their turrets, hoping for another shot at the persistent sniper.

Ten minutes later a large shell shot across the traffic circle and exploded in the road. In seconds the Amtracs scattered for the safety of the lee sides of the buildings. The tanks held their ground, as though it were beneath their dignity to move after one flat trajectory shell. The tank commanders stood up in their hatches while the main guns swiveled back and forth, pointing toward the rotary, their sensors trying to pick up the heat from the recoilless rifle that had shot at them.

McCoy and Howell began to rant and rave about misplaced machismo, and the tanks hastily pulled off the road into the defilade provided by the ditches. Not one of the four behemoths, however, made a move toward the better safety of the lee side of any building—each tank crew still hoped to deliver a swift return shot when the antitank gun fired again. McCoy agreed with Ray, though, that they had stayed too long in a static position. Besides, back at the overpass Bravo Company was still engaged, occasionally calling in volleys of 155mm rounds.

McCoy had Kilo and its attached tanks pull back while he drove to the overpass and we followed. From the overpass he watched through his binoculars as Bravo's .50-calibers plinked at two sets of targets—a series of berms in a palm grove about 400 meters to the northwest and a set of walls along the first row of buildings in the city proper, another 400 meters beyond the palms. Alongside one wall lay the charred hulk of the city bus that a few hours before we had seen at the traffic circle. Captain Lewis of Bravo tanks explained that a tank crew had seen men with weapons drive up and hop out of the bus, so the crew had hit it with a shell from the tank's main gun.

"I don't see a thing in that palm grove," McCoy said.

"They pop up every few minutes, like whack-a-moles," Lewis said. "They're out there all right, only they're dug in like ticks."

"Sounds like the Afak Drill to me," McCoy said.

The infantrymen attached to Bravo were lying prone, rifles pointed outbound. They couldn't see any targets at those distances, and as usual the tanks and Amtracs with their magnificent optics were taking all the shots.

"Ground's too soft down there for my tanks," Lewis said.

"Keep them here as the base of fire, and bring the infantry across the field," McCoy said. "I'll pull Kilo tanks around up north of the overpass. That way they'll have a clear field of fire at anyone leaving the palm grove and falling back on the city."

The infantrymen who were listening brightened. If they closed on those berms 400 meters away, for once they would have the first clear shots at killing ranges. No shrubbery or concealment stood between them and the grove—they would have to cross the wide-open area to get to the Iraqi positions. They were ready to go, frustrated with watching the tanks do all the shooting. Lewis exercised the right of command, even though he was a tanker, to move with the assault on the ground. The platoon commanders quickly arranged five squads on line. They stood erect, slipped down the slope off the overpass, and scrambled through the open fields. I went with the infantry while Ray drove the SUV behind Kilo's tanks.

When we stepped into the field, the brown ground was so soft that it stuck in the treads of our boots, as the Marines scrambled forward at a fast trot, rounds were snapping in, high but not heavy, not a fusillade. The cracks in the air made it obvious that some Iraqi soldiers had not run and were manning the berm. The Marines, advancing by fire team rushes, picked up the pace. Between McCoy's order for the dismounted Afak Drill and the troops reaching the halfway point across the field, less than fifteen minutes had passed. Bravo tanks didn't have to move to provide the base of fire, and Kilo tanks were swinging around the road, Ray following behind in the Yellow Submarine.

The PRC-119 radios worked well in the open space, and the Bravo and Kilo commanders had no trouble hearing one another and giving clear directions over the encrypted circuits. Kilo's tanks were coordinating with Bravo tanks about who would fire where. At the same time Bravo tanks were talking with Lewis, who wanted them to support the riflemen closing on the berms and then to shift fires away from the berm on his command. When tankers are monitoring several radio nets simultaneously, switching back and forth, hearing at least two conversations inside their headsets and responding to them in turn, they call it "having a helmet fire." As the infantry crossed the field, Bravo and Kilo tank commanders were having helmet fires.

Crossing a wide, flat space to close with an entrenched enemy, even with fire support from tanks, is risky, although it is taught in training because keeping control during an exercise is easier in open terrain. Early in the Vietnam War the infantry had tried to employ such textbook tactics for attacking a dug-in enemy. They abandoned them quickly because the North Vietnamese would hunch down in their thick dirt and log bunkers and deliver streams of grazing fire on the advancing riflemen. After suffering sharp losses in several fights, the infantry had learned to back off and pound the area, preferably with fixed-wing air dropping five-hundred-pound bombs. If that wasn't enough, the infantry would increase the dosage of high explosives until it was safe to move forward on the ground. In a five-hour fight at Khe Sanh, for instance, a single rifle company called in five thousand artillery rounds while moving less than 1,000 meters in a raid. To cross an open area in an infantry attack without calling in indirect fire support would be unusual. Against a skilled opponent, it would be suicidal.

At Diwaniyah, battalion 3/4 did not encounter such disciplined and tenacious opposition. The tanks were ready, but their main guns weren't needed against the berms. The Iraqi defenders were brave or stoic enough, but they did not know how to employ fires and were poor shots. The FACs with 3/4 did call in some air support, and the 155mm artillery did work some targets, but these targets were farther to the west. All morning the Iraqis had stayed hunkered down in their trenches behind the berms, occasionally poking up their heads to peep at the tanks, which promptly fired machine guns.

When it was apparent that the Iraqis intended to stay in the trench lines and neither surrender nor flee, the Marines went forward. The line of perhaps eighty Marines with rifles up to their shoulders advanced by rushes, M-16s crackling. Captain Lewis and his first sergeant were on the line with their 9mm pistols. McCoy walked with drawn pistol a few feet behind the advancing line. Lance Corporal Shealy tried, as usual, to run in front of the battalion commander, who kept pushing him to one side to see what was going on. Sergeant Major Howell, an excellent marksman, stayed off to one side with his M-16, waiting to take a shot.

The battalion had concluded that the Iraqis were not employing machine guns, did not have interlocking fields of fire, and couldn't shoot straight; they lacked both cohesion and fire discipline. Over the course of twelve days of continuous movement and sporadic contact, the battalion had taken the measure of the enemy. The Iraqis had harassed them every day with a few RPGs, a few snipers, and one or two incoming mortar shells. Their occasional successes depended on the law of averages, coming when they surprised the Marines. They relied on multiple firings of RPGs to hit vehicles that were more or less stationary on one road. The Iraqis weren't lacking in courage or individual armament—but they were lacking in teamwork, leadership, tactics, and marksmanship.

Now McCoy wanted the Iraqis to know that the Marines would not stay on the roads; they would come into the trenches after them. *[Picture 31]* As they approached the berm, the Marines increased their rate of fire. As long as the Iraqis were keeping their heads down, they weren't firing back. The Marines climbed over the berms, which were taller than a man, and entered the palm grove. It was lined with trenches and sleeping holes, most covered with palm stems and broad leaves. As we advanced, we passed blankets and plastic chairs, teapots and chipped dinner plates and canvas tied between the palm trees as awnings. The advancing Marines had to use only a few grenades—the Iraqi holes had no sharp angles or covered bunkers. The grove looked more like a Boy Scout jamboree under a lax supervisor; each soldier had hollowed out a comfortable hole, lined it with blankets, and brought along a change of clothes, a prayer rug, and some old dishes. There were campfires and rice dishes and cups for tea. There were even magazines.

The Marines shot them at close range. Some Iraqis shrank down in their holes, hoping the leaves would conceal them. The Marines shot through the leaves and kept walking. Other soldiers, in green shirts and trousers that looked like janitors' uniforms, leaped up, dropped their weapons, and ran toward the city. The Marines were surprised at how quickly they dashed across the road that was the kill zone the Kilo Company tanks were covering—they ran with the sprinter's speed of the desperate. Not one Iraqi was shot crossing the road, something the riflemen didn't let the tankers forget.

Once they reached the other side of the road, though, the Iraqis still had to cross several hundred meters of field. Some made it by dropping onto their stomachs and wriggling through the tall grass—some sort of long-stemmed grain—for many minutes. Those who tried to stand erect and run were cut down.

The smart ones had climbed out of the trenches and thrown aside their weapons and were now lying on their stomachs, arms outstretched in front of their heads, their faces in the dust. These were the instinctive supplicants, out of the fight, begging for their lives. The Marines ignored them as they swept through the palm grove. When enemy firing stopped, the Marines returned and prodded the Iraqis onto the hard-top, where their hands were bound behind them. Kilo Company sent forward four tanks to set in farther west and guard the road while the infantry consolidated and the prisoners were secured.

There were over a dozen Iraqi prisoners, more than the small EPW truck could hold. Two had to drape themselves over the hood like deer trophies hauled out of some backwoods, except that the eyes of these Iraqis were not opaque. They had their heads up, their hands cinched in plastic ties behind them, smiling at the Marines they passed. It was an article of faith among Iraqis that Marines did not take prisoners. Even Al Qaeda tape messages on Al Jazeera television singled out the Marines for special invective. These prisoners were glad to be alive and off the field of battle.

The Marines did a quick search of the bodies lying among the palm trees. Once the firing was over, few riflemen wanted to touch or look at their kills while the blood was still red and hadn't yet been absorbed in the dirt. That was too personal, and they told each other that if you looked too long on the dead, the images stayed with you when you got home. A pudgy officer in his late thirties had been captured with a sheaf of documents. He had a small wound in his right buttock and lay groaning on the ground that was sopping up his blood. A young Marine was trying to comfort him, patting his arm as a corpsman applied a pressure bandage. The wound wasn't bleeding much anymore.

"Don't baby him," a gunnery sergeant said. "Serves him right, getting shot in the ass. He should have surrendered. Get away from him, the stupid bastard." The gunny was angry at the wounded man, obviously a local militia officer who had stayed at his post.

"Doc," he yelled, "give me a read on this idiot."

The man lying on the ground was about as old as the gunny, but not as fit or ready for battle. The Iraqi should have had the sense to stay home, the gunny was muttering, as if he knew where the man lived and now he would have to do a lot of explaining about how the man had been seriously hurt at work when he shouldn't have been there in the first place.

The corpsman shook his head. "His pulse is fading."

"Get away from here," the gunny said to a group of Marines who had gathered to watch.

The man flopped, bouncing off the ground as if hit by an electric prod and spreading out his arms. The corpsman had loosened his belt and pulled down the trousers to tend to the fatal wound. Black flies enveloped the man's face, stomach, and testicles.

Ever since Cain killed Abel, killing another human being has fascinated and repelled us. We want to watch it, from a distance. Without scenes of killing, Shakespeare would not have been the greatest writer in history. On TV and in the movies, the police officer sooner or later shoots and kills an armed murderer. Depictions of war stress the same theme: the actors portraying American infantrymen in *Saving Private Ryan* and other movies routinely "shoot" dozens of enemy soldiers.

In six hours, the battalion estimated two hundred Iraqi soldiers and fedayeen had died, not an unusual number, for the length of the battle and the panoply of weapons applied. I didn't go around counting, and nobody else did either. Most of the killing was done at a distance by the tanks, the CAATs, and the indirect fires, beyond where the Marines walked that day.

In the sections of trenches that the riflemen had cleared on foot I saw about a dozen bodies, and on the other side of the road nearer the city scattered in the scrub grass were another dozen or so who had gone down before they ran very far. The odds were about one in five that any individual rifleman in the assault had killed another human being. In the excitement, fear, and fury of the moment, with the smell of gunpowder stinging the nostrils, the screaming of sergeants straightening out the line, the sound of firing blasting in the ears, the men running forward, flopping down, Kevlar helmet bouncing over the eyes, the sight picture jiggling, the finger squeezing before the aim post was steady, the aim point a puff of dust, a pile of dirt, or a green smudge—no one could sort out which bullet from which rifle ended a particular human life.

No one rifleman had killed another human being—they all had. One rifleman charging forward was not separate from another. Snipers and pilots separated out kills to count coup.

The riflemen were a team, and killed as a team. The trench line and the palm grove now belonged to them. In the movies, after the cop kills the bad guy, there is a fade-out on a high note. At Diwaniyah, the riflemen had trained for this close-in fight, imagined combat, and talked to one another about it. Now they had done it. The bodies were lying there. Yet they stayed away from them. They avoided the fat officer in his clean khaki green outfit, white undershirt, and underwear. He was too clean to be hardcore infantry and too old to be fedayeen. They stayed away from the head shots, too. Marines hit what they aim at. [Picture 34] Two Iraqis lay on their backs, the hard, cracked earth black instead of brown under each head. The two bodies had fallen almost touching hands, eighteen-year-olds in green cammies as clean as their officer's. The smart guys, those fedayeen dressed in black like ninjas, had run, and a few probably made it across the fields back to the city. The regular guys had stayed in the trenches, not knowing what they were up against.

The Marines' reluctance to examine the dead didn't reflect a reluctance on their part about the fight, or about killing in general. It was just that in this fight, no Marines had died, so they had no immediate anger or resentment against the other side. They took no pleasure in seeing the dead or recalling their deaths. If the other side had killed a Marine, their equanimity would have disappeared in a flash. It would have made no difference if they were ninja or militia—they would have been killed, and no Marine would be angry because they hadn't had the brains to surrender.

As the Iraqi officer lay in death's coma, McCoy was a few dozen meters away poking around what was left of a technical with a machine gun in back. *[Picture 32]* The pickup, still burning, had been hit by an AT-4 rocket, and the Marine who fired it was standing off to the side. The battalion commander congratulated him, and the Marine grinned his thanks. Howell pointed to three new motorcycles parked around the grove. McCoy walked over to a tan Kawasaki with red lights, glistening chromium, and a large black leather seat. *[Picture 33]* The odometer read 800 kilometers. It was so shiny and powerful that one expected a state trooper from California to step out from behind a palm tree and swing aboard. McCoy popped open a saddlebag and shook out three pistols and a shoulder holster.

It was ludicrous: probably a skinny eighteen-year-old in black pajamas and dark eye glasses, with a black and white checkered headdress wrapped bandit-style around his face, had driven up on an enormous motorcycle, pistol in shoulder holster, and yelled at the militia officer to gather his young soldiers and fight the American tanks approaching the overpass. McCoy didn't know whether the fedayeen had stayed to fight like the officer who died in the knee-high crop fields, or had abandoned his motorcycle and tried to run back to the city. Either way, one rumor was proven true: the fedayeen were arriving by motorcycle, and they did have the power to intimidate older soldiers. The militia officer could have shot the riders of the three motorcycles. Instead, he and his local national guard had stayed, fought poorly, and died as soldiers.

McCoy left the motorcycles and walked up to the road to talk with Captain Lewis, and Ray and I stayed to admire them. We suggested that McCoy take them back to the convoy, but he was concerned that a Marine would break his neck showing off. He was probably right.

A hundred meters to the west, another volley of RPGs exploded, one rocket grenade knocking the arm off an electric power pole. The fire support team responded with an 81mm mortar volley into the middle of the field where the Iraqi soldiers had fled. The RPGs had come from somewhere in the city, but Lewis decided not to fire back blindly. Since the 81s hadn't had any action, they were given the field as a target. Some of the fedayeen might still be out there, and besides, it was good practice for next time.

Gradually the firing died out. By early afternoon McCoy could no longer find a fight and pulled his forces back to Route 1 to fall in at the tail end of RCT-7. Colonel Hummer knew that sending battalion 3/4 to intimidate the fedayeen had been a hope, not a plan for ending resistance from the city of Diwaniyah. But the militia had been hit hard. When next the fedayeen drove up on motorcycles, shouting for them to form up and attack the Americans, the militia survivors might not answer the call. Time would tell.

On 1 April Hummer's main focus was on moving his regiment up Route 1 in trace of RCT-5. The pause was over, and RCT-5 was one day out in front as the lead for the division. Ray and I too were eager to move on. We said our good-byes and, together with an aggressive CAAT team that McCoy provided as an escort, raced north up Route 1 to avoid becoming ensnarled in the giant convoy creeping up from the south.

With battalion 2/5, across Route 27 to the Tigris River
1–2 April

North of the cloverleaf on Route 1 we saw no one. After crawling along in convoys it was eerie to race along at 60 miles an hour to keep up with two Humvees, whose drivers were enjoying the same pleasures, heretofore unseen, of the open road. The sun was out, the dust was down, and miles of flat, clear concrete stretched before them. You could almost think of the two ungainly khaki vehicles as quaint convertibles, each with a happy teenager standing up in the backseat, the wind whipping through his hair, finger on a .50 caliber.

Without slowing down, the Humvees dodged the usual debris, stones, black metal fragments hurled onto the pavement by exploded and charred Iraqi tanks, black boots, and an occasional body. Roadkill meant just that. And every highway on the main attack routes had its trail of black boots. Some Iraqi soldier imagines a tank steadily closing in behind or thinks back on the bomb that nearly hit his truck. He hops off, takes off his uniform, puts on his trusty *dishdasha* robe, and throws away the telltale boots—only soldiers wear boots in this part of the world. In sandals he heads out across the fields or down the road. It may take him a week to get back to his village, but he is on his way. His war is over.

Forty kilometers up the highway we caught up with the rear of RCT-5 at the elbow, where a secondary road, Route 27, bent right off Route 1. Every vehicle had its unit number painted in white on both sides, with a "forward," "main," or "back" symbol, referring to its position in the convoy. The simple system was invaluable to every soldier and Marine. Without it, sooner or later every one of us would have gotten lost and wandered forever among thousands of vehicles that looked identical because they were identical.

After waving our good-bye thanks to the CAATs, we snaked our way forward between enormous tractor-trailers that were towing bridging and supplies. Military Police were herding all vehicles onto the shoulders of the highway. They told us Maj. Gen. Jim Amos, commanding the 3rd Marine Air Wing, was up the road and his people were clearing this stretch of debris. I took pictures as the first C-130 landed on the highway with fuel for RCT-5. All together the division had up to eight thousand vehicles on the move, guzzling 200,000 gallons of fuel each day. Each fuel convoy averaged three days round trip, and they were running flat out. Before the war, based on their logistical feats in Afghanistan, Major General Mattis had expressed confidence in the C-130 crews and the wing and Navy Seabee construction crews. We watched the C-130 taxi off to the shoulder of the road. In a few minutes, Marines were hauling a huge rubber bladder out of the back, and vehicles were lining up to refuel.

Major General Mattis was not wasting a minute. RCT-5 was rolling, and it needed fuel. Last night Mattis had talked to its commanding officer, Col. Joe Dunford. "Be prepared to take the bridge across the Saddam Canal 20 kilometers east on Route 27 at first light on 3 April," the division commander had said, "and continue the attack to the Tigris from there." An hour later Mattis called back: "Take the Canal on 2 April." An hour later he called a third time, asking when RCT-5 could attack. "In four hours," Dunford said. "Do it," Mattis replied.

Now we were at the rear of RCT-5, stuck in a giant traffic jam at rush hour. No more vehicles could move down Route 27 until the bridge over the Canal was taken. At dusk on 1 April, as we were watching the C-130, battalion 1/5 was routing an Iraqi company defending the Canal. We heard about it within minutes. The main communications link in the division was the PRC-119 FM radio, highly reliable in open country over short distances. The word rippled back from unit to unit along the road: *We've taken the Canal.* Everyone knew what that meant: Mattis would have them across the Tigris in a day.

To get to Colonel Dunford, who was with his lead unit, all Ray and I had to do was weave in and out among a thousand vehicles in a yellow SUV without being accidentally squashed by some monster truck. The Military Police we were chatting with were mostly reserves, many of them cops in civilian life, and their major had once been a lieutenant serving under Ray. They decided to help us through the logjam. As with any police officer, no sensible person argued with them when they were doing their job, and in short order we were linked up with battalion 2/5, which was heading for the front.

I had visited with the commander, Lieutenant Colonel Donohue, when his battalion was training at Camp Pendleton, and now he loaned Ray a set of night-vision goggles for the drive. The battalion intended to halt short of the canal and to move past 1/5 at the canal at two o'clock the next morning. With priority to drive along the dusty shoulder, 2/5 rolled along at a steady pace and started down Route 27. We fell in behind Donahue's command trac.

The contrast between Route 27 and the highways we had so far taken during the campaign was striking. No berms or bunkers dotted the road, and no bulldozers had plowed long lines of trenches. Even the ubiquitous white sandbags, seen in every tiny village at some tiny intersection, were absent. No Iraqi military planner—not even Saddam's son

Uday and his fedayeen—had expected the coalition forces to leave Route 1 and turn east onto this secondary road. Civilians were going about their evening business at a steady pace. Most waved if they made eye contact, but none seemed awed or frightened by the hundreds of armed vehicles rolling by. Boys out in a schoolyard playing soccer did not interrupt their game to watch the Amtracs clatter past. The friendly and normal atmosphere made it obvious that the fedayeen were not lurking on this route. After driving for three hours, battalion 2/5 stopped in the dark and set in a hasty defense, with other units in front and behind. With only a few hours to grab some rest before moving again at two, guards were set out, and the troops fell asleep immediately, already having eaten while on the road.

Ever since Ray and I heard about the officer being killed when he was run over by the armored combat excavator in his sleep, we developed a routine, our own standard operating procedure. We would find a corner inside the perimeter where two berms came together and I'd roll out my sleeping gear. Ray pulled the SUV across the corner, blocking access to my "bed," and slept in the reclining passenger seat. During the daytime Ray did all the driving, while I navigated. I always slept outside because I preferred it. Ray slept inside with the radio, and with his old, tired, swollen grunt feet elevated on the dash.

Within a few hours battalion 2/5 was on the road again. With no city lights for 100 kilometers and with little wind to stir dust into the air, the stars stood out like piercing beams. The two-lane paved road ran northeast to An Nu'maniyah, where there was a good bridge over the Tigris. But as insurance 2/5 was to find a spot for a pontoon bridge. The battalion would follow Route 27 about halfway to Nu'maniyah, then find a route through the farmlands and come out at the Tigris 15 kilometers upstream, where the maps showed a good spot for laying down the pontoon bridge. The 2nd Tank Battalion would follow 2/5 down Route 27 and proceed straight on to attack Nu'maniyah. If 2nd Tanks seized the bridge at Nu'maniyah intact, good. If not, 2/5 would be setting up an alternate crossing site.

In the middle of the night Route 27 was wide enough for only one lane of Amtracs to move at a fast clip. Donohue's battalion had priority, and he made the most of it. Every driver was wearing night-vision goggles (NVGs), which looked like those small binoculars people used to take to the opera. A slot fitted onto a holder screwed into the front of a helmet allowing the goggles to flop down in front of the eyes. As you looked through the goggles, night became day. You could shoot a man 200 meters away or drive a tank or Amtrac as if it were early dawn, that time of day when the visibility is good enough to turn off your car headlights. NVGs were essential to the entire campaign, as convoys ran day and night without lights.

As the Amtracs of 2/5 headed for the Tigris, the drivers tried to keep a respectful distance, but an accordion effect inevitably besets any long line of vehicles. At times the road would be open on both sides and the Amtracs would accelerate, only to slow a few kilometers farther when a close shoulder or a possible enemy ambush site dictated caution. In our Yellow Submarine we were assigned a position with an Amtrac in front and another behind us—not a good spot for a sudden stop.

Ray was driving with one hand and holding his borrowed goggles with the other. Now he realized why the officer in 2/5's operations section had been so quick to loan them—they wouldn't quite focus without constant adjustment. And since his helmet did not have the mounting bracket, he had to hold them to his eyes. Still, they were better than nothing.

We were doing about 40 miles per hour when, without warning, the Amtrac in front of us swung hard right and lurched onto the shoulder. Before Ray could slow, another Amtrac loomed up directly in front of us. The idiot had parked in the middle of the road. Ray swung hard right too. Suddenly I saw our problem, three meters high and a few centimeters from my window. The driver of the Amtrac behind us, sitting two meters higher than we were, had seen the parked vehicle before we could and had slid right without slowing down. Now we too had cut right, but we had slowed down and were inside his blind spot, about to be crumpled like a used dinner napkin. So much for seeing Baghdad.

Ray gripped the steering wheel, downshifted into third gear, and shot us forward under the bow of the Amtrac. We skidded once, then the tires grabbed and we scooted ahead, coming once again into the driver's view. He abruptly slowed his trac, and we fell into our assigned place. After a few moments we remembered to breathe. Later we exchanged smiles and shakes of the head with the Amtrac driver. It's not only the bullets and bombs that can get you.

8

Across the Tigris

D + 12, D + 13

With battalion 2/5 at the Tigris River and battalion 3/7 at An Nu'maniyah
2 April

UNDER A SKY OF BRILLIANT STARS the Amtracs of battalion 2/5 clattered east along Route 27, the drivers in their night-vision goggles clearly seeing the road. On the horizon, we saw flashes of brilliant light from artillery prep fires near the town of An Nu'maniyah and the main bridge across the Tigris River. Battalion 2/5 was headed a few kilometers upstream to find a fording site, in case the Nu'maniyah bridge was blown.

About a dozen kilometers short of the Tigris, the Amtracs turned left off the hardtop and slowly started north along a dirt road that shortly narrowed into what the battalion commander, Lieutenant Colonel Donohue, called a "donkey path." It was an apt name for a track of packed mud that ambled alongside wide irrigation ditches, with occasional turns to visit the front yard of some farmer. In the first faint smudges of light we twisted, turned, and jounced in the Yellow Submarine, wishing we had treads like the tracs. Most of the time Ray was in first gear in four-wheel drive, and the new tires on the gritty Nissan with their deep grooves gripped the mud as we churned our way over one irrigation embankment after another.

We had a PRC-119 with us, its long antenna stuck out the window, so we could monitor the various nets—company, battalion, and sometimes regiment. At 6:30 Ray picked up a brief situation report sent out by RCT-5 to all its battalions: *"Iron Horse* [call sign for 2nd Tank Battalion] *has seized the Tigris bridge at Nu'maniyah intact and are crossing it now. They report destroying several BMPs, trucks, and tanks. [Picture 37] Have taken some RPG hits, but all tanks still in the fight at this time."* It was a major mistake for the Iraqis not to have dropped the bridge. Looking behind us, we marveled at the single-file line of two hundred vehicles, some with tracks and some with wheels, strung out across miles of paddy land and ditches, all snaking along the donkey path. If one vehicle slipped off and bogged down in the muck, the battalion would be stuck for hours in the middle of nowhere.

We were far from any road that showed on any map, out wandering among farms. To navigate, Donohue had recent overhead photos taken by a UAV and faith in his own piloting skills. Back and forth we went, never turning around but frequently executing wide U-shaped maneuvers to avoid low, squishy spots sure to snare the heavier vehicles. Our track, if drawn on a piece of paper, would have looked like the doodling of a three-year-old, utterly without a discernible pattern. But Donohue steered the column from one side of the paper to another, and by breakfast time we were looking at the placid Tigris. We were the latest in a long list of armies that had marched up the countryside of Babylon, cradle of the civilized world.

We had emerged from the maze of paddies onto a decent-sized hardtop, called River Road, that ran north 100 kilometers to Baghdad and south a few dozen kilometers to Nu'maniyah. On the other side of the road the land sloped down to the Tigris. From our vantage point, the view did not disappoint. What was obviously a floodplain was now lush green and dotted with palm trees and thick undergrowth. The brown waters of the river were wide and tranquil. There were no houses.

Donohue had found a suitable bridging spot and called back to bring up the pontoon bridging. It was not without irony that in a desert campaign the greatest terrain impediment to Marines was water. On the march up the 1st Marine Division had to cross the Euphrates, the Tigris, and, near Baghdad, the Diyala River. At each river floating bridges were put across in one day. Few units equaled the bridging companies in their patience to endure weeks of crawling along at the rear of convoys, out of the action and seemingly out of the mind of any senior commander. Yet few units possessed such a singularly focused and special skill. They did only one thing, and they did it exceptionally well.

They were also remarkable drivers. By taking the road that the battalion had found, the bridging companies were due to arrive at the fording site by noon. But it was late afternoon before the first truck emerged from the paddies to find the RCT commander, Colonel Dunford, waiting. Dunford understood the delay; he had been standing there looking out at the paddies, so innocent in their bright green top cover that concealed lakes of mud. He was glad they had made it through at all. [Picture 35]

When you first met him, Dunford seemed quiet, almost reserved, but you soon realized that that impression was misleading. Totally self-confident, he had an active, imaginative mind—in staff meetings he was the commander most apt to pick up on Mattis's invitation to offer alternatives to the division's planned scheme of maneuver. His regiment, with more than a thousand vehicles and six thousand men, had been the division's Main Effort since crossing the Euphrates. RCT-5 was now to lead the division across the Tigris and up to Baghdad. When Ray and I met him that morning, he was pressing all of his subordinates to close up fast; he wanted to consolidate the bridgehead across the Tigris and throw the pontoon bridge across as insurance.

Dunford suggested to Ray and me that we join 2nd Tanks and battalion 3/5 the next day. They would be continuing the attack up Route 6 to Baghdad, he said, by "this time tomorrow, before light on the fourth at the latest." Battalion 3/5 was clearing behind 2nd Tanks along the main highway. RCT-7 was closing up on Nu'maniyah and would clear the rest of the town and, he understood, do pacification work in the town as well. When we voiced some interest in seeing that, he suggested we drive down and join RCT-7, then link up with 2nd Tanks or 3/5 the next morning. Before you go, he told us, get your "rubber duckies" on.

"Rubber duckies" were the overboots, part of the chemical protection equipment carried by every Marine. The intelligence community considered the Tigris crossing to be the area of highest chemical danger, because Iraqi artillery had zeroed in on the bridges and, the reasoning was, if coalition forces crossed the Tigris, the regime would know that Baghdad itself would soon be attacked. Walking in the overboots was cumbersome; running in them, dashing forward in fire and movement, made your feet pour sweat. Even the most agile Marine felt clumsy and slow.

We turned our borrowed radio and NVGs back in to 2/5, said a quick "Thanks, see you later," and drove southeast in our trusty Yellow Submarine to Nu'maniyah.

River Road below the pontoon bridge was deserted: no cars drove by, no people were out in the fields, no one was waving from farmhouses. When 2nd Tanks had rolled through Nu'maniyah in a series of running fights, its main guns had fired 160 heavy shells. When a tank gun fires, it produces a distinct, sharp crack in the air, like lightning striking close by. After hearing more than a hundred such cracks, the people seemed to be in no hurry to come out to find out what had happened. Uniformed Iraqis had tried to stand and fight but were overwhelmed by Cobra gunships, Abrams tanks, and the Amtracs, with their 40mm up guns. We saw blackened chassis along the sides of the road, several in a row on the outskirts of Nu'maniyah. Some were so ripped apart that we couldn't tell whether the vehicle had had treads or tires. Others looked like they had been squashed by a giant hammer. They were most likely aircraft kills, two-thousand-pound JDAMs probably—even munitions exploding inside a vehicle didn't do that.

As we approached the town, we saw a Marine roadblock in front of us and went into our standard procedure. I got out, took off my hat, put my arms out at my sides, and walked slowly forward, allowing the Marines on the machine gun to see that I was dressed as they were, had no weapon, and looked very much like an old fart American-type. Shooting me would be a professional embarrassment (I hoped). Ray drove ten meters behind me. Once the weapons were pointed away from us, we chatted with the machine-gunner, who directed us to RCT-7's command post. He laughingly said we could follow the smell.

We found Colonel Hummer in his command tent pitched near town on the edge of a garbage dump. This was the second time we had seen this, and the reason for it was more tolerable than the smell. Each day an advance party, usually dispatched in late afternoon, had to find a flat open space for two dozen vehicles and heavy tents to be hauled up in the dark. Most flat open spaces in populated areas were occupied by buildings and people. That left the undesirable places like garbage dumps. RCT-7 had pulled into Nu'maniyah, to ensure that the town did not become a threat to the rear as the division moved through. Turning to his ever-present map board, Hummer gave us a quick brief. [Picture 36]

He had tasked 3/7 to search the town. Their psychological operations team was broadcasting to the population and the rifle companies would patrol every street, accompanied by interpreters and human exploitation teams. At the same time, 1/7 was clearing a military airfield to the southeast that the division planned to use to fly in fuel, and the MEF intended to move in there in a day or two. Battalion 1/7 would then cross the Tigris and turn southeast, together with 3/4, to attack the Baghdad Division, the Republican Guard division stationed at Al Kut about 30 kilometers away.

While Hummer's battalions attacked the Baghdad Division from the west, RCT-1 under Colonel Dowdy would move against them from the south. While avoiding going into the heart of Al Kut themselves, the regiments were to hit the Iraqis there so hard that they could not later regroup and attack the division's supply line from the rear. The body blows inflicted against Al Kut were to be fast and furious. Mattis wanted both regiments to be on their way north in trace of RCT-5 within a day.

Hummer suggested we spend the night in Nu'maniyah, take a look at what 3/7 was doing in the town, and join RCT-5 the next morning, so we left Colonel Hummer by the garbage dump and joined 3/7 in Nu'maniyah.

A fair-sized city of 75,000, Nu'maniyah had stout concrete buildings and broad avenues that provided redoubtable defenses for any determined enemy, even one afoot with infantry weapons. The streets were wide and paved, lined with thick wooden telephone poles that could easily be toppled to provide ready barriers to block armored vehicles. Many of the buildings were several stories tall, with multiple hiding places for two-man teams armed with the ubiquitous RPGs. The river protected one flank, and along the outskirts of the town stood several large industrial buildings built of concrete. In physical structure, Nu'maniyah was formidable.

Yet resistance there had been scant, less than anticipated. As usual, because they were in the lead, the tanks and LAVs encountered RPGs and some machine guns, returning a volume of fire that discouraged sustained opposition. Battalion 3/5 had quickly held open a lane through Nu'maniyah while the tanks and their supply trains went across the bridge. There had been some scattered fighting, especially in a palm grove near the bridge, but the tankers had squelched most opposition by the time 3/5 came up behind them to mop up. Some of the prisoners said they were from the Baghdad Division and that their officers had left them and fled to Baghdad.

The only known rifle-versus-rifle engagement had fallen to the tanks out in front—to the disappointment of the infantry. Capt. David Bardorf of 2nd Tanks had been standing next to his Humvee when a bullet smashed the side mirror. Bardorf turned around to see a soldier raise his head up from inside a bunker. Bardorf fired back with his M-16, striking the man. That was the whole engagement. The sole chance to exchange direct rifle fire had fallen to a tanker. Life was not fair to the grunt.

As we drove along the main avenue in late afternoon, smoke was curling out from an upper window of a warehouse that had been hit by several tank rounds. In the city we joined Lt. Col. Michael Belcher and battalion 3/7. The city was a strange mixture of urban and rural poverty. The center core looked strong and well built up, with lines of small stores on the ground floor, most with their glass fronts intact and shuttered behind iron grating. The town square held a roundabout where dozens of people were hanging around, looking down the street toward the Marine positions.

The side streets off the main boulevards, though, were a slapdash of tar laid on top of dust and used for walking more than driving. Large puddles that smelled like cesspools lay on either side, and the homes were one-story adobe or brick and mortar, with stout walls. Not a blade of grass or a shrub of greenery was visible anywhere—just dust, dust, and more dust. Chickens clucked and squawked and scurried about, pecking in the dirt. Donkeys brayed from behind walls, their owners wisely keeping them sheltered from any stray shooting.

The 3/7's intent was to make contact with the people and, through the psy ops speakers and human exploitation teams, find out what actions needed to be taken to ensure that the townspeople—as well as Marines passing through town—were secure. The Marines' hearts were in the right place, but their heads were still in attack mode.

While the loudspeakers blared a message of friendship and asked for cooperation, the infantry Marines set in, employing sensible infantry tactics, with interlocking machine-gun positions, some fortified behind Iraqi sandbags, for each infantryman, and Amtracs and tanks in strategic over watch positions. A no-man's-land of about 200 meters stretched between the alert Marines, who had arrived expecting a serious fight, and the townspeople, who wanted to greet them but were abruptly turned away. A small car approached from behind the Marines' line; the driver waved a white towel out the window, beeping on his horn to be let through. A machine-gun crew, gun threatening, gestured for the driver to turn around. The driver hesitated, not wanting to obey. A woman was huddled in the backseat, holding a sick infant in her robe. It took a while, but eventually the machine-gun crew were persuaded to let the car pass, and it continued on its way toward the center of town and the hospital.

When we awoke at daylight on 3 April, Ray and I discovered that the 3/7 Marines had sent out patrols throughout the night, and despite having only a few interpreters had made good progress. The troops were tired and disappointed that a real fight hadn't developed, but they carried out their orders. It paid off; they were able to obtain ledger books listing those imprisoned and interrogated by the local Baath Party police, and to uncover three arms caches of RPGs and mortar rounds. As usual, two caches were inside schools. They had raided four houses and captured fourteen Baath officials. In the morning the people at the market were smiling and were friendlier than they had been the evening before. Whatever rumors had circulated through the population during the night, they helped the standing of the Marines.

Then the Marines arrested a Shiite imam who had appeared on television and praised Saddam, and the attitude of the people turned distinctly hostile. When his followers threatened to riot, the Marines released the man. They did not know whom to arrest, or on what charges. The Marines were fighters, not police. Battalion 3/7 was anxious to hit the road, as were we.

With battalion 3/5 at Al 'Aziziyah on Route 6
3 April

Shortly after dawn we drove across the broad concrete bridge spanning the Tigris. We had the bridge to ourselves and had to admit it was a historic ride, even for a couple of old veterans. The river itself wasn't particularly remarkable, certainly no Mississippi or Ohio, but it was the river of the "cradle of civilization."

In the distance a slight mist softened the dreary tan color of the houses along the riverbank. The sooty smear of low-hanging clouds might have been mistaken for ordinary smog, unless you knew it meant that oil fires were burning alongside Route 6, a sure sign RCT-5 was out in front of us in the attack, a day ahead of the schedule Dunford had given us. You just couldn't trust Major General Mattis to relax for a moment; he never took a day's rest. If we were going to keep up, we couldn't stop to reflect on ancient history, we had to move.

Before we could catch up with RCT-5's forward battalion, though, we had to find gas. Humvees, tanks, Amtracs, helicopters, aircraft, and all sorts of military engines take JP-5 or diesel fuel. But the Nissan Corporation hadn't thought of that, and our Yellow Submarine needed unleaded gas in the middle of a war zone. So we drove along the highway and after a few miles, to our complete amazement, found a friendly gas station. We had stumbled on what was probably the only service station open for business north of Kuwait. Two Iraqis were sitting on crates under a broad cement umbrella that shaded a single row of pumps. More than a hundred military vehicles on their way to war had streamed by them that morning, and one Iraqi had probably said to the other, "Doesn't anyone need gas?" Then we arrived to answer his prayer, and he answered ours. It was a fair deal—all the gallons our two gas tanks could hold in exchange for twenty dollars U.S.—not Kuwaiti, thank you—and two MREs.

A few kilometers farther up the road the fates balanced the scales: we ran over a metal sliver, thrown from a destroyed Iraqi tank that was lying off the side of the road. Our lug wrench couldn't be found, so I rummaged through the ruins of the tank for one, found nothing intact, and trudged up the road to the next wreck. I flagged down a passing CAAT Humvee with a few captured Iraqi soldiers in green uniforms stuffed in back, only to learn that military lug wrenches are standard American; Nissan was metric. The captain said he would come back to help after he found someplace to deposit his prisoners. He was distinctly out of sorts. His unit was charging north, and these soldiers, instead of taking off their uniforms and running away like everyone else, had run out in front of his Humvee waving a white flag. Looking for a unit willing to accept more prisoners while in the attack was like looking for a gas station. We sympathized with each other's plight, and I returned to discover that Ray had found the wrench. We were on our way again.

At the intersection where Route 27 joins Route 6, we caught up with Lt. Col. Jim Chartier, commanding the 1st Tank Battalion attached to Hummer's RCT-7. Chartier had two companies of his tanks assigned to battalions in both RCT-1 and RCT-7. In return, he had a company of infantry from 3/4 attached to his battalion—mounted in Amtracs. Chartier had been leading RCT-7 for the past few days, including up to this intersection, but he had been following RCT-5 as he did. So he was a little frustrated and envious of 2nd Tank Battalion— it had been getting the action, while, right now at least, his main concern was getting enough spare parts. The maintenance crews were working with scarcely any sleep and tank upkeep was good, although the thermal sights were experiencing some degradation. As a corporal from motor transport quickly plugged the flat tire that we now had on our spare rack, Chartier told us that the weapon most often fired over the course of the campaign so far had been the 7.62mm coaxial machine gun, with its remarkable accuracy. He suggested we move up the road as fast as possible; Dunford wasn't slowing down, and he had been refueled.

All together the division had up to eight thousand vehicles on the move. Air had provided the supplement for Colonel Dunford's fast-moving column. Yesterday at dusk, as we hooked up with 2/5, the Military Police had stopped the convoys and we had watched the first C-130 land smack on the middle of Route 1, taxi off to the shoulder, and unroll a huge rubber bladder full of fuel. Since then, the workhorse C-130s had been cycling into the airfield that 1/7 had seized at Nu'maniyah. Each aircraft brought six thousand gallons of fuel, with over 100,000 gallons flown in over the past twenty-four hours. That had provided enough supplement for Dunford to roll north immediately.

With our own seventy-gallon tank of gas, another borrowed military radio, and a patch on our tire, we swung out and up Route 6, a flat four-lane road with a small dividing median, bordered by a string of short wooden telephone poles. The surrounding land was flat and less rich and green than the south side of the Tigris. The roadside villages were few and small, a smattering of one-story huts.

We were beginning to wonder where all the Iraqis were when they began to walk by us. At first we saw three or four males walking east on the other side of the road, keeping the median strip between them and us. Then ten more appeared, then twenty, then thirty. Soon we were passing fifty. After that they came in a steady column. About half wore full-length robes, and half had on trousers and long-sleeve shirts. Not one in ten wore any head dress, yet it was noon and the sun was strong. Most were wearing slippers or sandals and carried sacks or balanced rolled-up bundles on their heads. There were few women. No one waved or smiled or gave us the thumbs-up as we drove past. We hoped among these hundreds of deserters that there wasn't a sore loser with an AK-47. [Picture 39]

Soon enough we passed several Humvees. The Marines had dismounted and had their rifles pointed loosely toward the passing crowds; the Iraqis ignored them. The Marines didn't have room in their Humvees for the thousand or more who had quit the battlefield. So it seemed a stand-off. The Marines stood, and the Iraqis walked by, heading somewhere, or perhaps with no destination, satisfied just to be walking away from death.

Forty kilometers northeast of the bridge where we had crossed the Tigris, we finally caught up with Lima Company 3/5, at that moment the rear of Colonel Dunford's fast-moving column. Our first sign of it was a line of Amtracs that were well dispersed and far off the hardtop. As we approached, we saw that the troops were lying prone, facing west (to our left). They gestured to us to pull over behind an Amtrac. Artillery was working to the west, and columns of dust were rising after each boom, interspersed with a few solid columns of black smoke. The executive officer of 3/5, Maj. Jason Morris, came over and explained the tactical situation.

The enemy was dug in ahead at the town of Aziziyah. As in Nasiriyah and in Nu'maniyah, the main route skirted the edge of the town, but a branch road went over a small bridge and through the town. Republican Guards from the Al Nida Division were putting up a stiff fight. The Marines had experienced incoming, either artillery or mortars, and a heavier dose than usual of RPG fire. The Abrams tanks at the front of the column had blasted through on the main route, but it would be foolish to run a gauntlet of RPGs and automatic weapons with the Amtracs and Humvees. The battalion had dismounted and the rifle companies were fighting their way up to the bridge leading into town.

They had to check each culvert, ditch, and berm for hidden groups of Iraqis and it was exhausting work, moving forward by bounds, keyed up, bumping into Iraqi soldiers at short distances and in unlikely places. The companies were taking turns at the lead, with their Amtracs moving up behind them to provide supporting fires from the up guns. The fight had begun around one P.M., and we had arrived ninety minutes later. The 81mm mortar platoon was dug in on the left side of the highway; a twelve-foot-high cement wall sheltered their position from direct fire. There was some sort of industrial complex on the other side of the high wall, and an earlier fire mission into that complex had ignited a pair of oil fires. There was scarcely any wind, and the pillars of black smoke rising straight up provided excellent reference marks for the forward air controllers. We watched as F-18s rolled in to drop thousand-pound bombs on targets to our west, where there was a grove of palm trees. As we stood beside the highway getting briefed by Major Morris, a couple of rounds impacted between us and the grove. It could have been mortar or artillery fire—it wasn't hitting near anyone—but it wasn't Marine fire, not with air overhead at the moment. Ray commented that some Iraqi mortarman had probably dropped a few rounds down the tube before calling it a day and deserting. Morris was waiting for a medevac for two wounded Marines. So far forward had the RCTs moved that forty minutes passed before two CH-46s reached the battlefield—the helicopters were coming all the way from south of the Euphrates. Every battalion traveled with ambulances, a doctor, and highly qualified corpsmen, and they attended to the wounded in the meantime. When the CH-46s arrived, they circled the area unconcerned about enemy fire, then landed on the highway.

Gradually everyone on the front lines seemed to be developing skepticism about, if not disdain for, Iraqi marksmanship. At Najaf Iraqi defenses had stung the Apache attack helicopter assault on 23 March. But there had been no repeat of that early Iraqi success, and the Marines' caution was gradually diminishing. Marine pilots were forever trying to strike a balance between reacting aggressively to calls from the infantry and keeping their helicopters intact while they did so. Left on their own to choose, the pilots would opt for aggression. The equipment accountability system, however, was another matter. Marines might be as mean as junkyard dogs, but they also had about as much money. At the end of the day, the pilots were supposed to bring their birds home.

As the regimental combat teams moved forward, transportation helicopters played a minor role, with the exception of medevacs. The thirty-six-year-old CH-46 helicopter was worn out and limited in the number of troops it could carry. The risk-reward ratio to employ helicopters to move troops forward to seize road intersections or bridges

1. Battalion 2/5 C-7 Command Amtrac, RCT-5, 19 March 2003. Note the old-style maps and Post-it notes. High tech goes first to the Pentagon high command.

2. Charlie Company brain trust, waiting, D-Day, 20 March.

3. Battalion 1/7, gas warning, D-Day, 20 March.

4. D-Day. There were six gas warnings and three missile-launch warnings within ten hours.

5. If a pigeon dies, put on a gas mask—quickly.

6. The Crown Jewel pumping station; 2.2 million barrels of oil a day went through the turbine-driven pumps in this old metal building—saved by Corporal Garcia's squad of RCT-7 on 21 March.

7. Captain Lacroix (upper right) at the Crown Jewel, 21 March.

8. Battalion 1/7 Marine in a firefight just west of the Crown Jewel, 21 March.

9. Lieutenant Bates, CAT Red commander, with one of his prizes, 22 March.

10. Abandoned Iraqi tank at the Crown Jewel, 22 March.

11. Colonel Dowdy, commanding RCT-1, outside An Nasiriyah, 23 March.

12. Major McDonough at the Az Zubayr oil fields with Major General Smith.

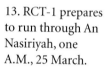

13. RCT-1 prepares to run through An Nasiriyah, one A.M., 25 March.

14. RCT-1 taking fire from a town, Route 1, early afternoon of 25 March.

15. Deploying as a dust storm increases, Route 7, midafternoon of 25 March.

16. A typical Shiite village persecuted by Saddam, Route 7, 27 March.

17. Miserable prisoners, Route 7, morning of 26 March.

18. Lieutenant Colonel McCoy, commanding battalion 3/4 of RCT-7, sketches the attack plan for Afak, Route 17, 28 March.

19. Major General Mattis briefs his commanders, 250 kilometers northwest of the Kuwait border, 28 March.

20. Marines trying to find the location of Baath Party headquarters, Route 17, 29 March.

21. A Marine sniper takes a shot at fedayeen, Route 17, 29 March.

23. Lieutenant Colonel McCoy inside the police station, center of Al Budayr, 29 March.

22. A squad advances through Afak, Route 17, 29 March.

24. Marines blow a hole to enter the Al Budayr police station, 29 March.

25. People ask for release of prisoners at the Al Budayr police station, 29 March. Marines released twenty prisoners.

26. The core of the mounted campaign, Amtrac (left) and M-1 Abrams tank (right).

27. Dragon Eye UAV with video camera, Route 17, 30 March.

28. Major General Smith watches video from Dragon Eye UAV, 30 March.

29. Sergeant Major Howell takes an Iraqi prisoner in the middle of a firefight, Ad Diwaniyah, 1 April.

30. This militiaman said he was forced to fight. Marines told him to get dressed and go over to a waiting truck. Ad Diwaniyah, 1 April.

31. A Marine clears the trench line, Ad Diwaniyah, 1 April. The average range of fighting was sixty feet.

32. Trench clearing: a burnt-out technical with machine gun in back, Ad Diwaniyah, 1 April.

33. Lieutenant Colonel McCoy examines a fedayeen motorcycle, Ad Diwaniyah, 1 April.

34. Many Iraqi soldiers fought bravely and died in trenches, Ad Diwaniyah, 1 April. They were terrible marksmen.

35. Colonel Dunford, RCT-5 commander, on cell phone bringing up his units, Route 27, 1 April.

36. Colonel Hummer, RCT-7 commander, at An Nu'maniyah, 1 April.

37. An Iraqi tank killed by the 2nd Tank Battalion, east of An Nu'maniyah, 2 April.

38. Battle of Aziziyah, 500 kilometers northwest of Kuwait, Route 6, 3 April. Major General Mattis at the front, on cell phone, orders all RCTs to roll on Baghdad.

39. Iraqi soldiers leaving the front, fleeing Al Aziziyah, Route 6, 3 April.

40. Battle of Tuwayhah, 20 kilometers outside of Baghdad. Here the 2nd Tanks were in a "run and gun" battle versus the Al Nida Division, Route 6, 4 April.

41. Marines of battalion 3/5 pause for water as they move up into the fight at Al Aziziyah, 3 April.

42. Warnings about gas, east of Saddam City, 6 April.

43. After the battle, (left to right) Corporal Weighe, Gunnery Sergeant Cheramie, Corporal Brown, and Corporal Moorehead, Route 6, 4 April.

44. Major General Mattis, Lieutenant Colonel McCoy, and Colonel Hummer at Baghdad Bridge under incoming, 7 April.

45. Marines clear the city side of Baghdad Bridge, 7 April.

46. Sergeant Major Howell (foreground) yells orders after incoming artillery hits Amtrac, killing two Marines and just missing the division, regimental, and battalion commanders, 7 April.

47. Major General Smith inside the Atomic Energy Center with relaxed Saddam, 7 April.

48. Russian torpedoes in a Baghdad warehouse, 8 April.

49. Poster of a safety-conscious Saddam in the warehouse, 8 April.

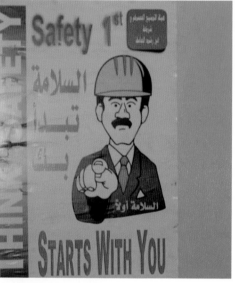

50. Sergeant Perolio, a battalion 1/7 sniper, seconds before he killed an enemy sniper, Baghdad, 9 April.

51. Fighting at Baghdad University, 9 April.

52. Inside Tariq Aziz's palace, (left to right) Lieutenant Colonel Conlin, Captain Lacroix, and Sergeant Major Bergeron, Baghdad, 9 April.

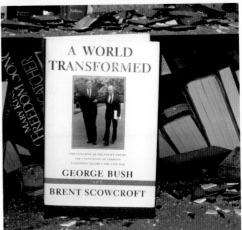

53. A book by President Bush in the destroyed library of Deputy Prime Minister Tariq Aziz, Baghdad, 9 April.

54. Saddam's palace under new management, Baghdad, 10 April.

55. Marines of Charlie Company, battalion 1/7, at Tariq Aziz's palace, 9 April.

56. Bing West and son, Captain Owen West, First Force Recon, south of Baghdad, April 12.

57. The end of a tyrant's reign, Baghdad, 10 April 2003.

58. Corporal Ferkovich (with M-16 under the flag) and his squad, 1st Battalion, RCT-7, April 2003. They captured the Crown Jewel on D-Day and twenty-two days later stood on the roof of Saddam's palace. "No better friend, no worse enemy. Semper Fi."

51. Fighting at Baghdad University, 9 April.

52. Inside Tariq Aziz's palace, (left to right) Lieutenant Colonel Conlin, Captain Lacroix, and Sergeant Major Bergeron, Baghdad, 9 April.

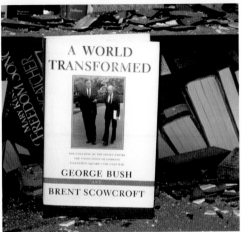

53. A book by President Bush in the destroyed library of Deputy Prime Minister Tariq Aziz, Baghdad, 9 April.

54. Saddam's palace under new management, Baghdad, 10 April.

55. Marines of Charlie Company, battalion 1/7, at Tariq Aziz's palace, 9 April.

56. Bing West and son, Captain Owen West, First Force Recon, south of Baghdad, April 12.

57. The end of a tyrant's reign, Baghdad, 10 April 2003.

58. Corporal Ferkovich (with M-16 under the flag) and his squad, 1st Battalion, RCT-7, April 2003. They captured the Crown Jewel on D-Day and twenty-two days later stood on the roof of Saddam's palace. "No better friend, no worse enemy. Semper Fi."

did not make sense. The dual risks of a crash or of the troops being surrounded on the ground were too high, versus the comparatively small amount of additional time the tanks and LAVs needed to get there on the ground.

Once the CH-46s had picked up the wounded, we gradually eased our way up the column. It was hard for the yellow Nissan to be inconspicuous, and soon we were flagged over and motioned into a ditch on the right side of the road, safe in defilade and not a nuisance to the advancing troops. Smack on the highway above us were two parked Humvees, with a map board propped against a rear tire. Colonel Dunford and Lt. Col. Sam Mundy, commanding battalion 3/5, were nose to nose trying to hear each other over the din of M-16s and 240 Golf machine guns. Ahead of them was a platoon of Marines in a semicircle, and 150 meters farther ahead was a narrow bridge with steel support girders on either side, like a trestle on a railroad bridge. On the other side of a river—which looked more the size of a moat—was a row of two-story buildings. Mundy's mission was to push across the small river and enter and clear the town, which extended for three kilometers. There was a bridge over the Tigris on the southern edge of the town, and Dunford wanted it seized if possible.

In single file, troops walked up the ditch where we stood watching. All were wearing their armored vests with the ceramic plates, Kevlar helmets, and web gear bulging with ammo and a few canteens. Many had Camelbak water sacks on their backs, with a rubber tube dangling under the chin strap. About half were carrying small rucksacks with more ammo. Some still had on their rubber overboots; others had taken them off and shoved them in the rucksacks. All looked worn. For Ray and me both, we knew from slogging through the paddies in Vietnam how tired these Marines were this late in the fight. The gear they were carrying wasn't that much different than what we had carried and as they trudged by us along the side of the highway they seemed to both of us to be the same Marines we had known thirty-five or forty years earlier—we both felt like we could call out a name from our past, and someone there, in that column, would answer. Ray was encouraging them, slapping them on the shoulders as they passed by, and when I looked at him I could see tears running down his face.

The temperature was about 80°F, and they had been in the attack for about four hours, lying prone, doing nothing for long periods, then being told to get up and get moving, shuffling along at a good clip, hearing some rounds snapping overhead, getting down, throwing some rounds downrange, checking the fields of fire to the left and right, getting up, shuffling forward again, and again, and again. Except when he has walked unsuspecting into an ambush, an infantryman in a firefight can sense when his side has definite fire superiority, so he can get up and trot ahead without too much fear. Rounds have a different sound when they are zipping by you than when they are cracking over your head. When the rounds begin to zip, the rifleman flops down and crawls. Earth is his best friend. When the rounds are high, he can move forward at a walk, usually bent over a bit out of habit, trying to make himself smaller. At Aziziyah, the troops of battalion 3/5 were moving steadily forward, walking in that hunched-over way.

After a while this sort of workout in a firefight becomes exhausting, yet it is also exhilarating. As he passed by me, one Marine with a machine gun on his shoulder paused to sip some water, then took a full look around, as though noticing his surroundings for the first time. [Picture 41] "This is like Full Metal Jacket," he said approvingly. "Smoke rising, arty coming in, machine guns."

He was right. Pillars of black smoke rose on every side. The 155mm shells with their distinct whisper, like cloth being quickly ripped, were whizzing by on their downward trajectory, hitting with a series of deep crump, crump sounds. Resting their bipods on the hardtop, gunners manning two pairs of 240 Golfs were taking turns "beating a tattoo"; the sound bounced off the macadam like a jackhammer. Practically no rounds were coming into our sector now that the Iraqis had fallen back. The Marines surged forward. Some stood on the hardtop as if to prove they couldn't be hit—or maybe they had been out in the sun too long. The machine-gunner was right; the scene did have a certain surreal edge to it. I half-expected to see Robert Duvall fly by in a Huey, playing Flight of the Valkyries, and dismount with his surfboard.

Instead, Ray and I saw Major General Mattis. He was standing by a Humvee with a large map board with red and blue square stickums pasted along the route we were on. He was listening on an iridium cell phone and staring at the map, oblivious to the shooting and shouting around him. [Picture 38] On the hardtop Dunford and Mundy continued their discussion, as if it were an everyday occurrence to have the commanding general—Mattis—in battle with them, and he was doing his thing while they did theirs. In military textbooks the theorists stress that the ideal location for the general is one where he can observe the battlefield firsthand, gauge the fighting condition of his troops and the enemy, and still communicate directly with his key subordinates so that he can exploit what he is observing.

It is rare in modern war that all four conditions can be filled simultaneously. By being on scene during this battle, Mattis was employing what theorists call the coup d'oeil, when the commander is able to select and focus on the battle's key elements. He could see that the Marines, although tired, were continuing to press forward, while the enemy had retreated into the town. He could see with his own eyes that his troops had the initiative.

And Mattis always had a sense for the troops. As he was studying the map, a Marine stumbled by him breathing hoarsely in the dust.

"Want some water?" Mattis said, gesturing at the gypsy rack that every Humvee carried with five-gallon water jugs.

The Marine refilled his canteens, took a deep gulp, and patted Mattis on the shoulder. "Thanks, man," he said, trotting off, apparently unaware that he was talking to his division commander.

Mattis and Conway had discussed the overall situation around ten that morning, when Mattis had driven forward to observe RCT-5 in the attack. Conway had told Mattis to "go for it" if the opportunity presented itself. MEF and division intelligence agreed that the only organized defense that stood between the Blue Diamond and Baghdad was the Al Nida Division, and RCT-5 had that division reeling backward. If Mattis could push enough power forward now, he could be at Baghdad, 70 kilometers ahead, within a day. Dunford, the RCT-5 commander, had with him infantry battalion 3/5 and 2nd Tank Battalion.

They might be able to go another day, but after forty-eight hours they would have to rest. Each long infantry fight is like a marathon. A good runner can push himself and complete two in two days, but that is the physical limit. To exploit the opening he was about to make, Mattis had to bring up reinforcements.

The iridium satellite cell phone with an encrypted channel provided him with the linkage. Mattis called 100 kilometers back to the division's main command post and spoke with his assistant division commander, Brigadier General Kelly. "Tell Steve to come up here right away to his friend Joe's location. Make sure he knows I want him to bring all his friends with him." The cell phone was encrypted, but Mattis wasn't sure he trusted it.

Col. Steven Hummer understood he was to bring immediately his thousand vehicles and six thousand men up Route 6. That morning he had sent battalions 3/4 and 1/7 across the Tigris and east 30 kilometers to attack the Baghdad Division from the west, while RCT-1 attacked from the south. Whatever residual fighting spirit had remained in the Iraqi division was punctured when 3/4 and 1/7 slammed into it. Hummer told McCoy and Conlin to reverse direction; they were headed for Baghdad.

That quickly it was done. After the meeting on 29 March at Camp David, General Franks contacted his major subordinate commands and made it clear that there was to be no continued pause. The objective of the ground campaign remained to seize Baghdad as soon as possible. On 30 March the word had gone down the chain of command that the pause was lifted, and late that day Mattis informed Dunford to retake the elbow at the junction of Routes 1 and 27. On 31 March RCT-5 had fought and reseized the elbow. On 1 April C-130s were flying in fuel, landing initially on Route 1, while RCT-5 executed the division's deception plan and advanced down Route 27, seizing the Saddam Canal. On 2 April Dunford's battalions seized the cement bridge across the Tigris at Nu'maniyah and added a pontoon bridge upstream.

Now on 3 April Mattis had his pieces on the chessboard aligned to finish the march up. Dunford had 2nd Tanks still rolling toward

Baghdad as 3/5 cleared Aziziyah and would continue the attack the next day. He had to get the rest of RCT-5 closed up, but he was working on that even as the 3/5 fight continued. Hummer would follow on their heels with RCT-7. Back at Al Kut, RCT-1 was south of the Tigris, having fixed and engaged the battered Baghdad Division as battalions 3/4 and 1/7 were slamming into it earlier that day. If it moved fast, RCT-1 could cross the Tigris at Nu'maniyah and be only a day behind RCT-7. To do that, Mattis made the gut-wrenching decision to change commanders in RCT-1.

The division's G-3 Operations officer, Col. John Toolan, was thoroughly familiar with the plan that the three RCTs were now executing and could reorient RCT-1 while it moved, saving the time that otherwise might be spent planning before moving. With speed of the essence, he replaced Dowdy the next day. Toolan took over the regiment while Dowdy became the senior officer airborne in a specially equipped four-engine P-3 aircraft that had extraordinary optics. Loitering overhead, it enabled a commander to survey hundreds of kilometers of the battlefield, zooming in on small objects with an astounding clarity. With his ground experience, from that vantage point Dowdy provided the division an overview that permitted rapid reaction to enemy movements across a broad front.

All across that front, as Saddam's control was crumbling, his minions persisted in denying reality while secretly preparing to flee. While Mattis was at Aziziyah gathering his forces to go to Baghdad, inside the city Deputy Prime Minister Tariq Aziz was holding a news conference to assure the reporters that Saddam Hussein was "in full control of the army and the country." *Saturday Night Live*'s favorite character, Information Minister Mohammed Saeed al-Sahhaf, did not disappoint. He agreed with Aziz, saying reports of U.S. advances on Baghdad were "illusions." If Mattis had his way—and commanders and staff throughout the division were straining every sinew to ensure he did—those "illusions" would become hard reality for Aziz and the rest of the Saddam Hussein regime in a matter of a very few days.

* * *

After issuing his cryptic orders at the front at Aziziyah, Mattis drove back down the column a little ways, taking his combat family with him. His driver, Sgt. Yaniv Newman, joked that his job was to peel red squares off the map. Actually, Mattis entrusted him to keep constantly up to date on all relevant enemy and friendly locations. His communicator, Sgt. Ryan Woolwort, joked that his job was to recharge the batteries for the iridium phone. Actually, he had to ensure that Mattis was never out of touch—no small matter with a boss always on the move. Mattis's aide, Capt. Warren Cook, made the trains run on time, as all aides must do. This was no small feat, especially since the division commander was moving so fast to the point of battle. Mattis had used one piece of modern communications technology—a satellite cell phone—to exploit the single most major opportunity in the campaign of the Blue Diamond. He now needed more robust communications, and so he had called for his "jump" command post—an LAV with a full suite of communications—to come forward.

At the same time, RCT-5 continued in the attack. The tanks had crashed their way through Aziziyah, led by Capt. Todd Sudmeyer's Alpha Company. The Iraqis had massed many more units than they had previously, trying to employ artillery and T-55s as well as RPGs and foot infantry. This array provided the Marines with more targets than before and slowed their advance, but for the Abrams tanks it did not alter the pattern. They eventually rolled through the town, their main guns and coaxial machine guns pointed mainly to the left. Aziziyah was a typical town, with storefronts set back from the road and a long row of cement buildings without paint or color bisected at right angles by wide side streets; it stretched north of the bridge for over two kilometers, then gradually petered out into smaller and smaller clusters of isolated buildings. While moving through the town, many Marine tank commanders did not button up. Like the TOW gunners on the Humvees, they stood erect, their shoulders and heads protruding above the armor, their hands on the .50-calibers, daring an Iraqi soldier to dart out with an RPG. Iraqis were trying to shoot at them with rifles, too, of course, and later Capt. Jon Luder dug a bullet out of the sandbags he had placed around his turret hatch. The armor passed through the town unscathed.

Colonel Dunford had expected that result, but Aziziyah still had to be cleared so that the hundreds of soft-skinned vehicles of all three regiments could pass through in the next two days without stopping. A repeat of Nasiriyah, where the drivers felt they were running a gauntlet and traffic jams held up convoys for dozens of kilometers, was unacceptable. Dunford told Mundy to push battalion 3/5 through the town, clearing as they went.

On the night of the great storm of 24 March, Mundy's battalion had fought and routed an Iraqi force on Route 1. He had by now concluded that the Iraqi soldiers could not stand up to a determined Marine assault. At Aziziyah dusk was coming on, and Dunford wanted the town cleared. If Mundy waited until dawn and then attacked, the regrouped Iraqis might hold up his battalion for another five or six hours, while the highway became clogged with vehicles waiting to move through. The Iraqis were already shooting from the first row of houses on the other side of the bridge. Kilo Company, which had taken three wounded so far, pushed across the bridge into the houses. The residents who were hiding in backrooms told them the Iraqi soldiers had fled when they saw the Marines running across the bridge. In the dark Mundy brought up his other two companies; they divided the town into a rough search grid and pushed from block to block.

Mundy had calculated correctly. The Iraqis fought from the outskirts of the town but lacked the training and small-unit leadership to dig in around houses and set up interlocking fields of grazing fire. Far from being the defender's natural ally, city blocks that split up a force invited desertions, and the Iraqi regular army forces and Republican Guards avoided them. Once the Marine companies pushed beyond the town's frontage, there was no more shooting. Followed by their Amtracs, the Marines worked their way down side streets and alleys, trotting from block to block, banging on doors and shouting back and forth to spook any lurking ambushers into giving away their positions. The Amtracs' diesel engines screeched and growled in the background; the din probably petrified the residents of the town. If any Iraqi soldiers were in town, they stayed hidden and did not let out a peep.

The only casualty was the pack belonging to Lance Corporal Pickering of India Company, who was highly upset. During a tight turn in an alley, it had been scraped off the side of the Amtrac. Gone was all his gear, comparatively clean socks, toothbrush, penlight, sleeping bag, soap, coffee cup, and a diary in which he had laboriously written each day. All he had left were his rifle and gas mask. His sympathetic fire team told him that was all the gear any good rifleman needed.

9

Run and Gun

D + 14

With 2nd Tank Battalion
Along Route 6 to Baghdad
April 4

WHILE BATTALION 3/5 WAS SWEEPING THROUGH Aziziyah, Ray and I had hopped into our Yellow Submarine and followed Colonel Dunford in his Humvee through the town and up Route 6. We raced along at 60 miles per hour, seeing nothing but open road and a few burnt-out Iraqi tanks. Dunford had told 2nd Tanks to find a bivouac north of Aziziyah and set in. Instead, we seemed to be following the highball express into downtown Baghdad. "I'm going to have to put a bit on Iron Horse," Dunford said over the radio, Iron Horse being the call sign for the 2nd Tank Battalion.

Fourteen kilometers farther, we pulled into a shot-up Iraqi military camp, a commandeered cluster of cement-block school buildings with a pale beige stucco finish, adorned with neat round puncture wounds from 120mm tank rounds. Startled Iraqi soldiers had literally fled out backdoors when 2nd Tanks drove up, and the Iraqi flag that had flown over the compound was now folded in a tank commander's pouch. While Ray sat with Dunford studying maps, in the dark I ate an MRE dinner with First Sgt. Edward Smith of Fox Company, battalion 2/5, which was attached to the tank battalion. First Sergeant Smith had served in both battalion and force reconnaissance, where my son Owen was currently serving with the MEF. Smith was well known in the recon community as Horsehead Smith (Marines don't necessarily care if their nicknames are flattering), and he was "one of those NCOs people think should be a colonel, physically and mentally on top of things, the way he takes care of his men." Horsehead Smith was sitting with his little family: the company commander, Captain Johnson; the driver, Lance Corporal Mikolas; and their TOW gunner, Staff Sergeant Zamora, a reservist who was a cop in Florida. After we opened our MREs, we traded items—Mikolas gave me cocoa beverage powder for nothing in exchange—and swapped tales of the campaign, sitting in the dirt, filthy and comfortable at the end of the day.

Horsehead smiled and shook his head about life in armored vehicles, something his recon training had not prepared him for. Fox Company rode in a dozen Amtracs, following the tanks. The day had been a beaut, he said—all the way up to Aziziyah they had seen little knots of Iraqis out behind the berms at 200 to 300 meters, "low crawling with RPGs, RPGs flying over our heads, the Iraqis running, taking off their uniforms, and we're going by so fast that the tanks are shooting only at enemy main systems, like other tanks."

If he could make a suggestion, Horsehead said, it would be to buy each squad a small radio, like the ones some of the reporters had, in order to keep up with the sports scores and what was going on in the rest of the world. He liked the messages the tank commanding officer, Lt. Col. Mike Oehl, called in by satellite phone to his office back at Camp Lejeune, North Carolina. A family member could call that number and hear the colonel giving an update on what the battalion was doing and how well things were going.

The tank philosophy was to steamroll over the trouble spots. Horsehead hadn't seen an Abrams tank stopped by anything. Antipersonnel RPGs bounced off the armor. His main problem, he said, was keeping up the morale of the infantrymen. All the riding was hard on the troops. Hunkered down inside, they felt they didn't control what was happening. They wanted to be outside on their own two feet. They wanted action.

"I tell the young devil dogs," Horsehead said, "don't get discouraged if you don't get in a real fight. We've done our job if Saddam goes and we all go home in one piece."

While we were talking, Major General Mattis drove in to go over the attack plan with Colonel Dunford. The plan was for the division to reach the outskirts of Baghdad the next day, take a day to break down into small infantry-tank teams as necessary, and then go on in. It looked like First Sergeant Smith would shortly be moving his troops out of the Amtracs and into a real fight.

That night, for the first time in the campaign, we felt the power of the American air arm. We lay in our bags in the dirt looking at the bright stars and listening to the steady roar of invisible planes passing overhead. The horizon toward Baghdad, 60 kilometers away, blinked with flashes of dim yellow light. It was like sleeping on the runway at JFK International Airport.

On the morning of 4 April Colonel Dunford delayed the attack while the supply train for Lieutenant Colonel Mundy's battalion, 3/5, caught up. Mundy had left it 40 kilometers behind the day before, when he sprinted to keep up with the tanks. He was now down to a quarter of a tank of fuel in many vehicles, and low on water and MREs, and the troops had to rehydrate before starting out. Just as vexing, Mundy's companies had captured fifty Iraqi soldiers yesterday, and he was stuck either transporting them, leaving them behind with a force to guard them that was large enough to protect itself in the middle of a battlefield, or dropping them by the side of the road. Dunford said the RCT would roll before noon, and Mundy assured him that battalion 3/5 would be saddled up and in position.

Dunford asked about the status of the tanks. Capt. David Bardorf, the supply officer, said his tanks were in the best shape he could hope for in the absence of spare parts. Bardorf was the son of my close friends from Newport, Rhode Island, and his parents were immensely proud of his dedication to the Marine Corps. David loved tanks, a quirk that I as a former infantry officer could not understand. He also shared Colonel Dunford's reservations about the supply system in the rear, and replacement parts were a particular sore spot. The tanks were ready, though.

Ray and I asked Dunford if we could ride up front with the tanks, assuming that the Al Nida Division had had enough after yesterday. Dunford turned us over to Mike Oehl, the battalion commander, who passed us on to Alpha Company's Captain Sudmeyer, who had led the 2nd Tank Battalion dash of the day before. Today Alpha Company would be second in the battalion's movement, following Charlie Company. Sudmeyer had enlisted in the Marines after high school, rose to the rank of sergeant in the infantry and recon, and was sent to Penn State, accepting a commission and agreeing to serve at least five years. Ray, who was normally willing to calmly fall into a column with the Yellow Submarine wherever he was told, was asking a lot of questions of Sudmeyer's executive officer, First Lt. Douglas Finn, whose tank we would be behind; Ray was double-checking radio frequencies and call signs.

When I asked Ray what was bothering him, he looked at me as if I had two heads. "These tankers think they're invulnerable," he said. "And they're right. But we're not. If that young hard-charger gets into a fight, he's liable to forget all about us in this soft-skinned vehicle behind him. If he's going to lead me into a fight like I was in a tank, I want to be sure I have my shit together."

Refueled and rearmed, the 150 vehicles formed up in two columns. To the right, or northeast of the median of the four-lane highway, was a row of thirty-five Humvees, a few with .50-calibers and most with TOW rockets. To the left of the median thirty-four Abrams tanks lined up, with a scruffy yellow SUV about midway back. Ray conducted a last-minute radio check with Sudmeyer and Finn. At eleven on the morning of 4 April 2nd Tank Battalion, leading RCT-5, began to roll down Route 6 on the 55-kilometer drive to the outskirts of Baghdad.

The countryside was a flat expanse of tan dirt interspersed with scruffy green shrubs. Scattered up the highway were various clusters of adobe houses and mud huts and a few industrial parks with high cement walls. Along both sides of the road were extended trenches and berms, a common enough sight. The double column, which extended in length for 14 kilometers, had just straightened out and hit a cruising speed of about 25 kilometers an hour when the battle began.

To our left was a group of cement buildings and a wire fence, and farther up the road a grove of palm trees. The Iraqis let the Marines' lead tank company go by, and then as Alpha Company was passing, there was a loud *woosh*, as if a jet had passed only a few meters overhead, and an explosive blast to the right that seemed as big as a 155mm shell, only with more flame and red sparks. There was another *woosh* and another *boom* and another red fireball to the right of our SUV. The company net came alive as the tankers tried to identify the weapon.

"SAM! SA-7 malfunctioning! He's aiming for the Cobras."

"Negative. Those are Saggers. Repeat, Saggers."

More back-and-forth followed, as the tankers tried to determine whether a heavy-duty antitank guided missile had been fired at them. The warheads had been heavy enough to rock even an Abrams.

"This is Alpha Six. Pick up the pace. Pick it up. Open some space between us and those palm trees."

The commander of a unit over the radio is called "Six." Captain Sudmeyer wanted his tanks and Humvees to speed it up. The lead tanks had opened fire to our left with their 7.62s. A Humvee with a .50-caliber was firing to our right. Sudmeyer, Finn, and the other tankers had their hatches closed and were scanning to the left with both their thermals and day optics. The TOW-mounted Humvees on the right were on their optics as well, but the gunners in the top turrets were exposed from the chest up.

The Al Nida Republican Guard Division had not folded. All along the road there were puffs of dirt from behind the berms: some were caused by our own outgoing fire, and some by the muzzle blast from Iraqi small arms. The column rolled past an occasional burning military vehicle, roasting on the side of the road. It passed more berms, some sandbagged, and more exchanges of machine-gun fire. The Iraqis were well coached about the thermals and were staying away from the apertures in their bunkers, lying flat and safe, unseen, until they worked up the nerve to jump up and shoot an RPG or an AK-47. That was the chance for the tankers and TOW gunners, who were mainly using their M-16s. An Iraqi would fire, and Marines in four or five vehicles would return it. Once in a while, when two or more Iraqis were seen in one bunker, a tank main gun would fire.

I turned on my digital camera, and the battlefield cooperated with continuous action, kilometer after kilometer, growing in intensity. The TOW gunners saw some tanks moving in a tree line 1,500 meters east and let loose a flurry of missiles. At the front of the column a T-72 and two BMPs with crews inside were hit as they sped toward Baghdad, trying to outrun the M1s of 2nd Tanks. All along the road vehicles were burning, and the smoke was dense. In the slight wind the black plumes from fires at oil storage sites hung and thickened. Nearer the road the Iraqis had lit off trenches filled with oil; the flames were a bright orange, and the smoke arched and curled over the road. The tanks drove through black waves that crested and looked about to break.

An Iraqi truck by the side of the road went up in a tremendous roar, and the radios crackled with warnings of truck bombs. From then on the tanks and Humvees veered to swing around the now-numerous Iraqi military vehicles that were burning alongside the highway—ammunition was cooking off in nearly every one of them. Every 500 meters or so we passed another flaming vehicle. Corpses were few—the drivers had fled when they heard the tank guns behind them. In the near trenches, here and there, were scattered dishes and teapots. It was impossible to gauge the amount of damage being done by seventy-two tanks and Humvees bristling with weapons. The first tank might miss, and the second, and the third, but sooner or later, if an Iraqi persisted in shooting, he would be hit.

We had some concerns about our position in the run and gun. The AK-47 fire was high but uncomfortable. First Lieutenant Finn did forget about us when he saw movement in a bunker to our left. I saw the main gun swivel and drop several inches—a sure sign the gunner was aiming in—and yelled at Ray, who was trying to get into the median strip to the right of Finn's tank, but before he could react, there was a sharp *crack!* The Yellow Submarine veered for a second, Ray firmly gripping the wheel, then straightened out. The windshield had been split down the middle by the concussion. Ray let loose a few salty remarks over the radio, and the next time the main gun fired, Finn gave us fair warning. When the firing became too heavy, Finn moved left to allow us to pull alongside, and we drove on the median, with Finn in the Abrams on the left and a thoughtful TOW Humvee driver on the right. The rounds cracking overhead stayed high as we continued down the highway.

"It's a good thing they can't shoot worth a damn," Ray said.

Unfortunately that would not hold entirely true. Too many Iraqis were shooting, and they had come to fight. Ray and I, tracking our location on two Garmin GPS receivers, saw that we were now in the vicinity of Tuwayhah, at least on some maps. [Picture 40] As we approached the 64 easting—the point on the military map where the highway crossed the 64 north-south grid line—a tank was stopped, and we swung around it to the right. Over the battalion radio net we heard that the tank of Charlie Six, Capt. Jeffrey Houston, was a mobility kill, meaning no casualties but the tank couldn't continue to move. His executive officer reported that he had command, and Charlie Company, less the commanding officer and one tank that had stopped to assist him, continued to lead the fight.

The Humvees to our right were working over a small shop, hammering it with .50-calibers; a cloud of white dust swirled around the door front. The Iraqi shooters were crouched somewhere back from the storefronts, picking their moments to fire, looking for an exposed target. Over the din of the tank engines, the churning of the treads, and the stutter of first one 7.62mm machine gun and then another, no one could hear an Iraqi firing. The Marines couldn't see a heat contrast on their thermals, so they drove by, waiting for a flicker of light, a flash somewhere in the corner of a building.

Then we heard the grim news over the radio.

"Scout Six is down."

First Lt. Brian McPhillips of Pembroke, Massachusetts, was dead, shot in the head while leading his TOW Humvees through Tuwayhah. He was close friends with Captain Bardorf, the son of my friends in

Newport, and, although I hadn't met him, McPhillips and I had attended the same high school, Boston College High.

Iraqi firing didn't seem heavier now, but it was more confined, with targets close at hand. Ray was monitoring the radio, listening to reports that we had accidentally passed by our turn. On our own GPS receivers the displays showed that we were continuing northwest toward Baghdad. Capt. Sudmeyer, however, had shown us on a map that we were supposed to turn north on what was called Route Green. One of the tanks in the lead wasn't answering up, and later we learned that a volley of RPGs had killed the loader and knocked out the tank's radios and GPS. We were all following a tank that was headed in the wrong direction and we had already passed the right-hand turn onto Route Green.

The column slowed as the lead tanks and the RCT command group talked on the radio, sorting out where we were and where we should be. The Marines' firing was steady, not overwhelming but constant, as first one and then another tank would spot something and cut loose. Few main gun rounds were fired, mostly the 7.62, intermixed with the .50-caliber. The tanks were buttoned up, but the Humvees' gunners were standing erect. Immediately behind Ray and me the Amtracs of Horsehead Smith's Fox Company had pushed up, tops open, and Marines were firing.

Then the word came over the radio for us all to turn around. One tank—Captain Sudmeyer's—cut out of the firing line and roared forward. We heard Scout One check in, saying they had Scout Six's Humvee with them and confirming that Scout Six Actual was KIA. About 500 meters farther on Captain Sudmeyer's tank had stopped broadside in the road, blocking any farther advance in the wrong direction and shielding each vehicle as it turned around.

As we completed the turn and started back the way we had just come, we saw that an Amtrac behind us had pulled over to the side, and Captain Bardorf had pulled up in a Humvee with an ambulance behind him. They lifted a Marine from the back hatch of the trac and put him on a stretcher. As we pulled back past the ambulance, we saw that the

Marine's face had lost all color. He had been shot in the head. Three Marines had been killed in the last half-hour.

While the main column untangled itself and we stayed close to Finn's tank, Bardorf and the ambulance turned around and zigzagged back to Captain Houston's stalled tank. Since we had passed him, Houston had taken a bullet in the jaw, and another tank and Colonel Dunford's three-Humvee command group had stopped to help. With sitting targets, the fedayeen who had been hiding in the ditches and behind the berms began crawling forward, firing RPGs and AK-47s. Lance Corporal Peixotto, Houston's driver, was holding a compress to Houston's face with one hand and firing his 9mm pistol with the other. Colonel Dunford had taken control of the overall fight, and we listened as Dunford, or "Grizzly Six" over the radio, told Lieutenant Colonel Mundy to dismount his battalion and clear both sides of the road. Corporal Jones ran over to help Peixotto with Houston. A descendant of Sam Houston, the Marine captain liked to tell how his famous ancestor ordered that an arrow be jerked out of his leg. Now he was fully conscious, watching his comrades fight the hostiles who wanted to take his life. Dunford's turret gunner, Corporal Moorehead, was hit in the helmet by shrapnel as big as his fist, suffering only a welt. Dunford's sniper, Gunnery Sergeant Cheramie, dropped an Iraqi in green trousers who was running in a crouch toward the tank. Cheramie hit him three times before he went down, later telling Ray and me that he believed the man had to be "hopped up" to take those hits and stay on his feet. *[Picture 43]* The regimental gunner, Chuck Colleton, kept up a steady rate of fire on the attackers as Dunford directed the overall battle.

Two tanks and Dunford's Humvees were providing a tight protective circle around Houston, spraying the area on both sides of the road with M-16 and machine-gun fire. The attackers were a mixture of fedayeen in civilian clothes and soldiers in green uniforms. They didn't lack for courage, slipping in close to use the trenches and irrigation ditches. An iron horse had been wounded and hobbled, and they saw they had a chance to kill it—only they couldn't close those last 20 meters. The firepower was too relentless.

Bardorf and the battalion doctor, Lieutenant Webb, pulled up with the ambulance, which already held five wounded. They were helping Houston, who had stayed conscious through the fight, crawl into the vehicle when the ambulance driver, Corporal Holden, was shot through the hand. Webb now had seven patients.

By now the two lead tank companies had found their turn to the north and made it but were held up while the action around Houston's tank was being resolved. Stopped on the road heading north, we couldn't see Houston's tank, but we could hear the action. A section of four Cobras was buzzing up and down the sides of the road, one or another of them peeling off to fire his 20mm cannon or loose rockets at some cement building or at any of the countless light-brown berms out in the fields. Their acrobatics, their sudden dips and swoops, then their dead stops in the air, hovering while the rockets poured out in bright white streams, made me hope we wouldn't see a midair crash. We watched the ambulance come back toward our position, and after a while two CH-46s that had been circling overhead landed on the road, which was filled with dust and churning vehicles, all firing. The column waited while the wounded were evacuated, forming some sort of huge cocoon around the ambulance. The firing was so unremitting that you grew to accept it as normal background noise.

Just as the CH-46 was lifting off with the medevac, Sam Mundy's 3/5 Marines were beginning their dismounted attack to mop up behind the tanks. The 2nd Tank Battalion had broken through, destroying the Al Nida Division regulars as they went, but there were still plenty of enemy fighters alongside the highway. Mundy's Marines still had their work cut out for them.

Mundy told Lima Company to clear the northeast, or right side of the highway, while India went to the left, where the ground was more broken up with lumpy irrigation ditches and berms. Mundy thought the troops, who had fought for ten hours advancing through Aziziyah yesterday, had looked tired when they started out that morning. Now they knew that they had to sweep forward at least four kilometers to clear all of the ambush. Four kilometers of fighting, sprinting, and flop-

ping, lay ahead. It was going to be a long day for the hoplites, but they went about the task with determination.

The Marines crossed the roadside ditches at a trot, beginning in two columns, then fanned out and walked toward the first berm, about 70 meters out in the field, shooting a few Iraqis in green uniforms who were cowering in shallow cover. When they climbed the berm, to their surprise they were looking down on a row of Iraqi soldiers, most running away, many raising their hands. There wasn't much fight in them, and many were old—thirty-five- to fifty-year-old—militia types. The Marines cinched their hands with the plastic ties and prodded them over the berm onto the road.

The Iraqi American interpreters in Mundy's human exploitation team talked to any Iraqis they happened upon. Yesterday in Aziziyah and now at an intersection where there was a row of houses, the HET heard the same stories about buses with fedayeen and foreign fighters. The divisional command had passed the same warning. Last night foreigners staying at the Sheraton Hotel in Baghdad had boarded buses to join the Al Nida in its fight.

India Company, in column to the southwest side of the road, started seeing random dust puffs from bullets. The troops flopped down along the road, and the company commander, Capt. Ethan Bishop, sent a platoon at the double time over a solid wooden footbridge spanning an irrigation ditch that was half filled with water and bordered by bulrushes. The orange-tan earth had been turned over many times and was now furrowed and ruffled. To the left of the bridge was a berm not as tall as a man; a wide, chopped-up field lay on the far side, and a high berm 300 meters out stood on the other side. Thinking the shooters were behind the far berm, the platoon ran straight out several hundred meters. The incoming fire only increased, and the platoon was unable to locate the source.

An exasperated Captain Bishop called for Lt. Casey Brock, who looked like a football lineman, a large target on the infantryman's battlefield. "Brock, get out there and show them how to do it," Bishop said.

Brock brought up Cpl. Larry Russell and his squad, who had a reputation of being characters; Russell was called "Staff Corporal," a play on the rank of Staff Sergeant, because he had led the squad for thirty-two months, despite being reduced in rank at least once. He was totally confident of his ability to lead Marines in the field—and the Marines in his squad had equal confidence in him. When the redheaded Russell gave his squad an order, they knew it was a good one and that he would be in the thick of it with them. Russell knew how to fight, both in the field and on liberty; the "on liberty" part explained his still being a corporal.

Brock suspected the Iraqis were in tight, hidden in the folds of the earth. He led the squad over the footbridge and turned them on line to sweep the close-in field. Immediately the firing increased, and the squad went flat. Brock and Russell split the squad into two teams and advanced by short rushes, getting up, running, dropping down, sighting in, looking for a target, then getting up again, repeating the drill over and over.

Everyone in the division had become accustomed to seeing abandoned Iraqi military equipment, blankets, tents, sleeping bags, and—of course—boots alongside every highway. This area was no exception, except that here foreign fighters and fedayeen were hiding under that abandoned equipment. The Marines saw some Iraqis at 30 meters and others at five, hidden under blankets, snuggled in culverts, lying in the weeds and in ditches. Behind a low berm they saw rags and items of clothing and tents collapsed on the ground, beneath which men stretched out flat, peeping out and shooting. Wherever the Marines looked carefully, they saw another young man in dull civilian clothes or half-military dress tucked against the earth, the camouflage crude yet complete. The fedayeen were hiding in plain sight, so close to the road they could have hit the passing tanks with rocks.

The problem for the foreigners was that every time one of them rose to fire an RPG, two or three tanks or Humvees fired back. So as the tanks roared past, they either fired from under their cover, hitting nothing, or didn't fire at all and let the tanks pass. Now, with 3/5 Marines among them on foot, they no longer had the option of lying low. Many surrendered, including most of the Iraqi militiamen and Al Nida soldiers mixed in among them. A few of the foreign fighters surrendered, but most did not—they had come to Iraq to die, and die they would. They were poor shots for the most part, some even firing from under blankets without looking. But three Marines were dead, and several more were seriously wounded, and men like Russell and Brock knew the difference between these jihad fighters and the militia. Consequently the Marines shot them in the ditches and in the field. They threw grenades into the bulrushes and shot the fighters when they ran out. They threw grenades into the drainage pipes running under the road. If one shot didn't put a man away, and many times it didn't, the Marines shot him again and again. The few foreigners who were captured appeared to be drugged. One in particular, a Syrian, had a gunshot wound in the chest; blood bubbled from a lung wound, yet he showed no sign he even knew he was hit.

Around four in the afternoon, after three hours of fighting, Mundy radioed to Dunford that the firing had petered out. Brock and Russell and the others waited out in the fields for another hour, but no more foreigners came to fight. Battalion 3/5 had collected one rifle with a night-vision scope and three with sniper scopes and had captured two Egyptians, seven Jordanians, and six Syrians. They didn't bother counting the dead.

While Mundy was clearing along Route 6, Ray and I waited with the lead tanks and Amtracs on the cutoff road. The plan was for RCT-5 to swing north around the outskirts of Baghdad. RCT-7, coming up the next morning, would go straight ahead to the Baghdad Bridge, where we had been accidentally headed before being turned around. As soon as Mundy reported that Route 6 was clear, we continued our move north.

Beyond the farmlands we drove by a huge military complex of long multistory buildings with high walls and wide parking lots. There was a shot-up car and a body on the pavement outside the main gates, and firing started as we went by. A 40mm up gun started it by hosing down a mural of a smiling Saddam, and then others lit off. With all the outgoing, it was hard to tell who was returning fire from where. The complex had a thousand nooks in which a sniper could hide and in the main building heavy ammunition began to cook off, the explosions bright and red in the dusk. We stayed near the tanks at the head of the column, and Fox Company was behind us, standing up in the Amtracs, rifles at the ready in the growing dark. As they passed the large building with explosions rumbling deep inside and firing crackling on all sides, First Sgt. Edward Smith, Horsehead—the Marine's Marine—was struck in the head and killed.

10

Ring Around Baghdad

D + 14 to D + 16

With RCT-5 along the Diyala River
4–6 April

IT WAS DARK WHEN WORD CAME UP the column that First Sergeant Smith was down, struck in the head. Any head injury sounds bad, but earlier that day in the tank fight three Marines had been hit in the helmet, and none were hurt badly enough to be evacuated. So at first it wasn't known that the wound had been fatal. Ray and I had driven a half-kilometer farther up Route Green to a large intersection that marked RCT-5's objective and would be its stopping point for the night. The usual assortment of drab and dirty storefronts, set well back from the road, marked all four corners of the intersection. It seemed most of the shops repaired cars, trucks, or tractors, which wasn't unusual since Route Green was the dividing line between town and country. Just past the intersection was a large repair facility that obviously was in operation—for the Iraqi army; there were tank and truck parts in organized stacks and disorganized heaps all around the facility. The tanks pulled in on two corners of the intersection, and Colonel Dunford's forward command post element had claimed another corner. A stream of Amtracs and a battery of towed 155s were jockeying for space and spreading out from the center of the intersection. The sky flashed red like a huge blinking neon light as artillery shells, fired back at the military encampment, cooked off in tremendous roars, and streaks of red and orange rockets and burning shrapnel sprayed the sky.

Into this organized chaos drove a civilian mini-bus—the driver either did not hear the shouts to halt over the din or was oblivious to the danger. Over the deeper sounds of the other explosions, we didn't hear the Marines' inevitable firing at the car, but we saw an ambulance with a hole in its windshield pass us, the doctor walking alongside. Later we talked briefly with an exhausted Lieutenant Colonel Oehl, who had just led his tanks for 70 kilometers in the division's longest sustained fight. He had lost two of his men, but he did not have time to look back. Already his men were repairing the battle-damaged equipment, and he was calculating his fuel requirements for the next day. Colonel Dunford, who under fire had helped to rescue Captain Houston, had ordered that disabled tank destroyed. As tired as Oehl, Dunford was now planning his move into Baghdad, too.

Once the explosions from the burning Iraqi ammunition ceased, the area was remarkably quiet. Marines fell asleep in the tanks, or on the oil-soaked macadam outside the storefronts, or off the shoulders of the road. Out in the fields perhaps the sergeants had the troops dig in, but at the crossroads there was no earth. Fatigue claimed everyone who was not on watch. The only sound was the noisome yapping of a pack of curs driving off a strange dog.

Sometime around ten P.M. the Iraqis woke everybody up. The first rocket hit at the crossroads with a sharp *bang* that brought everyone awake. A sentry near our recently scraped SUV said RPGs were incoming.

"That's no little RPG, Marine," Ray said. "You'd best get down."

We were flat when the second 122mm rocket came in. For a second or two there was a *whoosh*, long enough to register fear, then the next *bang*. The first rocket seemed to hit to the left, where the regiment had its command post. The second sounded like it hit in the middle of the road. *Whoosh, bang*. The third hit on top of a store. They were all around us, and the BM-21 launcher that the Iraqis had bought from the Russians held forty rockets. We could do nothing but wait. Somewhere not too far away the 11th Marines had their anti-artillery radar on and sweeping. It picked up the blip of the rocket in midflight, then a computer projected the back azimuth and spat out the coordinates, which were fed automatically to a firing battery of six 155s.

Soon artillery shells were burning across the night sky, silent orange comets brighter than the stars. They chased one another until they seemed to form up like a flight of geese. Flight after flight flew overhead, each a bright yellow dot fading out seconds before impact. In all, three Iraqi rockets had hit the regiment, and seventy-two RAPs, or rocket-assisted projectiles, hit the Iraqi rocket-launch coordinates; each shell contained 108 bomblets, each as lethal as a hand grenade. The arithmetic was daunting. The Iraqis had fired three rockets—the Marines answered with 7,776 bomblets.

In the morning Marines pointed at the impact points, marveling that a total of 140 pounds of Iraqi high explosives could smash into a congested command center and not hurt a single soul. I could barely distinguish the impact points from all the other scars and scrapes around the intersection, which was heavily trampled by treads and explosions.

Across an irrigation ditch from our now-scruffy Yellow Submarine and on the side of the road opposite the RCT command post sat a clean white Mercedes with shiny aluminum hubcaps and only a few M-16 pinpricks in the front windshield. An Iraqi man in a green uniform lay on his back with one knee up. Next to him a body lay facedown with a robe hiked up, exposing fat thighs and white underwear.

The lance corporal in a sentry hole asked if I wanted to upgrade our transportation. Late the previous afternoon the Mercedes, instead of stopping at the checkpoint, had accelerated. The driver and passenger had been killed. A search revealed that he was a lieutenant general, chief of staff of the Republican Guard. Sheer panic must have enveloped the man. It was insane to have tried to drive across that intersection.

As we were chatting, an old woman and a middle-aged woman towing two small children walked across a field and stood gesturing at us from a safe distance. In pantomime they were placing the children's hands in their mouths, then rubbing their bellies and pointing behind us. Behind them stood the man of the family, occasionally prodding them to better performances. Next to our Nissan SUV were a few civilian cars parked at odd angles. I looked inside a minivan and saw the keys still in the ignition and sacks of food and bottles of propane in the rear seat. The sentry and I talked about it, and he asked permission of his corporal. Then he escorted the women to the vehicle. They filled their arms with more than they could carry and started to wobble away. The sentry suggested they be allowed to drive away.

"They can come back after we've left," the corporal said. "I'd be doing them no favor letting them drive right now."

It was a wise decision. Three civilians in cars had been killed during the night, driving into battalion lines from side roads or ignoring warnings to stop. As for the Mercedes, it would soon be claimed by looters, who would probably bury the bodies.

Colonel Dunford had invited Ray and me to join him at the command post of 1st LAR Battalion. Before leaving, I walked over to the colonel's Humvee to retrieve my laptop; its battery had been recharged by Corporal Weighe, driver and plenipotentiary in charge of keeping all critical items within arm's length for the colonel's fighting family of four. The Humvee was Dunford's real command post while on the move. Here Weighe kept at hand a military GPS receiver called a Plugger; a two-hundred-dollar commercial Garmin GPS; an iridium satellite phone; two PRC-119 radios; one Blue Force Tracker monitor screen; a roll of toilet paper; six canteens; foot powder; two dirty towels; a converter strip for AC plugs like those on my computer; four red lens flashlights; two compasses; one small stove; two jugs of coffee; four metal cups; a dozen maps; four night-vision goggles; three M-16s; and one .50-caliber machine gun.

After I removed my computer from this mobile office, Ray and I drove the short distance north on Route Green to the LAR battalion. Dunford told the battalion's commanding officer, Lt. Col. Duffy White, to find before dark a fording place for RCT-5 over the nearby Diyala River. The Diyala flows down from the north, runs along the eastern edge of Baghdad, and joins the Tigris at the southeastern corner of the city. We were on the east side of the river. Across the river, eight kilometers to the west, was the impoverished Shiite section of Baghdad called Saddam City, a rabbit warren of adobe huts and squalid apartment buildings teeming with two million poor people. According to the division plan, RCT-5 was to clear Saddam City from the north.

Dunford dealt in what was called "mission-type orders." While the RCT had momentum, detailed, written orders were rarely given. Dunford assumed that his commanders knew how to go down checklists and contact his staff for specifics. He told his battalion commanders what he wanted done, not how to do it. Today his intent was to have a bridge company working at a crossing site somewhere along the Diyala by 10:00 P.M. But first a site had to be located, and the bridging equipment had to be put on the road to it by dusk.

A map study showed several potential crossing sites along the river. Lieutenant Colonel White told his staff to launch a Dragon Eye, a UAV the size of a model airplane. [Pictures 27 and 28] A flight path was programmed into the UAV's computer, and it was hurled into the air by a long elastic band, then controlled via line of sight through a handheld box, much like the model airplanes that hobbyists buzz around city parks on Sunday afternoons. Flying at 90 meters for about an hour, the Dragon Eye's internal camera sent good-quality video back to a monitor in White's command post.

While White gathered his commanders to allocate search sectors along the riverbank, Warrant Officer Mike Musselman gave me a quick tour of a typical LAV, which looked like a sleek armored car on eight wheels. Protruding from the turret was the narrow barrel of a Bushmaster 25mm chain gun, which fired anti-armor and high-explosive rounds. Its seven-power stabilized day sight was superior to that on the Amtrac but not as good as that on the Abrams tank. The thermal sight could pick up a vehicle at 2,000 meters. The sights were connected both to the 25mm and to a 7.62mm machine gun. Musselman said that at night they could tell at 1,500 meters if a vehicle was civilian. The PRC-119 radio worked well, the crew members told me, but they preferred commercial GPS receivers to the military version. A standard crew would be a driver and gunner/vehicle commander up front and in back a four-man fire team—called scouts—who had a set of immediate action drills for dismounting. They needed—but did not have—a radio to connect the scout team leader to the LAV commander.

Musselman said that the procedure for the LAVs was to roll along, and when Iraqis fired, a line of them would answer. The Iraqis preferred to hide on the reverse side of berms and popped up and down, so he usually saw them for only a second. The day before yesterday at Al 'Aziziyah, though, behind a berm 500 meters to the west, he had seen about a dozen Iraqis shucking off their green uniforms. One had fired an AK-47 at the LAV, turned, and run away. Musselman said that was nuts. He hit the man in the back with a burst from the 25mm, saying he watched the tracers go downrange, and the man turned "misty." He fired at three more soldiers, and they all fell on their faces, waving their arms. Two Marines then walked all the way out to bring in about a dozen Iraqis who surrendered, one an old man with only two teeth.

Lt. Col. White joined us, and Musselman asked about his shorts. White unhitched his antichemical bib overalls to show that he was wearing black boxer shorts with Saint Patricks's green shamrocks. To bring them all good luck, he had promised his Marines he wouldn't take them off until they were in Baghdad or they disintegrated, whichever came first. The LAV crew consisted of Mike Musselman, Nieves Avida, Ryan O'Mara, and Q'wame Kleckley. Each had a name for their LAV. *Shamrock* was now painted on the side. Musselman suggested there had been undue command influence, and Lieutenant Colonel White grinned.

White recommended that Ray and I drive to the river with the weapons company, commanded by Captain Hudspeth. The most likely-looking crossing site that the Dragon Eye flight found was in the zone assigned to the weapons company, so that was our best chance of predicting where the action might be. While they were forming up, we walked up the road to where some townspeople were gathered around an irrigation ditch. Last evening, as the Abrams tanks roared into the intersection, a T-72 tank, pride of the Russian army and purchased by the Iraqis for a goodly sum, had fled down the road, turned while crossing a culvert, and flipped over. The first tank in history to capsize on dry land, it now lay treads-up in six feet of water, its crew entombed.

In a rice paddy near the submerged tank, a blue and white Greyhound-size bus was stuck nose-first in the muck. The middle-aged driver, who had pulled a sharp left turn when the T-72 claimed right of way across the culvert, stood near us, holding his small son's hand. He watched glumly as his life's savings settled deeper into the paddy. Soon looters would pillage the bus's interior, and after that the dusty winds would peel off the paint. Brown rust would form after a few rains—another derelict claimed by yesterday's battle. Ray walked over and spoke with Warrant Officer Musselman. Then we met with Captain Hudspeth and found our place in the line of LAVs. As we were driving away, an M-88 tank retriever was attaching cables from its derrick to the stranded bus. The M-88 looked like a locomotive on treads, with the power to pull a city block. As it pulled the bus out of the paddy, the bus driver was waving his arms like a rabid fan cheering on his favorite football team.

To reach the river, which lay seven kilometers to the west, we followed a line of LAVs along the top of an irrigation ditch that on the map was marked as a road. I had concluded that Iraq's secondary roads had been dug by wandering herds of water buffalo and paved by sheep and cows. We certainly passed enough of them—with shepherds smiling and their herd dogs yapping—and Ray explained how to tell the difference between brown long-haired sheep, Angora goats, skinny Holstein cows, and Brown Swiss. Once we were 200 meters from the hardtop, we had left the war a world away. Moving at slow speed, we passed a mud village where most of the people were friendly, although some were glaring. We bumped our way past scattered farms where whole families came out and waved. We passed green field after green field, and a few farms with riding horses, including an expensive black Arabian hobbled in the courtyard, with a bright blanket on its back to ward off flies.

After about an hour we hit a decent road, one that was actually paved, that intersected yet another decent road that ran along the river itself. In the farm fields near the intersection of these two paved roads, Ray and I saw a line of abandoned dug-in tanks and bulldozers; we hoped the dozers would remain un-hit and available for reconstruction after the war. Hudspeth's column turned left along the river road and, within 200 meters, found the crossing site it was seeking. Near the intersection of the two decent roads, bridge abutments had been built on the high banks on both sides of the river; the bridge itself had never been constructed. However, just to the left, or south, of the bridge abutments, the high banks had been cut away and graveled roads constructed, again on both banks, down to the water's edge. On the far bank two sand-colored bridging pontoons sat beside the gravel road. Obviously this bridging site had been prepared—and perhaps previously used—by the Iraqi army.

The Diyala River was the cleanest and most welcoming body of water we had seen since leaving Kuwait. Fed by a large lake far to the north, the river flowed green and clear, reminding Ray, he said, of the Shenandoah in Virginia. With a strong arm you could almost throw a rock to the far side, indicating to Ray and Captain Hudspeth—another country boy—that it was certainly less than 90 meters wide. They agreed on the width of 60 to 65 meters. Except for the cuts down to the crossing site, both banks of the Diyala were sharp and steep. The far bluff was open and grassy, with a grove of palm trees along the bluff to the right of the gravel approach road; the road led from the water's edge up through the palm grove and intersected with what appeared to be a paved road about 200 yards from the river. A low wire fence paralleled the road halfway up the hill.

The water was deep, stirred by a slight current that pushed any flotsam downstream at one or two kilometers an hour. It was noon, and the sun was bright, with only a slight wind. With its high banks and green fields, the site looked like a swimming hole. And judging by the maze of hoofprints in the mud along the road, hundreds of water buffalo, sheep, goats, and dairy cattle came here regularly to drink. This would be an excellent bridge site—if Hudspeth and his Marines could find a better way to get to it than the route they had just taken.

Shortly before one P.M. Captain Hudspeth completed his preliminary engineering survey and radioed to his battalion command post a precise report indicating the site was suitable for a pontoon bridge. He asked permission to proceed north in his assigned recon zone to look for a road wide enough for the RCT convoys to cut across from their current locations to the crossing site. At the same time Delta Company of his battalion was calling a fire mission several kilometers to the south of the site. The battalion CP responded that Delta Company would conduct any recon required after completing its fire mission. Delta Company was supposed to be north of the weapons company but was actually to Hudspeth's south. The battalion staff couldn't seem to grasp that Delta Company was out of its assigned zone.

While Hudspeth was diplomatically trying to persuade the CP to look at a map, I wandered over to chat with the crew of an LAV that was mounted with a TOW missile. The lieutenant in charge bragged to me again about the optics on the LAV. "There's no reason to shoot any soft-skinned at long range," he said. "We can identify who's who. We're waiting for a tank or BMP." He complained that the Abrams tanks took all the shots.

I laughed, saying the infantry complained about the same thing. It sounded as though the tankers were guilty of establishing a monopoly or indulging in predatory pricing or other anti–free market business practices.

Then I walked back to where Hudspeth was patiently trying to persuade the battalion CP to let him get on with his recon. I remarked to Ray that this was an example of the rigidity of the military chain of command getting in the way. Dunford had made it clear that all units on the recon were to look for a crossing site and a suitable route to it. Waiting for Delta to finish up down south and then move north of us to check out a route would mean wasting several hours. I ranted about how the private sector gives subordinates more freedom to get the job done, but Ray defended the military, saying the CP was mixed up but was not intentionally ignoring the purpose of the day's mission.

Finally Hudspeth cleverly detached his LAV and a few others and headed north up the highway, telling the CP that he was going to check out some movement. Indeed, there was steady northward movement of civilians walking and driving on the road, all heading away from Delta's fight to the south. By going north, of course, the LAV captain could also keep an eye open for routes that the RCT might use to reach the crossing site.

Ray and I argued back and forth, maybe over how many angels could dance on the head of a pin. We had nothing to do, sitting in an SUV on top of a bluff in a row of four LAVs, as the river flowed by below. For a while we watched the people walking past our vehicles. A few dilapidated old Hondas and Nissans drove by, most painted white with wide orange stripes, one of the few splashes of color in the landscape. Herds of buffalo ambled by at their own slow pace, ignoring the switches of the little boys driving them. Skittish sheep pranced by, following goats or donkeys with bells around their necks. A white calf and a black-and-white Holstein cow broke away from two young girls and began snatching quick mouthfuls of fresh greens from a tiny vegetable patch surrounding the house beside the crossing site. The owner was out in a flash with a stick, swatting at first one cow and then the other. But these animals were practiced thieves, and when he went after one, the other one grabbed another mouthful. Ray got out of the SUV and blocked the garden while the man drove the beasts away and yelled at the girls. This was not your typical war zone.

Ray got back in the vehicle, sweating in his antichemical suit. With nothing to do, we left the four LAVs on the bluff, drove the few meters down the slope to the crossing site, and parked next to a fifth LAV that was watching over the river. We took a bar of soap and started for the water. A Marine standing behind the LAV next to us told me to be careful. The bank on the other side was open, running back for several hundred meters. I assured the Marine I had confidence in him and the situation. We walked the few remaining meters through the mud, stripped, and sank into the green water. Refreshed by its coolness, we traded dry dirt for water-filled dirt—a terrific deal by my standards.

Barely had I assumed the floating position when a Marine ran down, clearly excited. "There are four Iraqi bodies," he said.

"Screw this," I said, remembering the Ben Hai at the DMZ in Vietnam, with its stink and the North Vietnamese corpses bobbing like blown-up dolls. Putting my face in the water lost its appeal.

"Bodies as in 'bodies' or bodies as in 'live human beings'?" Ray asked. This generation of Marines tended to use the word for any being, alive or dead.

"Bodies," he said. "Live bodies."

"Well," Ray said, not wanting the Marines to think they had to baby us, "you're not responsible for us two old assholes if anything happens. You remember that."

As the Marine turned away, three mortar rounds hit on the other bank, about 200 meters up the river to our right. The LAVs had set up 81mm mortars back on the bluff, and they had fired at something.

"Back to the car, Bing," Ray said. "They think they see something, and I think they're worried about protecting us."

We hurriedly pulled our MOPP suits back on and started through the mud a few meters toward the car, relaxing a little as the firing appeared to stop.

Just then, across the river, a white Iraqi tanker truck pulled off the paved road and headed down the gravel approach road toward the water. Ray, worried that the Marines would destroy the truck and so foul the crossing site, immediately yelled, "Don't shoot that truck! Don't shoot that truck!"

The driver, apparently seeing us or at least the several LAVs sitting along the riverbank, pulled the truck off the gravel road and into the palm grove, stopping before he got to the low wire fence. We relaxed, thinking the crisis was past, and resumed our trek back to our SUV, Ray a few steps in front of me.

Ray reached the vehicle and turned and looked back—and saw that two men, dressed in civilian clothes, had gotten out of the truck and were walking toward the river. They stepped over the low wire fence and came down the middle of the gravel road. Just as I reached the SUV and turned to look back myself, the LAV on the high bank beside us opened up on them with its 25mm chain gun. One man went down immediately, and the other turned to run. He got only one or two steps off the road before he went down as well.

Ray was screaming, "No! No! Cease fire!" as the gun was turned on the truck itself. The Marine who had come down to the riverbank to warn us earlier was behind the LAV. He and I were also yelling "Cease fire!" A quick burst into the side of the truck set its side fuel tank—called a saddle tank—immediately on fire. Then the gunner—or maybe it was another gunner—returned to the two men down in the road and hit them several more times.

Later that afternoon two F-14s made a low pass over the river, making no radio contact with the LAVs. That absence was a source of concern to the LAVs, although their friendly marking panels were displayed. Two other LAVs were on the road to the south. Before anyone could establish communication, one F-14 came back from the west in a dive angle and let go a five-hundred-pound bomb. Luckily it hit behind a berm, beyond the weapons company, and short of the LAVs on the move. With no one hurt, the company turned its attention to consolidating its position.

We stayed out on the dike, within the defensive perimeter but in our own space. The firing to the south petered out before dusk, and we watched the people, cars, and herds come back down the dirt road past the company position. Ray and I had seen that same behavior often in Vietnam. How savvy civilians know when the fighting is over is a mystery, but word gets around somehow. Fifty people of all ages and three hundred farm animals of all descriptions walked by the cut leading down to the site, homeward bound.

We looked out to the east, our backs to the river, and through binoculars we watched a family slowly walk across the series of dry fields with numerous irrigation ditches and scrub growth. The head of the household, a tall man in a black and white turban and tan robe, led, followed by a boy and two girls in their late teens, the girls in bright red and long yellow dresses and the boy in a T-shirt with some English letters. They were herding several cows and laughing. Lagging behind was a fat old woman who had difficulty climbing over the rough ground. She was holding the arm of another woman in a black dress with yellow designs like butterflies. Every now and then the man would stop, and they would catch up.

It was a clear day, and dusk was lingering. We boiled coffee and watched as the family entered the courtyard of their comfortable-looking farmhouse. The main brown brick building had two floors and several windows, and inside the courtyard were two smaller buildings. A telephone and electric line led to the house; the ground showed the tracks of several cars, hidden away somewhere. The house was surrounded by forty acres of land, some of it green paddies, some scrub dotted with sheep and cows. The girls went out to tend to the cows, while the boy let loose the dogs and the man turned on a water spigot that Ray said was a pump they used to irrigate the vegetable garden beside the buildings. The boy climbed a tree in the yard and shook the branches, while the girls and woman gathered up the figs. Then the woman shooed them into the house and called to her husband.

We saw that the woman had blond hair and ruddy features, and we joked about the German engineers who had been in Iraq since the 1950s. The man ignored her and walked away from the spigot so that he was in full view of us. He squatted on his haunches next to his brown brick wall, lit a cigarette, and looked at us looking at him. He probably was concerned. Maybe he was trying to show that he was a man and would guard his family.

I thought about why Ray and I were so disturbed this afternoon. We knew combat and sudden death—that wasn't it. This was it, looking at that man with the home he had built and the love and happiness therein. Life is sacred, even for those who choose a profession of taking lives. Sparing a life in a combat setting often involves some risk. The best that could be said about the incident was that Ray and I weighed risk one way, and the gunner on the 25mm weighed it another way.

I thought about First Sergeant Smith. Only two nights ago, Colonel Dunford had sent me over to get Smith's opinion of the campaign. A man in superb physical condition, Horsehead had lived to train, yet was fun on liberty. He didn't see himself as a tough guy, although the rest of the world did. One night in a restaurant a man was lying to some friends about being in Marine recon. Seeing the first sergeant listening in amazement, he asked Smith if he was a Marine. Horsehead, who was in his sixth year in recon, said yes, he was a Marine and proud to drive a truck. He shook the man's hand and wished him luck. Later he told the recon Marines with him that they should treat everyone with respect. E-Tool Smith and Horsehead Smith were the same kind of Smith. The two Iraqis across the river weren't coming back, and neither was Horsehead.

The deaths were the same, equal in God's eyes, but not in mine on this earth. First Sergeant Smith was a warrior in my tribe who led others into battle and protected us. The Iraqi men were from another tribe. We had come to liberate their people. President Bush really believed that, and I had seen enough to know it was true. If Saddam posed an inevitable threat to our American tribe, then we had to remove him before American civilians died. Liberation, though, was a trickier idea. I looked at the well-to-do farmer dragging on his cigarette and looking back at us. I couldn't help but wonder if he had been an Iraqi who had seized Kuwait thirteen years earlier.

After full dark fell, we watched the light show over Baghdad as targets were hammered at regular intervals. It was amazing how many fresh places in a city could be hit with thousand-pound bombs. More amazing to us was the traffic leaving the city. We could see a steady line of headlights on Routes 2 and 5 leading north out of the city. No bombs were dropping on them. Clearly the Central Command intelligence system had the sophistication to identify mainly civilian traffic and had decided to let the vehicles go untouched, even knowing that many of those in the traffic flow were Saddam supporters and Baath officials. In the march up to Baghdad under Gen. Tommy Franks, there was no Road of Death, as the press had called the 1991 mauling from the air of Iraqis fleeing Kuwait on a highway. The Iraqis who fled Kuwait had participated in its rape; the Iraqis now fleeing Baghdad might be getting out before the regime made a last stand.

In the morning we followed the LAVs away from the Diyala River site. The engineers had decided that no approach road could sustain all of RCT-5's vehicles there without a major snafu. The search for a pontoon crossing had turned elsewhere. So no Americans crossed the river to determine if there were weapons with the Iraqi bodies. The division's judge advocate general later conducted an exhaustive investigation. The testimonies of those interviewed were in conflict, and no objective evidence about weapons at the scene was available.

We put the incident at the crossing site behind us as best we could, and we left the LAVs to join Colonel Dunford's mobile command group, which consisted of him, his executive officer, and several engineers splitting up to investigate possible crossing locations. Along with the entire RCT, Ray and I joined the search for a way to cross the Diyala River. In our SUV we wandered the highways (such as they were), the byways (which were numerous), and the donkey paths on the northeastern banks of the Diyala. The vaunted U.S. Marine Corps, soldiers of the sea, masters of far-flung oceans and exotic littorals, were blocked by a tiny river in the middle of a land cut by canals and ditches with no decent roads. The ignominy of the day was relieved only by the solace of knowing that the U.S. Navy was 800 kilometers away and with luck would not hear of our plight until after a successful crossing. I don't mean to treat it lightly, but the search was not without a humorously ironic side.

While we were bumping along the cow paths, Ray switched from one tactical net to another on the PRC-119. He had spent the year 1972 coordinating fire support for Vietnamese Marine battalions as the North Vietnamese poured south. He had called in perhaps a thousand air, artillery, and naval gunfire missions and had become accustomed to listening to many radio nets. Throughout this campaign, he kept a list of call signs and frequencies, skipping around to pick up who had contact and where we should drive. Now he had picked up "Highlander," who was Lt. Col. Duffy White. It took me a moment to accept that this was the same voice that had been so jocular yesterday with his Marines. That was before the F-14 had dropped the five-hundred-pound bomb by mistake near the LAVs. Now Duffy's voice had a hard edge to it. A section of Cobras were on station—we could hear one of them buzzing around—and were shooting up the tanks and dozers we had seen near the farm with the Arabian horse. Duffy told them they were interfering with his LAVs and to cease and leave. It was a quick, terse transmission, and that was the end of it. Duffy appreciated the aviators' efforts but saw the current situation a little differently than they did.

The 1st Marine Division used equipment destruction charts as an indicator of the cohesion of enemy units. Some air advocates took a different view, preferring that aggregate statistics be kept to buttress claims of effectiveness after the war. Using this method analysts had determined, for example, that in Desert Storm U.S. armor had accounted for the large majority of Iraqi tanks and other vehicles taken out. Now the question had come up at the divisional command as to whether the ground forces should keep a count of vehicles destroyed. The division didn't want to collect memories of dead hulks—it maintained that since attrition was not the goal, road kill wasn't a valid measure. The goal was to destroy the cohesion of the enemy divisions and to get on to Baghdad.

To tally enemy equipment destroyed daily, the 3rd Marine Air Wing and the MEF kept color slides in PowerPoint. So too did the coalition forces air component commander (CFACC), who controlled and apportioned all fixed-wing aircraft in the theater. On most days 120 Marine aircraft attack sorties, in addition to another hundred Cobra attack helicopter sorties, were allocated to support the Marine ground forces. When a major ground unit advanced, the dozens of kilometers to its front were safeguarded by a no-bomb line. Inside that line no aircraft could bomb without permission. Each day the Tactical Air Operations Center at the MEF established "kill boxes"—large areas that contained no friendly units. Attack aircraft in sectors with no targets would radio the center or the forward air controller airborne, fly into the kill box, and expend their ordnance there. For an attack helicopter or aircraft on an attack mission not to destroy at least one enemy vehicle was a professional embarrassment. The result was that within the Marines' zone the equipment of the eight Iraqi divisions was destroyed and more than five million pounds of high explosives were delivered. More important, the threat of air strikes drove many Iraqis to abandon their equipment. The division's staff was perfectly willing to credit air with every destroyed enemy vehicle.

What did concern a ground commander like Lt. Col. Duffy White was air that hunted close in during the late stages of a campaign. The Iraqis abandoned their vehicles in two waves. The first wave happened early, when they feared the air threat; the second came later, when they knew the American ground forces would soon be on them. Every pilot flying close to friendlies was supposed to be on somebody's radio net with eyes on the target. But slip-ups did occur. A Marine tank was hit on D-Day; Amtracs were hit at Nasiriyah; now there had been a near miss on White's LAVs. White demonstrated the sensible solution: since awareness of air, with its devastatingly lethal weapons, was everybody's business, any Marine with a doubt and a radio was well advised to call the fire support team and voice his concern.

For Ray and me in our Yellow Submarine, our concern was less with avoiding Cobras than with determining how RCT-5 would ever get across the Diyala, which with every passing hour was looking more like a giant moat guarding a fortress. All the good roads out of Baghdad ran parallel to the river. None of them crossed the Diyala, except within a few kilometers of its confluence with the Tigris in Baghdad. The bluffs along the river were steep, and crossing points like the one we found yesterday were few. UAVs, helicopters, and overhead photos were looking for unmapped crossings but finding none. The roads—or as battalion 2/5 called them, the donkey paths—ran along the tops of the irrigation ditches, which was logical enough. The farm animals drank several times a day, and over the decades the paths they used had become firm enough for vehicles. An occasional bulldozer would fill in a few low spots, and then the province engineer would trace it as a road on a map he sent to Baghdad. As Saddam looted his country, all infrastructure construction was neglected, and life went on as usual—until Colonel Dunford showed up with 90 kilometers of vehicles, some weighing seventy tons. RCT-5, with all its heavy equipment, needed a real road, one that, if not paved, was at least wide enough and straight enough for the column to keep going if a breakdown blocked one lane, or if one tank or another piece of heavy equipment slipped and got mired down.

All the roads that the Marines found running west to the river were one-lane dirt tracks. Any of them posed a substantial risk of tying up the entire RCT midway out in farmlands. We were driving out of one of those farm roads when Colonel Dunford drove by, and we pulled over for a quick chat. Ray suggested unloading the enormous earth movers at the rear of the convoy and widening a side road, kilometer by kilometer.

Colonel Dunford was tired, frustrated, and a bit testy, indicating that we didn't understand the underlying issue. He didn't have time to build a new road to the river, he said, and if he did, there was no guarantee there would be a usable road on the other side. He was considering leaving his trucks and Humvees behind and, with his Amtracs and LAVs—all of which could swim—going on across "light." The tanks would cross at the southwestern bridge and swing around to meet them.

"The Iraqis have nothing that can really hurt or stop my Marines," the colonel told us. "Yesterday, while 1st LAR looked for a crossing site, I had a complete review with my battalion commanders. We all agree that the Iraqis have no organized unit above a company, if that. They have no observed indirect fire, no coordination among units, no individual marksmanship. I don't need all our heavy stuff to take Saddam City."

Ray asked him why he didn't just go back to where the Diyala joins the Tigris and cross on Route 6. "RCT-7 and RCT-1 will do that, but C-flick [CFLCC] wants us to encircle the city and conduct armored raids into it before we go in to stay," Dunford said. "I need to get across to the north side of Saddam City and complete the encirclement so the rest of the division can do that."

Almost as we were talking, the 3rd Infantry Division was conducting the first armored raid into Baghdad from the southwest, having taken Baghdad International Airport the previous day. A column of tanks and Bradley fighting vehicles were driving in a loop through the southwestern sector of the city, guns blazing, destroying vehicles and any enemy exposing themselves, then driving back out again. This strategy of mounting raids and encircling Baghdad was the plan of the CFLCC, whose headquarters were in Kuwait. The CIA had informed the CFLCC that a redoubtable defense line had been established in secret inside Saddam City. Thus the CFLCC's strategy was based on an assessment of the enemy much different from that of Dunford and his battalion commanders.

Joint war games conducted the prior November had not resolved underlying differences within the coalition on how to go about taking Baghdad. In those war games the Army had favored raids to attrit whoever chose to come out to fight at that moment. This approach fit a force that was mechanized, heavy in armor, and light in infantry to protect the armor. In these raids Abrams tanks would venture in and engage whatever defense fired upon them. The Abrams would then drive back out and repeat the process the next day, and the next, until the defenders were attritted. A raid by definition includes a plan to withdraw; to swoop in and then back out of the city. Concepts like "containing" and "encircling," when thousands were fleeing the city, did not constitute a plan for taking control of downtown Baghdad.

The Marines, for their part, intended to go into Baghdad, wrest control, and stay. Their tanks would be broken down into tank-infantry packages: the infantry would go to the front to protect the tank, which would be brought up for direct fire support. This approach fit a force with substantial infantrymen per tank. The danger was that a head-to-head slugfest might result in many casualties. In the battle for Hue City in 1968 the Marines had attacked on a linear front, advancing block by block, giving and absorbing punishment. In Baghdad the Marines intended to advance on two narrow corridors, protecting their flanks by occupying the buildings on both sides of the street up which they were advancing, going for the command and control heart of the enemy, and bypassing many enemy strongpoints. This approach assumed that the Marines would be able to locate and fix the key centers of the enemy's defense.

The British, based on their experiences in Northern Ireland, preferred a more deliberate approach, combining careful on-the-ground intelligence-gathering with well-planned strikes at the opposition's leadership. The British would encircle, then select their targets.

The CFLCC and the Army, the Marines, and the British thus held different concepts about how to fight in a city. Not only had the differences been unresolved in the fall 2002 discussions and war games, but they were still unresolved now, as Colonel Dunford and RCT-5 were looking for a route to complete the encirclement of Baghdad.

The CFLCC had designated V Corps as the Main Effort, with the 3rd ID poised to be the main American unit to seize Baghdad. The problem was that the 3rd ID actually had few infantry. Over the years it had become heavy with mechanized units, and budget pressures had led to cutting the infantry to fill the mechanized slots. So the 3rd ID would be going into Iraq with many fewer dismounted infantry than the 1st Marine Division, with over six thousand riflemen. Normally, to seize a well-defended city, dismounted infantry are at the heart of an attacking force. Tanks and all other vehicles hang back and come forward under the infantryman's instructions to provide fire support. Then the vehicles go back again to the protected rear. This was the opposite tactic from the one used in the march up to Baghdad. For the past seventeen days the tanks and armor had led, and the infantry had been behind them.

During the planning stage some on the CFLCC staff had suggested that the 1st Marine Division could attach a regiment or two to the 3rd ID once it was on the outskirts of Baghdad. The MEF and the division planners had responded with a countersuggestion: rather than pull apart units that had trained together, it seemed more sensible to assign the 1st Marine Division itself to take the city. The CFLCC wasn't about to do that, so the matter of how to take Baghdad had been dropped. As with the dog that chased the car, the question was what it would do when it caught it. Now that the CFLCC's forces were encircling Baghdad, it faced the question of what to do next.

As we stood in the dirt near the Diyala River and looked at an endless line of bulldozers, bulk fuel haulers, tank transporters, and the rest of the RCT-5 vehicles, it was clear that getting all this equipment across the river and encircling Saddam City to the north would take a few days. Colonel Dunford said that since he didn't have a magic wand, persuading the top of the command hierarchy to go for his lightening-up option would be hard. We should keep in mind, he said, that he wasn't the only one thinking about ways to persuade the CFLCC. The division was working on several creative ideas.

He suggested we contact RCT-7, which had a battalion waiting to seize the Baghdad Bridge. We called Colonel Hummer, who told us to proceed toward the bridge until we couldn't go any farther. He would alert the battalion commander, Lieutenant Colonel McCoy, that we were coming.

11

Assault into Baghdad

D + 16, D + 17

With battalion 3/4
Assault across the Baghdad Bridge
6–7 April

WE THANKED COLONEL DUNFORD FOR ALL HIS courtesies and, on the afternoon of 6 April, headed south back down Route Green. We drove at slow speed against the traffic: hundreds of Amtracs, Humvees, and trucks in RCT-5's train were trying to inch forward, unwilling to accept that they were going nowhere until new roads were built to the Diyala River or until RCT-7 crossed to the south, whichever came first. We drove through the intersection where the Iraqi rockets had slammed in two nights before, and sure enough, the white Mercedes of the Iraqi general was gone, probably hidden under a fig tree in some farmer's courtyard. A few hundred meters on we passed the military complex where First Sergeant Smith had been fatally wounded. In the smoke-filled dusk this complex had been a blazing cauldron of fire and explosions, with a body sprawled at the gate and desperate Iraqis shooting and Marines firing, not knowing where to shoot. In the bright daylight the building looked harmless, simply another overbuilt office building designed by an architect with more cement than taste.

I was becoming impatient with our turtle pace, and Ray was becom-

ing impatient with me, and no one had ever accused either of us of ret-
icence. Soon we were moving past the Amtracs at a higher speed, Ray
expressing his disbelief at my refusal to acknowledge the danger. As we
were amicably settling our difference at Marine decibels, we missed a
Marine on an Amtrac yelling to us. Soon another Marine waved a semi-
stop with his hand as we drove by. In a nanosecond a third Marine was
out on the road with his M-16 half raised. A sudden tap on the brakes—
two foreheads almost slammed the dashboard—and we stopped. Dead
stopped. Not moving. The young Marine peered at us and decided we
looked American enough. The muzzle slid away.

"Were you going to shoot us, Marine?" Ray asked in what he probably thought was a neutral voice.

"Somebody yelled 'stop that car,' sir," the young Marine said. He
caught on fast, adding the "sir" and not answering the question.

A Humvee pulled up, and a sergeant leaned out.

"Major General Smith, my CO's back up the road. If you have the
time, we'd be glad to have you drop by, and we'll snap you in on what
we've been doing."

Ray declined, and we sat there for a moment, collecting ourselves.

"Bing, you know how dogs react to a rabbit?" Ray said, employing his
avuncular tone. "In this car we are a yellow rabbit, and suicide bombers
are loose in our midst. I don't fear the Iraqis shooting us, but I sure as
hell fear a United States Marine with an M-16."

On the other hand, if we'd proceeded at a snail's pace, it would have
taken us hours to get clear of all the Amtracs, and we were definitely not
driving alone after dark. Our dilemma was solved by a passing CAAT,
going to the bridge. We were welcome to tag along. CAATs have two
speeds, fast and reckless. Weaving in and out among the convoys, before
dusk we made it to the street approaching the bridge. We were now on
the outskirts of Baghdad and the street was lined with drab shops, all
closed and locked. We had radioed ahead, and Sgt. Maj. Dave Howell
was waiting to guide us in.

During the run-and-gun tank fight two days before, this street was
where we would have ended up had we kept going straight after we
missed our turn. Battalion 3/4 had battled up the street yesterday,

Howell told us, and some serious firepower had been exchanged. A few hundred meters in front of us, directly north, we could see the crisscross trestle supports to a bridge, which Howell assured us we could study as carefully as we wished in the morning.

The street was wide and empty, bearing the first sidewalks we had seen in Iraq. On both sides were lines of small stores, most with locked iron grates. Spent shells and black scuffmarks littered the pavement, and overturned tables and chairs were scattered about, signs of sudden fright and flight. I could imagine the people out walking, doing a little buying, smoking their cigarettes, and lingering over tea at the outdoor tables; the soldier guarding the bridge would be swaggering and swearing to kill the infidels. Then Captain Lewis and his Bravo tanks were heard, or probably heard just as they were seen. Over went the tables as the soldiers ran to the other side of the bridge, and the shopkeepers hastily closed the shutters over their doors and exited down the side alleys.

Howell said it had been the usual kind of fight, with incoming RPGs and outgoing tank rounds. Artillery had chipped in. They could have rushed across the bridge then, Howell said, but the regimental command had to check with the higher-ups, and last night the Iraqis blew the crossing. There were two bridges side by side. One was a small two-lane bridge and the Iraqis had blown a ten-foot hole in it. Howell was sure it could be crossed on foot by throwing across some long planks. The main crossing, called the Baghdad Bridge, would hold four lanes of car traffic. But the Iraqis had blown up the center span, at least fifty feet in length. No one could get across the Baghdad Bridge until the engineers brought up a new center span. The battalion was preparing to assault across the pedestrian bridge in the morning. Howell assured us we had arrived at the right time.

The street had a forlorn and foreboding look—not one Iraqi was in sight. Not even dogs were skulking about. Smoke as thick as a heavy mist hung over the scene, and the smell was of garbage mixed with cordite, rotten and sharp. Rocks, cans, papers, and metal were scattered everywhere, as if a great wind had blown through. The few Amtracs and Humvees I could see were well spread out as a precaution against incoming shells. If one vehicle were hit and its load of ammunition exploded, the other vehicles would not be damaged. Members of a gang in L.A. or Detroit would take one look at this street and happily fly back home. This was one mean street.

As in most urban fights, the firing had been aimed straight up and down the street and so had spared the shops on either side. We walked by a store with chicken wire across the open door. Inside on the shelves were a few dozen eggs, jars of pickles, matches, a box of crackers, cheap sugary candies, loaves of bread, and a few packs of locally made cigarettes. The store's inventory cost less than ten dollars. A few doors up was a shop with one barber chair and a sink. Beyond that a confectionery. Some of the foreign press reporters were hanging about, one man with a mouthful of food, trying to grin as Howell glared at him. A little farther on we paused at a shop with an aluminum panel that rolled from top to bottom like a garage door. The grating had been pried open from the bottom and was propped up a few feet by a short board. The sergeant major looked around at the nearest Amtracs herringboned off the street. A Marine was just disappearing into a rear hatch, and Howell yelled at him to stand fast. The Marine stood up sheepishly, his arms full of soda bottles.

"Goddamn it, that's someone's property!" Howell shouted. "Put it back and secure that door. Where's your platoon sergeant? You tell him I want to see him, goddamn it."

The foreign press sauntered back to their vehicles before Howell could turn his wrath on them. We followed Howell through a set of iron gates into the parking lot of an abandoned medical clinic. McCoy had set up his CP next to his Humvee, and no looters would venture in while we were there. Inside the clinic the layout was like a small hacienda—patients' rooms on all four sides opened onto a courtyard. We were looking forward to catching up—over an MRE dinner—with the command group family, but McCoy was preoccupied with the next day's assault. For the first time in weeks we sat in chairs out of the dirt, happily sharing our noodles and pressed turkey with a million flies and mosquitoes.

John Koopman of the *San Francisco Chronicle*, a former Marine, and

Simon Robinson of *Time* joined us. Koopman had discovered that some water still dribbled out of a few faucets, so we were able to clean off the first of five layers of dirt before picking up our food. Previously Robinson, an Englishman, had asked if Ray and I were CIA assassins, suggesting we had that look about us and that he'd heard his fellow Brits were employing such a team down south in Basrah; perhaps we were the Baghdad equivalent. But he had since come to accept that our fighting days were behind us and that all we were doing was consulting and researching for a book about the division.

The two journalists were pleasant company, but Howell wouldn't eat, said he wasn't hungry, and went off to check on various Marines. Staff Sergeant Moreno, the sniper in Howell's little family, dropped by. He was pretty sure he had had a kill yesterday at 800 meters on the fly. The electronics intelligence team riding in a specially equipped LAV had a momentary fix on two men in a taxi who were directing some of the RPG teams. The taxi had parked in the same spot too long, and Moreno was called up. As he was lining up the shot, the taxi took off. Moreno took a lead and fired. His spotter said he saw the passenger lurch forward as if he had been punched hard in the back. We congratulated him on an impressive shot. He had used a 7.62mm rifle, a ten-power scope, and match grade copper bullets with a slightly hollow tip to improve their flight ballistics.

That night I hadn't yet seen the driver, Cpl. Mark Evnin. Howell made frequent short trips around the companies and usually Evnin waited with Moreno for Howell to tell them where they were going next. Moreno said Evnin had been killed two days ago at Kut.

Howell walked back in and sat reading two pieces of mail he had just received. When he finished, he lit them and watched them burn. That was by the book—you weren't supposed to keep mail, in case you were captured and the letters were used to break you down.

A Marine on the roof was looking down at us in the courtyard. Annoyed, Howell yelled up at him. "When you're on guard, Marine, you look out, not in," he said. "Who do you belong to?"

"Sir?" the young Marine said.

"Who's your platoon sergeant, damn it."

"Staff Sergeant McDuffy, Sergeant Major."

"Well, tomorrow you remember to do what McDuffy tells you to do."

"Yes, Sergeant Major."

Who do you belong to? That was what was bothering the sergeant major. He was angry and frustrated about Al Kut. He had played it over and over in his mind, thinking how it could have ended differently.

Two days ago, while Ray and I were at Aziziyah as battalion 3/5 pushed through that town, Colonel Hummer had sent battalions 1/7 and 3/4 south to Al Kut to pummel the Baghdad Division so it could not threaten the division's rear. Lewis's Bravo tanks were shooting up some vehicles on the outskirts of Kut, which was as far as they were to advance. Sitting behind the tanks were three Amtracs with infantry. McCoy told them to dismount and get into the fight. Next to the road were some bunkers and palm trees, and soon the infantry were firing. Howell, sitting in his vehicle with Moreno and Evnin, asked what the firing was all about. The infantry said they could see Iraqis in a trench under the palm trees. Just then an RPG hit a trac, skimmed off, and spun around on the road like a flaming top. That got everybody going.

Howell jumped out of his truck, and began to fire a 203 grenade launcher, lobbing 40mm explosive shells with the bursting power of small hand grenades out toward the trench line. A few incoming rounds snapped by from a mud house about 100 meters to his right. To eliminate the threat of enfilade fire coming down their exposed flank, Howell grabbed an AT-4 rocket to hit the house and got up to go. Evnin, crouched next to him, asked if he could use the 203 while Howell was gone. Howell handed him the weapon and told him to stay behind a small berm to their front. AK rounds were spraying around the area, but none seemed to be accurately aimed. Howell hadn't crawled 15 meters when Moreno yelled that Evnin was hit. The sergeant major dropped the AT-4 and ran back. Then he realized rounds were snapping all around them, so he dragged Corporal Evnin behind a small berm and cut open his cammies.

An AK round had hit him in the lower stomach, below his armored vest with its life-saving ceramic plates. There wasn't much external bleeding, and he was conscious but in deep shock. A corpsman rushed up and probed the wound. Evnin winced in pain and Howell sent the corpsman sprawling.

"I'm trying to do my job, Sergeant Major," the corpsman said.

"You better do a damn good job," Howell said.

The wound wasn't bleeding heavily, but Howell wasn't fooled. The bullet had struck deep. Placing his men on a skirmish line, Lieutenant Stokes of Kilo Company moved forward by bounds to clear the area for a medevac. They used up all their grenades killing six Iraqis in the trench line, while the 60mm mortars suppressed the fire from farther away. A CAAT team sped up and they drove Evnin to a CH-46 medevac bird, but Cpl. Mark Evnin of Burlington, Vermont, succumbed before reaching the hospital. Every Marine on an expedition belongs to two families, his loved ones back home and his fellow Marines in the field. Sgt. Maj. David Howell, the complete infantryman, the source of knowledge about tactics and aggressiveness, had lost a member of his little family and it hurt.

Howell left to meet with McCoy about the next day's assault. Outside in the parking lot the Marines were resorting their gear and fastening their packs along steel rods on the outside of the Amtracs. Tomorrow they were attacking on foot, and it might be a day or two before the Amtracs caught up with their gear. Marines carried their gear in a large rucksack with deep pouches and a small detachable day pack. On their web gear and in the day pack they packed their fighting gear: ammo, compass, gas mask, knife, penlight, goggles, water, and so on. This twenty-pound load, which was carried over the armored vest like a carpenter's belt, comprised the everyday tools of the trade, what the rifleman needed to kill. Before the war, if anyone had compared what the Iraqi soldier carried in the sack over his shoulder—a few ammo clips, underwear, prayer beads, a teapot, an old magazine—with the items the Marine carefully packed, the comparison would have predicted the outcome in battle.

Among the gear a Marine carried were the following items: a tough-fibered camouflaged chemical-protective jacket and hood with drawstrings; bib trousers with no fly; three wads of toilet paper; rubber over-boots; a gas mask (that never left the Marine's side); four atropine injec-tors (in case he was slimed); socks fragrant as a skunk; desert boots; an inch of dirt; a dog tag in the lacing of a boot; a penlight with red filter lens; a sleeping bag filled with dust; a folding knife; an entrenching tool; an electric shaver; five quarts of water; night-vision goggles; toothpaste and toothbrush; two T-shirts (never worn); two pairs of desert cam-mies (although one was enough); Handi Wipes; a clean weapon; and 120 rounds of ammunition.

At four the next morning I was awakened by an Islamic cleric who stood on the balcony of a nearby minaret calling the faithful to heed the first prayer of the day. The high-pitched mnemonic chant sounded clear and reminded me I had heard no firing. That would begin soon enough on this day. I wondered if the clerics would thank us for freeing them from Saddam, or curse us, or both.

A few hours later everyone was moving in preparation for the as-sault. Later we were told that American forces had not conducted an as-sault across a bridge against opposition since World War II and, before that, since the Civil War. We were told to put away our antichemical suits; Saddam wouldn't let slime loose inside the city where he was holed up. Everyone was happy to shuck the hot, stiff, stinking suits and get back into the light cammies that allowed some air to circulate and sweat to dry.

This was a strange kind of raid; Marines were going from the out-skirts straight into the city and not planning to come back out. The Marines moved in alongside of the shops, giving the open streets a wide berth. The Iraqis were staying well clear behind the shops, back in the slums surrounded by fetid water. The main activities on the road were the comings and goings of the press, mostly the unembedded from sev-eral nations who traveled in a small caravan. Koopman and Robinson stayed near Howell, off the street—a wise move.

Ray too stayed close to the buildings as we moved up, so I did the same. I understood fields of fire and traps both in the bush and in villages, but I hadn't fought in a city, while Ray had made it through one of the toughest street fights in our nation's history. He didn't like how this assault was shaping up. RCT-7 had been here for a day, bringing up engineers and bridging. The night before we arrived, Lieutenant Colonel Belcher's battalion 3/7 had teamed up with OGA operatives and the Army's ODA, or Operational Detachment Alpha, a bland name for tough special ops soldiers. They had seized an airport to the south—Howell, smiling, told us Colonel Hummer had gone in with Belcher. Hummer thought McCoy took too many chances—now he was out there on a night raid. It would have been foolish to assume that the Saddam regime did not know the Marines were at their door and were not going to knock. If there were any remnant of command and control left in Baghdad, the Iraqis knew the Marines were coming across, and they had the exact coordinates of the bridge. There was nothing for the Marines to do but cross it.

On the left side of the street we followed Sergeant Major Howell past Kilo Company, which was gathered in the shadow of a building listening to Capt. Kevin Norton, the company commander, go over the final plans. To the left was an Abrams tank, and in front of us was a small house on the river's edge. If you pushed past the sniper team and leaned too far out the broken windows on the north side, you would fall down a 12-meter cliff into the Diyala River. The river looked deep, and the far side, the Baghdad bank, was about 30 meters away; it too was a sheer cliff, with what looked like a garbage pit at the top, all kinds of rocks and debris and churned-up dirt, with bits of cloth and paper strewn about. It seemed a perfect place for foraging crows and rats. To the right of the house was the small bridge, perhaps six meters wide, and next to it the four-lane concrete Baghdad Bridge.

About five meters to the left of the small bridge was a one-room tan brick building, scarcely larger than a tollbooth. Shells had ripped it apart, enlarging its single window into a spacious door. Standing behind the flimsy bricks and peering around the corner to look across the river were Major General Mattis, Colonel Hummer, and Lieutenant Colonel McCoy. [Picture 44] All were dressed in desert cammies with goggles on their helmets. On Mattis's helmet was the metal slot for attaching night-vision goggles—it appeared Hummer wasn't the only one who had gone out on a night op. Mattis's armored vest was jungle green, but everything else in the scene was a monochromatic light tan: the bridge trestle was caked with tan dust, the dirt was tan, the bricks were encrusted with the dirt, and the Marines were khaki tan. A few dozen feet behind them, behind a brick wall, the lead platoon of Kilo Company clustered inside a small courtyard, where AT-4 rocket launchers, machine guns, and 60mm mortars rested on top of packs in the dust. The weapons were spotless, the men were filthy. Long boards and metal piping were propped against the wall, to be used—along with a large metal gate they had found—to span the gap blown in the bridge decking. The radio operators fiddled with frequencies and constantly asked for radio checks from one another. The officers and staff NCOs stood in a knot and glanced at their watches. On the roof of the building inside the courtyard, eight members of Kilo's fire support team were manning several radios, maps spread out in front of them.

No fire was coming from the Baghdad side. Beyond the garbage at the edge of the cliff, a row of houses, some with tall exterior walls, extended along the left side of the highway. On the other side of the highway was a grove of palm trees at least three football fields long. Down the road at the end of the grove, I could see a cluster of apartment buildings, maybe 300 meters back from the riverbank. Kilo Company was to clear the houses to the left while India Company swept through the palm grove.

The 1st Tank Battalion, a few kilometers upriver to the north, was repairing another bridge that had been blown. But if that effort failed, then the Baghdad Bridge would be the only fast way for the division to enter the city. Major General Mattis was making sure McCoy understood that he would get whatever fire support he needed. Word of the assault across into Baghdad had spread among the press, and more than a dozen journalists and photographers were pressing forward. They sensed the senior officers didn't care what the press was doing. The Marines and the press each had a job to do. The journalists stood back taking notes; the camera guys constantly jumped out from behind a building, snapped a few pictures, then hopped back to safety. To a watching Iraqi, it probably seemed the Americans were zapping them with silent rays to give them cancer or make them impotent.

It was risky because the final artillery prep was firing a "danger close" mission, meaning friendlies were only a hundred meters from where the shells were landing. The gun-target line, where the shells from the howitzers passed overhead on their way to the target, was only 50 to 100 meters to our right. We could hear each round as it passed by, a cloth-ripping sound as the shell pushed aside the air and thundered into the earth. One slight misalignment, and the photographers would be lanced with burning shrapnel. I wasn't sure they understood the random killing power of 155mm shells. Yes, most of the shells were striking on the far bank, but the nearest shells were bursting not 100 meters away from us, and shrapnel flew, not swam. The river didn't make any difference.

Major General Mattis and Colonel Hummer walked back to say a few words to Kilo's Marines. Hummer shouted something to McCoy before leaving, and McCoy laughed. Since I was taking notes, he shared the remark with me: Hummer's parting words of encouragement were "McCoy, don't fuck up."

Whether an artillery mission was needed at all could be debated, given the absence of enemy fire at that moment. But plenty of RPGs had whizzed over the river, and once the Marines were packed tightly together running across the pedestrian bridge, one RPG would wreak havoc.

The shells were chewing their way through the palm groves when there was a large splash in the middle of the river. Hearing, above the racket of the explosions, was difficult, but Ray had his radio handset next to his ear, and we were crouched alongside Howell and McCoy's radio operator. Over both radios came an excited warning from the electronic intercept team that an Iraqi general, in a taxi on a cell phone, was calling a fire mission on our position. A round hit to our right on the riverbank near an exposed Amtrac, and the crew hastily climbed out and ran back toward the slum behind them. Ray had walked around the left side of the small building and was gesturing to me to join him. Howell was looking around, trying to get McCoy's attention.

The next blast shook us all. It was a sharp crack, as if lightning had struck behind us with no warning—a sound so loud, so splitting, we knew something dreadful had just happened. For perhaps two, maybe three, seconds the shock was so stunning that no one did a thing except look at the dust and smoke rising several meters behind us. Then the Marines in the courtyard began yelling and running around, not sure what to do but not liking one bit being trapped and packed in behind walls that had no fighting holes.

Howell rushed into the courtyard. "Shut up!" he screamed. "Only the chain of command talks! Sit down along the walls. No one stands up!" [Picture 46]

Behind the courtyard an Amtrac was smoking, its turret peeled back like the top of an open can of soup. The back hatch was flung open, and Marines were pulling out the bodies. The radio net was crackling with raised voices.

"Turn it off! Turn it off!" Kilo Six was shouting loudly into his radio.

"Enemy incoming! Enemy incoming! Continue to fire!" someone countermanded him over the radio.

"You continue to fire, and I'm going to shove this handset up your ass. That fire gets turned off now. Do you read me? Now!"

Captain Norton was seething. McCoy was ordering all artillery to cease immediately. Some Marines were screaming that our own artillery was hitting us. Others were yelling that it was incoming Iraqi arty. The Marine artillery battery radioed in, insisting all six of its guns were in alignment and that we were under fire from the Baghdad side. The electronic intercept team insisted that the Iraqi forward observer had been shouting into his cell phone, screaming at someone to fire. The Marines spread out and found some cover, though not all that much.

The Amtrac that had taken the hit had transported Kilo's fire support team and, when struck, was empty save for the four-man crew. The trac was smoking, with blood-splattered maps scattered in the dust, along with torn packs and twisted shards of metal. Inside three minutes two wounded crewmen were being driven to the battalion aid station, only a few hundred meters down the road. In five minutes the bodies of Cpl. Martin Medellin and Lance Cpl. Andrew Aviles were covered with camouflage bivvy sacks and carried away on stretchers to an ambulance. Aviles was eighteen, the youngest Marine to die in Iraq. The tragedy came within a few feet of being a catastrophe. Had the shell not hit the turret, the Marines clustered in the courtyard and the senior commanders of the division would have been hit.

But the Marines weren't thinking in those terms. They were angry and upset, unsure what had happened. It made little difference. Incoming and outgoing were both part of war's package of death. The bridge had to be crossed. Captain Norton gathered his men, and Howell gave final instructions to those carrying the metal gate, reminding them to test three times before stepping out on the planks over the chasm where the bridge had been blown apart. The Iraqi general acting as a forward observer was smart: the electronic intercept team heard him yelling at his driver not to stop, so he couldn't be fixed and fired upon. Kilo started across the pedestrian bridge while the Iraqi was still yelling for fire.

In single file the Marines ran onto the pedestrian bridge, careful not to trip over an Iraqi soldier who lay at the entrance, face up with his shirt open, exposing a belly that was round, either from lack of exercise or from the buildup of gases after death. Two fire teams and a machine-gun team went first to provide cover fire for the plank carriers. The scene wasn't much different from movie scenes, showing the storming of a castle in the Middle Ages—some attackers shot arrows to cover those who were throwing boards across the moat. The main exception was the crazy press photographers from half a dozen nations who were running alongside the Marines, snapping away with their shutters. They had no idea the danger they were in. On both sides the bridge was lined with oil pipes, steel railings, and thick steel girders crisscrossed to hold it up. One or two RPGs or a few bursts from a machine gun could careen and ricochet down the bridge and only scratch the steel but gouge the flesh. One photographer was so diligent, or nuts, that I made a note to look later at what he had taken. His photo is on the back jacket of this book.

From the cut in the bridge down to the rocks along the edge of the water was about a 15-meter drop, but the lead Marines threw the metal gate across the gap, slid planks across, and scrambled over. The rickety planks rested on what looked scarily like the metal frame for a double bed, but no Marine fell while going across.

Once it was on the Baghdad side, Kilo swarmed into the row of houses to the left while India headed into the palm grove on the right. Given what 3/4 had experienced so far in Iraq, we all agreed, the odds were high that India would get into it once inside the grove. But if defenders chose to fight from the houses, that would be harder to deal with. So McCoy cut left after Kilo, and Ray and I went with him. Firing came from one house right on the river, but that was it. Why one Iraqi soldier stayed when everyone else fled was baffling.

The riverbank was littered with what I had thought was garbage— deep fighting holes, blankets, food, dishes, canteens, web gear, ammunition magazines, AK-47 rifles, and RPGs assembled and ready to fire. Tank and artillery fire had shredded and tossed everything about, and one had to wonder about the tactical sense of soldiers who dug in where they could be seen from the opposite bank. The Marines were already moving rapidly from house to house, anxious to get beyond the first block and secure some cover before a firefight broke out. Captain Norton was a whirling dervish, shouting a profane string of cautions to his platoon commanders, squad leaders, and individual Marines, determined that there would be no more Marine casualties if he had anything to say about it, and as the company commander he was saying a lot.

We ducked into the first house on the block for a look around. It was modest but not uncomfortable, with high ceilings, fans, and cool tile floors. The Iraqi soldiers manning the fighting holes outside had displaced the family that lived there and slept in the parents' room in a high bed in a heavy stained wooden frame. They left a few loose 7.62mm cartridges in the rumpled covers and had ransacked the closet and the drawers, scattering lipstick, rouge, and cheap jewelry. They had shoved the refrigerator against the wall nearest the street, perhaps as a defense, and had fled before the Marines came to call.

Back out on the street, the Marines were already two blocks ahead of us, shouting "Clear!" back and forth as they ran from house to house.

Some cars and small trucks were on the main street, all shot up beyond repair, the dead drivers still in a few of them. In a white minivan with a shattered windshield a dead man with curly white hair was resting his head on the steering wheel; and a spider had woven a large web from his hair to the windshield, an ideal trap for the hordes of flies feasting on the congealed blood. Reporters and photographers were running alongside the Kilo Marines, snapping pictures. An excited French reporter in heavily accented English said to Ray and me, "They are so brave!" Since he was being sincere, Ray, who held an impassioned view of French politics, restrained himself and walked on in silence.

Across the street were bursts of firing, and along with a cluster of reporters we walked over to watch the Marines finish clearing the palm grove. In the hour that had passed since they took the bridge, they had advanced several hundred meters and were almost at the end of the trees. Behind them were several Iraqi bodies as well as a heavy machine gun on large metal wheels and a recoilless rifle on small metal wheels with holes from armor-piercing rounds near the top of its barrel. From their positions you could see back to the pedestrian bridge. Either of those weapons would have had a formidable effect.

At an entrance through a wall into the palm grove an Iraqi soldier lay facedown, the deep treads on his boots looking barely worn, a military radio and battery next to his right arm. *[Picture 45]* The electronic intercept team was now radioing warnings about mortars. Lieutenant Leeks of India Company had dispersed his men among the palm trees. He sent a Marine over to smash the Iraqi's radio, waited a few moments, then continued the attack. The radio operator was the last soldier killed. Both companies reported they had reached their designated limit of advance, about 500 meters in from the bridge.

Kilo was on the left side of the divided highway with a commanding view. Two Iraqi vehicles approached at a good rate of speed, and a machine gun fired several bursts at them. Both cars swerved to the right and rolled to a stop on the wide dirt shoulder. Marines advanced cautiously. In the first car—a nondescript small white four-door—two civilians lay dead. In the second—a reddish minivan—one civilian had a bullet in the leg, and five or six others were crying and sobbing. The Marines pushed the minivan off the shoulder and put the driver back behind the wheel. He hastily drove away in the direction from which he'd come.

McCoy was upset and asked Ray if he had any suggestions as to how to stop such killings. Ray said there wasn't anything the Marines could do if civilians drove into a firefight. If the Marines didn't shoot, on his advice, and instead were blown up, he would not forgive himself. I wasn't so sure. Surely some bright staff officer could come up with some better system, I said, some way of putting out a warning sign or something. Ray said maybe in time for the next war, but you couldn't stop operations now while someone tried to figure out what to do about civilians who drove into areas where there was shooting. Civilians continued to die due to fear of the suicide bombers.

With the bridgehead secure, McCoy's battalion settled into providing security while the center span across the Baghdad Bridge was repaired by the engineer. Ray and I walked back across the pedestrian bridge, got into the Yellow Submarine, and drove several kilometers south to RCT-7's CP. We found Hummer in a good mood. The 1st Tanks had repaired the bridge to the north of battalion 3/4 and moved across. A pontoon bridge was being laid next to the Baghdad Bridge, where the destroyed span would be replaced by a metal span within a day. Battalion 3/7 was filling in to the north of 3/4, and 1/7 was in 3/4's trace.

While we were talking, Colonel Toolan, commanding RCT-1, came up on the radio, asking to speak with Colonel Hummer. *"Ripper Six, this is Inchon Six. Three-one is in position and prepared to hold open the bridge to the north."*

"Inchon Six, thanks, but we're all set. We'll be finished by morning."

"Can't blame me for trying."

Hummer laughed good-naturedly. Traveling night and day, Toolan had moved RCT-1 in behind RCT-7, eager to get into the fight. With 3/1, which was superbly trained, in the lead, Toolan was hoping that one of RCT-7's battalions might be running a bit late, so he could cut ahead in line and slip into Baghdad.

As we talked on the afternoon of 6 April, three battalions were in East Baghdad, a fourth was crossing, and at least three others were waiting to cross. We asked Hummer if higher headquarters, the CFLCC, had changed the concept from encirclement and raids to attacking straight in and seizing Baghdad. Hummer told us that raids appeared to be the strategy still in effect, but division was in receipt of no written frag order from the CFLCC specifying what constituted a raid. After discussing the matter with the MEF, the division had settled on several targets whose importance deserved a sound raid, about twelve, possibly more. The number of sites kept growing every time they looked at the map: the Saddam Fedayeen Training Center, the Rasheed Military Complex, the Atomic Energy Commission, Baghdad University, the Ministry of Defense complex, Fedayeen HQ, Directorate of General Security HQ, and the Al Azamiya Palace. There seemed little sense in pulling back outside the city after a raid, only to have to move forward again for the next target. So the division had blocked out East Baghdad into three sectors, one for each RCT, and each RCT was assigning sectors to battalions. When a battalion finished seizing the key site in one sector, it would move on to the next.

We looked at the map. The three regimental sectors covered the whole Marine objective area for East Baghdad. RCT-7's sector was drawn in bright blue and had the same outline as the state of Florida. Inside the outline were eighteen numbered squares, with six assigned to each battalion. The regimental staff had selected at least one site worthy of a raid inside each square. One man's raid had morphed into another man's seizure of a city. Battle commanders at the front, who had a first-hand sense for the cohesion or collapse of the enemy, were coming up with imaginative ways to circumvent the guidance coming down from higher headquarters, whose technology conveyed a graphic but inaccurate picture of the battlefield.

After explaining his overall plan, Hummer told us Lieutenant Colonel Belcher's 3/7 was launching another night attack, but we couldn't get to his position in time to join him. He suggested instead we take a look at the Atomic Energy Commission that Lieutenant Colonel Conlin's 1/7 had captured, only a kilometer away. He pointed to a gigantic berm that we had thought was a hill. It had taken at least fifty thousand dump trucks of dirt to build a protective circle around the complex. Inside was a cluster of buildings with sandstone brick facades and large unbroken windows, separated by rows of rose bushes and winding concrete driveways. The setting was similar to a small campus with a modest endowment, trying to scrape by and keep up appearances. We could think of no rationale for the enormous berm around the complex. The library was tidy, with a small number of books, mostly in English and with publication dates from the 1960s and 1970s. There was a collection of oil paintings, as though the Atomic Energy Commission's real function was to serve as an art studio with only one model and one theme: Saddam in his many beatified roles, solemnly listening to earnest scientists, heeding the pleas of the elderly, embracing little children, studying the Koran, and sipping tea on a bucolic hillside. *[Picture 47]*

As we drove back to the Baghdad Bridge, Ray and I passed the first wave of looters, hundreds of people of all ages, men and women, rushing into government buildings outside RCT-7's perimeter, carrying off metal desks, plastic chairs, computer keyboards, lamp fixtures, parts of air conditioners, wastebaskets and empty picture frames. We drove carefully, as the only Americans on the road outside the Marine perimeter, surrounded by hundreds of happy looters, smiling and hollering at us, holding up their wares for sale. They were giddy, acting as though they had had too much to drink, carried away with grabbing anything. The looting was a pent-up release after decades of repression—it was also the first real sign that the population knew the Saddam regime would not survive. They knew the Americans would not shoot them, and there weren't enough Americans to guard every building in a country run by a punk government. Colonel Hummer and his regiment were fighting to seize Baghdad. Beginning on 6 April, we saw the looters move in lock step with the advancing battalions. Somehow that word spread through all of Baghdad.

That night we could not get back across the bridge because of the steady flow of fighting vehicles crossing it, so we pulled in again at the unoccupied medical clinic. The rear of 3/4's supply train had pulled out, and we had the sad little building to ourselves. Ray settled into the Yellow Submarine, and I tried to sleep in a patient's bed in the open courtyard. That wasn't smart. Half asleep, I semidreamed I was on an operating table, with an accusing Iraqi doctor looming above me, his patients looking on. I shifted to be outside under the stars next to the SUV.

Years ago Col. Bob Barrow, a Marine I admired tremendously, commented that he had never seen a crowded battlefield. In Vietnam, Ray walked into the fight for Hue City with 146 Marines and walked out with seven of the original group. Of the fourteen members of the squad I knew best in Vietnam, seven were killed. Since then the American military had learned how to use maneuver and lethal weapons to devastate an enemy at far less cost to itself. The cost is never zero, though, and when you travel with the grunts, those who die are those who were standing next to you. First Lieutenant McPhillips and First Sergeant Smith were gone in the tank battle; Corporal Evnin was gone, no longer driving for Sergeant Major Howell; and today 3/4 had lost two more, Corporal Medellin and Lance Corporal Aviles. The battlefield was never crowded. The Green Machine had crossed into Baghdad, and it had paid a price, modest by comparison to other wars, not so modest to the families of those who had gone. And their little families within the Marines—those they depended on and swapped turkey for noodles with and shook awake to stand watch in the dirt at three in the morning—would remember them. They might not talk much about it when they got back to the States and went to another duty station or left the Green Machine for civilian life. But they would remember.

12

Seizing the Snoozle

D + 18, D + 19

Clearing East Baghdad with battalions 3/4 and 1/7
8–9 April

ON THE MORNING OF 8 APRIL Ray and I decided to take the pontoon bridge over the Diyala back into Baghdad. The Baghdad Bridge, where yesterday the Amtrac crew had been hit by artillery, had been repaired, but that did not hold the same panache as a genuine amphibious bridge. For nineteen days the bridge company had eaten dust sitting at the rear of traffic jams. Now they had put their boats, which had seemed so anomalous in the convoys, in the water, floated their pontoon decking, dropped huge anchors to hold against the current, and bulldozed dirt ramps on both sides of the river. And we were the first semicivilian vehicle to cross. Our Yellow Submarine was no longer spiffy. It was encrusted with dust, the air panel was tattered, the back window was a piece of cardboard, dust was piled inches thick on the inside, a rear tire had been twice punctured and twice repaired, the front windshield was cracked, and a deep gouge crawled along the right side to remind us of the role luck plays in life. The bridge company waved us on before a line of Amtracs, and we cheered them, saying how terrific their bridge was, and they grinned back, a hard, thankless job well done.

In four-wheel drive and low gear, our plucky SUV spun through the mud at the top of the up ramp and popped back out on terra firma—six inches of solid dust. A corporal directing traffic had watched us slip and slide up from the river and nodded in appreciation. We stopped to chat, and he told us he thought his unit had forgotten about him.

"Not too shabby," he said. "Even some of the tracs have a hard time with that slope. I've been here directing traffic for almost twenty-four hours. This sucks so bad, I'm enjoying it."

We laughed and wished him well. Marines were easily entertained: a war, a night of miserable guard duty, and a chance to watch others who have it worse.

We drove on and soon caught up with McCoy and 3/4. His battalion was methodically checking the houses on both sides of Route 6, which runs northwest for several kilometers through the heart of downtown East Baghdad. If he proceeded by poking around each building on the route, his job should not take more than a year or two to complete. It seemed a succession of higher headquarters were discussing how fast the battalions should move; in the meantime McCoy was ordered to hold to a deliberate pace, some suspecting that he tended to charge ahead.

On his right flank battalion 3/7 had reported in from its night attack, together with the OGA and ODA, against the Al Rasheed Medical Center, where intel had reported American POWs were being kept. Lieutenant Colonel Belcher's Marines found U.S. Army uniforms there, but the POWs were gone. In the compound they also found three trucks full of bodies of Iraqi soldiers who had been killed the previous day or two. Evidently the Marines' bridge crossing had taken a heavy toll.

Scattered along the wide highway and on the dirt shoulders of Route 6 were a few bodies of males in civilian clothes, and it was hard to imagine what each man had been doing, out on the wide open roadway, when cut down. As 3/4 searched through the rows of houses, two tanks stood guard on the highway to the front. The houses looked like condominiums in any American city, with high cement walls and stout gates that opened inward. In the tiny courtyards were recent-year Japanese-made cars and mini-trucks, patches of Bermuda grass, small flower beds and garden hoses, a short flight of brick steps leading to the front door, neat rooms with tile floors, and clunky television sets and over-head fans. The brick and concrete work was rough but passable, with louver forms for decoration and red, yellow, black, and white tiles. Servant quarters were in the back of most of the condo-type houses. It seemed like middle-class living. But the residents had all fled—not an Iraqi was in sight. For the Marines, hopping over walls, ducking around corners, and covering each rush across another alley was hot, boring work by noon.

The tankers could see a kilometer up the street, and occasionally a car would head their way; they would fire a few warning shots, and the car would pull a quick U-turn. Around noon a dumpy white and or-ange car—apparently the only color scheme permitted on most cars in the country—headed down the empty street toward the tanks. We were standing next to McCoy's Humvee on the shoulder and paid no atten-tion to the first *bang, bang, bang* that warned the car to turn around. Suddenly there was much shouting, and Marines scurried to take cover as the car accelerated and headed directly at a tank. The Marine in the turret fired his 7.62mm machine gun in long bursts, and the nearest Amtrac joined in. A dozen meters in front of them the car veered to the right and stopped. The Marines hastily closed the hatches and waited for the explosion. Eventually, when nothing happened, the hatches were opened, and the engineers were called forward.

Two middle-aged men in faded blue work clothes lay bloody and dead in the front seat of the car. There was no identification, no tools, no explosives, and no junk in the car—only two dead men and a mys-tery. A reporter watching and photographing the event was mystified: he kept saying over and over that he had thought he was about to be blown up. The driver must have panicked at the warning shots, and driven toward the tank instead of away from it. Then he may have been hit and his foot stuck on the accelerator. McCoy was again upset. This had happened two days in a row. There had to be a solution. The rest of the Marines were less reflective, glad there had been no explosion.

The fruitless search along Route 6 resumed, and the Marines moved from houses into rubble-filled fields that were sprinkled with upper-class houses under construction in a neighborhood of slums.

If the secret to real estate is location, location, location, then this developer made a bad mistake. On all sides were squalor and decay, dumpy low-rise tenements, and fields full of trash. Since there was no free enterprise under Saddam, the location of the building project certainly had something to do with the politics of the Baath Party. The half-finished cement buildings would have provided excellent cover for interlocking fields of fire, but the Marines were encountering only stray shots from "shoot and scoot" snipers: they fired a few shots to assert their manhood, dropped the rifle, and left the field of battle—leaving, unfortunately, the poor civilians in the slum area behind the construction to suffer the consequences when the Marines fired back.

After one such brief exchange, as the Marines moved by, Ray and I entered the house where the firing had come from. Except for a cuckoo clock from Switzerland, the rooms were tastefully done, with fine rugs and comfortable, if heavy, furniture. On the roof behind a high, solid cement wall we found a few AK-47 shells, and downstairs in the courtyard was a dish of rice, some meat, black boots, a green shirt, web gear, and the bipod for a 60mm mortar. We found the mortar barrel a few hundred meters farther out in the junk-filled field, where the fleeing soldiers had dropped it.

The rows of cement apartments fronting open fields made ideal defensive lines for an urban stand, but nothing had been prepared. Outside the city bulldozers had plowed hundreds of kilometers of trench lines and berms, but here in the city no holes or trenches had been dug where the terrain favored the defender. After dropping the bridge span, the Iraqis had had a day to set in at least a hasty defense, but they hadn't done even that.

Every fighting force prefers a particular battle style, which becomes obvious to the opponent after a few battles. The North Koreans and Chinese first employed massed infantry assaults, then settled into trench warfare. The Vietcong were skillful with mines and sappers wriggling through the barbed wire at night. The North Vietnamese were deadly with mortars and dug-in bunkers with light machine guns that supported one another with cross fires. In Somalia the tribes swarmed to the battle with AK-47s and RPGs. In Gulf War I the Iraqis had tried without success to employ armor.

In this war Iraq had a choice of weapons—and it chose badly. The Iraqis had mortars and lucrative targets at every road junction, yet they rarely fired, perhaps from fear of the counterbattery radars. The Iraqis equipped an army with artillery and tanks that they proceeded to abandon. Even the machine gun, a staple since World War I, was not employed. The weapons they consistently employed were the AK-47 and the RPG, which had an antipersonnel and antivehicle warhead. Likely the RPG manufacturers benefited from the myth of Somalia and from the hope that an entire nation armed with RPGs could force an American withdrawal, as occurred in Mogadishu two years after Saddam's forces were driven out of Kuwait. The supply of RPGs seemed inexhaustible—they seemed as common as flies. Dependable and simple to use, they were ideal to dispense to the ill-trained fedayeen.

The Iraqis had ample weapons, but they did not have the will to use them. The plain fact was that in the countryside the Iraqi army had not consistently shown up to fight. The success of the 11th Infantry Division at Nasiriyah had been a surprise, and the Iraqi army had done well at Najaf, while the Al Nida Division gave Colonel Dunford's RCT-5 a stiff fight. But these were the exceptions. Overall it had been a paramilitary fight, meaning the Iraqis lacked military organization. Without such organization, a force cannot defend a city. Contrary to the fears of senior American staffs overseeing the battle, the Iraqi military wasn't digging in to defend Baghdad.

On 8 April McCoy's battalion fought a few skirmishes with stay-behinds, and only one was memorable. It happened about two in the afternoon, when the Marines were hot and not paying close attention because nothing much seemed to be happening. Ray and I were talking with a rifle platoon, when a tremendous burst of firing erupted from a tank a few hundred meters away, next to the road. The platoon looked all around, trying to pick up the enemy as the tank machine gun went on and on, stopping only when it was empty.

The tank commander (who will remain anonymous here) had walked out into the trashy field to relieve himself. Modesty on a battlefield can result in being shot by your own side, so the loader on the tank was keeping half an eye on his sergeant. The tank commander was paying attention to his own business when he heard a rustling in the trash pile next to him and watched, astonished, as three wild-eyed and disheveled Arabs clawed their way out from beneath some discarded blankets, AK-47s in hand. With his trousers around his ankles, the sergeant turned and ran toward his tank, yelling "Shoot! Shoot!"

The loader swiveled the 7.62mm machine gun and fired until he was out of ammunition. He then drew his 9mm pistol and emptied that clip as well. The sergeant was not hit. One fedayeen was literally pulverized; the other two lost their nerve and fled back into the field, where eager riflemen quickly closed and killed them. The battalion shared a good laugh, and the tank commander, who was popular among the troops, took it good-naturedly.

I wondered what the dead young men had been thinking, having watched their comrades run away a day or even hours before the Marines arrived, hiding in their miserable hole in the garbage, perhaps saying their prayers over and over, assuring one another that they would kill an American before they died, a foolish assurance. As Sgt. Maj. Henry Bergeron of battalion 1/7 said of the fedayeen much earlier, "This is the perfect war. They want to die, and we want to kill them."

As the endless block-by-block search wound down in the late afternoon, Ray and I drove to a large military camp on the west side of Route 6, where McCoy planned to spend the night. We passed through the gates and drove by office buildings until we noticed a giant warehouse, easily two football fields in length. Curious, we parked and pried our way in through a side door. Inside, the roof was several stories above our head, with a set of steel girders and enormous pulleys made in Germany. Posters on the walls featured Saddam in a hard hat cautioning the workers in English and Arabic that safety was their responsibility. It was an assembly plant for large military equipment, stripped bare except for sets of animal cages with metal mesh screening and four long

Russian torpedoes with red and white stripes painted on their attached warheads. [Pictures 48 and 49]

We left the warehouse and drove back to the office buildings, where we again looked around inside. Besides the obligatory three to six pictures or prints of Saddam, the walls and shelves of each room held one or more gas masks, some in new wrappings, with monocular face plates, like scuba-diving masks. They were every bit as well constructed as the American masks. The director's office held a bathroom with a shower, a bidet, and a ceramic toilet. Ray pushed the handle on the toilet, and it flushed with a great gurgle and swish. Ray declared that a working toilet meant the war was over. I wasn't so sanguine. Here we were standing among the inner machinery of the Saddam regime: cages for small animals sitting in a vast mechanical assembly line; safety signs in Arabic and English that suggested either sly caricature or no sense of the absurd; torpedoes, with explosive warheads attached, stored hundreds of kilometers from the sea in a country with no navy; a low-level manufacturing official with his own bidet; and sophisticated new gas masks in every office. The things you could reach out and touch made no sense as a set. It wouldn't surprise me if some Iraqi slimed us in the night or if there were no chemicals to fire at us. The regime was structurally psychotic.

We shared our MREs with the flies on the patio, chatting with a sniper team on its way to watch from a water tower for the night. A gang of looters sauntered up, asking about computers. We politely told them there were only 486-model machines inside, beneath their standards. They of course did not understand English, but they did understand the sniper team looking down on us, so they left. Ray and I were beginning to respond to the bizarre by being bizarre—not a good sign of mental health. Night settled in, and for a while we listened to the 3/4 battalion net. It sounded like the regiment was waiting for permission from the divisional command to accelerate the rate of advance and that Army units had moved in on the west side of Baghdad. That meant Saddam's troops didn't have much real estate left to occupy—they were being squeezed from both sides. We waited an hour for 3/4 to arrive at our comfortable patio before concluding the battalion wasn't coming at all.

As usual, it had been dark before the battalion coiled and McCoy had driven back to the regimental command. In his absence someone had decided that the battalion should stay where it was rather than move back to the agreed-upon bivouac, where we had cleverly claimed the choicest spot. Now half of 3/4 was confused, heading back to where the other half had set in. As for us, from the clanking of treads and the deep rumble of engines, we knew we were outside the lines of Bravo tanks. We might have stayed put and risked some fedayeen stumbling over us at three in the morning, but one burst from a .50-caliber from a nervous Abrams tank, and our Yellow Submarine would disintegrate, hurling us back into the crowded Amtracs for the rest of the campaign. That was a risk absolutely too great.

We radioed for help, and thanks to the GPS, a CAAT came out and escorted us back inside the lines. We spent the evening of 8 April in a drizzle under a makeshift awning with a dozen Humvees that were constantly recharging their batteries and testing their engines. The exhaust fumes hung a few feet off the ground while nearby the officers on watch talked loudly through the night. It was as interesting as listening to men yelling into their cell phones while waiting in line to board an airplane. Our tranquil patio with running water and a flushing toilet seemed like a mirage.

By the morning of 9 April Major General Mattis had most of the 1st Marine Division across the river and moving through East Baghdad from the southeast (RCT-7), east (RCT-1), and northeast (RCT-5, which had followed RCT-1 across the bridges). Ray and I heard that Lieutenant Colonel Conlin and his battalion, 1/7, had drawn an interesting mission. So we said temporary good-byes to our friends in 3/4 and drove down Route 6 to hook up with 1/7.

Conlin, who had just returned from the RCT-7 command element, showed us a map with a few dozen square patches, each about 70 square kilometers and containing about 100,000 people. Intelligence about enemy locations was nonexistent. The video feeds from the Predator and Pioneer UAVs had been unable to pick out the enemy from the civilians.

The electronic intercepts were gibberish; it sounded like widespread panic among Saddam's followers, but without rallying points. Colonel Hummer's staff could only provide red circles on a map, called "buildings of interest"—hospitals, mosques, schools, training sites, and the like—where opposition forces had been in the past. In the absence of any written instruction to the contrary from the CFLCC, each battalion was to keep pressing forward and expanding. The embedded reporters pitched in, telling Conlin that the Iraqi handlers and guards for the international press at the Palestine Hotel had not shown up for work that morning—not a single officer or enlisted man. Saddam's military had deserted en masse.

Conlin was happy; he had drawn a prize zone, a 60-square-kilometer peninsula where the Tigris veers abruptly to the west, then zigs back east and continues its southerly course through the center of the city. Called Al Karradah on a map—its outline resembled a penis or a long nose. Aware that it might be referred to later, the Marines prudently called it the Snoozle. It was actually Embassy Row, the rich suburb dotted with several of Saddam's palaces and the palatial homes of the Baath leadership. A secluded, palm-draped locale along the river, it was sheltered from the noise and smog of western, downtown Baghdad, only a few minutes' drive across the river. At the extreme far end of the Snoozle sat Baghdad University. The CIA had warned that the fedayeen were dug in there.

For Maj. John McDonough, the battalion's S-3 Operations officer, the Snoozle presented the opportunity to prove a concept. McDonough was intense, tough, and prickly. He did his homework and expected others to do the same. He was a charter member of the Maneuver Warfare movement, a controversial concept of operations that had revised strategic thinking inside the Marine Corps.

Like the Army, the Marine Corps had left Vietnam a discouraged institution. Deployed along the border with North Vietnam, Marine battalions had suffered the highest casualties, yet they had been forbidden to pursue the enemy when he retreated back across the border. By the early 1970s, Marine battalions in Vietnam were experiencing racial, drug, and alcohol problems, the disrespect of sergeants and officers, and a feeling that engaging the enemy only led to Purple Hearts and crippled bodies. Lacking a theory of victory, the Corps had ceased to be a warrior society for winners.

After Vietnam two successive commandants, Gen. Louis Wilson and Gen. Robert Barrow, both Korean War heroes with southern courtesy and iron wills, had reshaped the Corps and reinvigorated its morale. They encouraged battalion commanders to discharge malcontents; no questions would be asked by higher command. Fully ten percent of the force was sent packing—with no warning, no severance pay, no apology. Pack your sea bag, and take your attitude elsewhere, was the message. Drill sergeants on the grinder ensured that every recruit understood he was joining the Marine Corps and accepting its values; the Corps wasn't joining him. It was his fellow Marines who counted, not his ego. His sense of self-worth depended on accepting discipline, authority, and order. If he could not comply, if he could not meet the physical and mental challenges and pressure, he would be sent home. Never a rose garden, the Corps bore down even harder; shape up or ship out.

A renewed sense of values alone was not sufficient. The Corps saw itself as the Green Dragon, a fighting machine that came from the sea to defeat any enemy, in any locale, on any terms. The lives lost in Vietnam, however, had not brought victory. The enemy was not defeated. The Green Machine, often called "the Gun Club" and sometimes "the Suck," had not triumphed in Vietnam. Marine leaders did not blame President Lyndon B. Johnson (whom they did not trust) and the other politicians for the losses on the battlefield. To be sure, they intensely disliked the secretary of defense at the time, Robert Strange McNamara, who acknowledged that he felt the pain of the North Vietnamese and of the protesters back home, while ordering the Marines to hold senselessly along the Demilitarized Zone and making "body counts" the only measure of success on the battlefield. But the Marines also knew that they themselves, despite poor political leaders, had not fought smart enough in the jungles of Southeast Asia.

Marines were rightly known as shock troops. In World War II on islands like Iwo Jima the tightness of the terrain had extracted a trail in
blood as the Marines inched forward. And in Korea the frozen ridge-
lines had had to be taken and held, regardless of losses, so that those on
the road below could get back safely. As a result of those two wars and
the Washington bean-counters' body count mentality, in Vietnam the
Marines fought under leaders and principles based on finding the enemy, fixing him, and slugging it out toe to toe, strength against strength,
until by dint of personal valor and dogged determination the foe was
vanquished.

After Vietnam the Marines knew they needed a new doctrine for
fighting. The U.S. Army was out in front in the late 1970s, asking
whether Vietnam-style search-and-destroy tactics made sense. Eventually
the Army worked out a clever scheme for defeating any Soviet/Warsaw
Pact attack against NATO in Western Europe. This change in operations
was called the Air-Land Doctrine.

It could not serve as a road map, however, for the Marine Corps. The
Corps was required, by an act of Congress, "to be most ready when the
Nation was least ready." The Marine Corps was also tasked with maintaining and developing the nation's amphibious doctrine. To meet these
obligations, the Corps had to develop expeditionary packages to go
anywhere on short notice. It had to be lighter in terms of tanks and
heavy artillery than the Army, whose prime war-fighting forces were focused toward the border between East and West Germany. But the
Corps still had to be heavy enough to sustain itself in unimproved the-
aters of war. These dictates of equipment meant the Corps needed its
own war-fighting doctrine, to be able to come from the sea and quickly
build combat power ashore.

Meeting in restaurants and paneled basements in the mid-1980s, a
few dozen Marine majors and lieutenant colonels debated alternatives
to the attrition strategy of Vietnam. In many ways the Marines are like
the Jesuits, a closed society that insists upon monkish rules that seem to
an outsider to be rather rigid and to an insider to be quite rigid. More
traditional Marine officers fretted that changing war-fighting concepts
would endanger political support for some weapon systems or other-

wise shatter rice bowls. Despite the glowers of the seniors, the Young Turks persisted. They had logic on their side; many of the bloody fights in Vietnam had been head-to-head slugfests, devoid of deeper thought. They had been the company commanders ordered into those fights— one couldn't argue the contrary with them.

In the early 1990s, with Gen. Al Gray—the eldest of the Young Turks—now commandant, the Marine Corps published a new operational concept called Maneuver Warfare. It stressed determining the enemy's critical vulnerabilities and attacking his critical nodes. In Vietnam, in retaking Hue City in 1968, the Marines had advanced block by block; under Maneuver Warfare, the aim was to strike at the enemy's command and control center, leaving the soldiers on the bypassed blocks without leadership or cohesion. The doctrine also stressed the need for speed—speed of decision-making first and foremost, then speed of execution as well; since speed was always relative, it meant being faster than your enemy above all else. Almost a generation of Marine officers had grown up studying the new doctrine.

Now, inside Baghdad, Major McDonough had the chance to show that Maneuver Warfare was real, not just a theory and not only the province of generals. Conlin asked McDonough to design the scheme of maneuver for the Snoozle. Under the old doctrine, the plan would have been to deploy abreast two companies with tanks across the five-kilometer front and advance down the peninsula block by block, reaching the university at the western end by the afternoon of the second day.

Instead, McDonough proposed rolling through the center of the Snoozle, tanks in the lead, peeling off one company to secure the embassies and one platoon to guard the approaches to the central bridges, and sending the tanks on with one company to search the university. Conlin should ignore random RPG shots, McDonough urged, and concentrate on grabbing the three key pieces of real estate; he should rely on shock to crumble the resolve of any stay-behinds. He should finish taking the Snoozle in four hours and the next day move on to another sector. In other sectors, other Army and Marine battalions were planning the same type of nonlinear movement.

Conlin approved McDonough's concept. His brief to the company commanders at noon took twenty minutes, the essentials crayoned on one white board, supported by one large map and a two-year-old satellite photo map product provided by the National Imagery and Mapping Agency. The U.S. government has expended a great amount of money and effort in providing updated map products for U.S. forces in the past twenty or so years; but the widespread impression that maps can be made instantaneously is false. To an old-timer like Ray, who landed his battalion in Grenada without any maps at all, today's intelligence products looked excellent. To the younger generation raised in the "information age," the two years it took the system to process the imagery, produce useful maps with military grids superimposed on the imagery, and then distribute the maps to the infantry was much too long. Pentagon intelligence and communications agencies did not accord high priority to the Army and Marine infantry. The higher up the chain of command and the higher in the rear, the better the imagery products received. Some called this system a "self-licking ice-cream cone," a reference to staffs passing back and forth digital data that made them feel they were in the know but that did not benefit those on the ground moving forward.

The company commanders then had two hours to brief their people, and at two P.M., Conlin rolled out from the soft drink factory he was occupying, next door to a brewery. Not a case of soft drinks or beer had been taken. Veterans from World War II would have shaken their heads.

With tanks in the lead, Conlin's Hummer slowly bumped down a rutted dirt road toward Route 6, then quickly stopped. CNN's balky Humvee, rumored to be equipped with a Porta-Potty, wouldn't start. The Marines had come to conclude that the TV crew were good sorts, not responsible for the politics of Jane Fonda and Ted Turner. Getting to Baghdad was a big deal for the TV crew—superbig, as in staying employed. So Conlin fidgeted while Sergeant Major Bergeron hitched CNN's yuppie Humvee to the tow bar of his Marine Humvee. After ten minutes the convoy was again on the move. To the north was a low wall, and beyond that a few hundred meters were a few high-rise apartments. One rifle shot cracked over Conlin's vehicle, then another.

"I don't believe this," Conlin said, ignoring the fact that the sniper, if he was well trained, was shooting at him. If he did see himself as the target, Conlin didn't appear at all concerned. He seemed more irritated by the effrontery and stupidity of the sniper, who persisted in firing another shot from the same position.

The column, as usual, was lined up in single file: tanks in the lead; then fifteen Amtracs, all with the up gun station manned; then Conlin, Ray, and me; the sergeant major's Hummer with CNN's vehicle attached; and a line of sixty Amtracs. One idiot had taken a shot at a thousand Marines. To the left of the column was a brick wall, and a few hundred meters on the other side was an apartment building with about seven stories, the top floors having commanding views over the wall, looking down on the convoy.

Like most battalion commanders on the move, Conlin had a designated marksman in the backseat of his Hummer. Sgt. Tony Perolio, the best sniper in the battalion, hopped out with his telescopic 7.62mm rifle. After draping a sandbag over the hood of the colonel's Hummer, he and his spotter scanned the buildings with their scopes, looking for the sniper. Perolio had fired fewer than a dozen times in twenty days on the march up, and he had hit only two Iraqi soldiers, both of them in a melee and at close range. Shots like that didn't count for a sniper.

Before Perolio could find a target, from down the column a .50-caliber opened up, followed by a few machine guns. Bullets whanged, and dust poofs spurted from the cement side of the apartment. Two Amtracs at the front of the column wheeled south and screeched past a dumbfounded Conlin. Troops tumbled out and deployed along the wall, unable to see anything. Perolio looked appealingly at Conlin. This was supposed to be his target, and now Bravo Company was trampling all over the place.

"Stop this circus, Sergeant Major!" Conlin yelled to Bergeron.

The Marines did not want to stop—they wanted to kill the sniper. The march up to Baghdad hadn't been like the grueling, two-sided battles at Iwo Jima in World War II or the Chosin Reservoir in Korea or Khe Sanh in Vietnam. Conlin's battalion had met the enemy in spurts and heard the rattle of a few AK-47s and the zip of one or two RPGs overhead. The battalion was a killing machine, a thousand young men who shaved each day, said "sir" to their elders, held open doors for any woman, responded without resentment when sergeants yelled at them, cleaned their weapons five times a day, checked the links on the ammo belts, and tapped the magazines against their Kevlars to make sure the cartridges were seated. And practically every one of them wanted to shoot a fedayeen. At the airfield at Nu'maniyah they had been disappointed when the Iraqi soldiers fizzled and the sergeant major had made them take prisoners. Now there was a sniper out there, a real, live target who wasn't surrendering and who hadn't yet run away. Besides, in that high-rise with no connecting buildings, he had no place to run. This was killing time.

But no one crossed the sergeant major. Bergeron yelled, and the firing ceased along the line. The Bravo troops remounted, and Conlin had a few choice words with Major Healey, the company commander.

The burden now fell to Perolio. He and his spotter, Lance Corporal Alvarez, preferred to work as a lone team. They had spent hundreds of hours on the firing range. To go out and kill another soldier when he is unsuspecting and careless, as all soldiers are at different moments in each day—that requires the suspension of thought, the blotting out of feeling about another human being who is not an officer, not a leader, just another soul on the battlefield. There's little that's special about reaching out with a weapon that fires true to a thousand meters, mounted with optics that can see the wart on the enemy soldier's cheek before the bullet pushes his nose through the back of his skull.

But to encounter another sniper—another man hiding and trying to kill your commander—for a sniper like Perolio, that was the duel he had sought and would remember and be proud to recount. Conlin knew that. He had stopped to give Perolio his chance, trading off a few minutes from the mission. Everybody in the command party knew that Perolio had two, maybe three minutes, and then Conlin would be rolling again.

Alvarez had the lower right corner of a window in his scope and was calling out range and description. Perolio had draped his body over the Hummer's hood, rifle firm on the sandbag, eye against the scope. *Bang! [Picture 50]* The bolt went back, and the next round was in the chamber.

"Got him," Alvarez said. "His head snapped back."

"I didn't see," Conlin's driver said.

Perolio had forgotten to take off his sunglasses as he peered through his scope—he would be sure to hear about that. "Are you sure?"

"Yeah. I told you. The head snapped back."

"Let's get moving," Conlin said.

The convoy got under way again, turning northeast onto the main boulevard, accelerating past the sad orange and white car and the dead from 3/4's firing the day before, past shot-up and shuttered storefronts, a candy concession, an oil-smeared car repair shop with a porcelain bathtub filled with gasoline to clean off the grime, and tiny grocery stores with metal grilles. Three kilometers up the road the convoy followed CAAT Red on a sharp left turn into the Snoozle, then barreled down a narrow street lined with warehouses. It swerved at high speed onto a wide boulevard with trees, neon signs, and restaurants whose signs were hung over the wide, intact glass windows fronting on the street—restaurants with a bit of color and a lot of normalcy. With no warning, the convoy had burst onto a normal city block, a block untouched physically by nineteen days of war—a block lined with cheering, welcoming crowds of Iraqis.

Conlin's thoughtfulness to the embedded reporters now paid off in another way. CNN was filming as 1/7 went down the street, and Lieutenant General Conway, who was watching the live feed in his combat operations center, was so impressed by the wide-open friendliness and lack of opposition that on the spot he approved the division's request to let the battalions roll until they hit a defense; there would be no more map objectives, and no more deliberate advances—they would just roll through East Baghdad. Similar video was coming back via Fox News with Rick Leventhal, who was with 3rd LAR Battalion to the northeast. Conway got together with other generals for a video teleconference. They would forget the plan for methodical advance, they agreed. "That's OBE—overtaken by events," Conway said. In the next war every battalion will probably be required to carry a video camera or a reporter with a live feed.

The 1/7 convoy was several kilometers long, and as it rolled through the Snoozle, residents ran up from side streets and stood on street corners, waving and smiling. No battle damage could be seen anywhere. Europeans from the embassies—Swiss, French, Belgian—stood among the Iraqis. Some of them waved, some didn't, but most of the Iraqis did. They clustered at the street corners, some waving white handkerchiefs or cloths. There weren't many of them—hundreds, not thousands—but all seemed friendly.

According to plan, Charlie Company executed a smart turn to the west and headed to the river to secure the embassies. There'd been talk of the battalion swinging by for a group picture in front of the French Embassy, perhaps pissing on the steps. But Conlin was hoping to continue his career, and so Major Healey and Baker Company proceeded straight for the university, leaving behind the downtown section and, a kilometer on, rolling past tasteful houses with manicured hedges, some done in curlicues and none suffering from a lack of water or gardener care. No people were out waving in the fancy section.

As the tanks rolled by, on the right were the expensive houses, and on the left a brick wall, and beyond that the expanse of the Baghdad University campus, with some small vegetable gardens, overgrown sports fields, low-rise campus buildings, a prominent mosque, and a large high-rise in the distance. The tanks rolled up to the ramp for the bridge leading into West Baghdad and stopped. From there they had a commanding view of the university.

As the first Humvees and Amtracs followed the tanks by the houses of the discreet rich, an RPG whizzed by from the university grounds to the left. After a few seconds a second RPG flew by, again high. Then came the desultory crack of a few AK-47 rounds. Ray and I were following Conlin, whose vehicle stopped, and he hopped out as the Amtrac rear ramps went down and troops poured out. Ray pulled over in the lee of the university's brick perimeter wall, and I got out, video camera in hand, to catch the dust puffing up from a berm about 200 meters out in the university grounds, on the other side of the small garden.

The troops crouched along the wall, which had wrought iron inserts through which they could peek and see fields and shrubs ahead, and beyond the twenty-story complex and the mosque. Any heavy return fire against the berm from the tanks or the Mk-19 40mm Amtrac up gun would hit the mosque. I wasn't convinced the shooters had planned that. Four hundred meters away to the right were several dorm buildings. The CIA had it right—some fedayeen had chosen to make a stand in the center of the university. The troops didn't know what they were expected to do. Usually the tanks fired before anyone else could detect a target. This time the tanks were past the action, and Conlin had not called them back.

"Knock down that wall!" Conlin yelled.

An Amtrac took a running start, hit the seven-foot brick wall, and bounced off. It backed farther off, then charged again at higher speed. This time the wall buckled slightly. A third ram, and the wall crumbled. Bravo's 1st platoon ran through and started across the tilled field, stepping on rows of what looked like small lettuce heads. Conlin trotted after them, Healey swinging two other platoons around to the right. Startled at being left behind, Sergeant Major Bergeron roared at his driver to follow Conlin and the trac that had rammed through the wall. The bricks at the break in the wall were strewn two feet high. The sergeant major's driver took a running start and slammed down on the accelerator, forgetting that CNN's vehicle was attached. The Humvee jounced across the loose bricks, jerking hard and breaking the tow bar. The fifty-thousand-dollar CNN Humvee hit the bricks, leaped skyward, and slammed nose-down into a ditch.

Ray was laughing and shouting at me, "Get that! Get that!"

I trotted along after the platoon, which moved across the garden in a skirmish line, until the platoon commander remembered that the area had been prepped by Army artillery with dual-purpose improved conventional munitions (or DPICMs). These are savage little explosives, about the size of a baseball, perfect for tearing off a head or shoulder as they fall—or for removing a foot or a leg if stepped upon. A gunnery sergeant had lost his foot earlier in the campaign to a DPICM. The Marines had refused to fire them into Baghdad. The platoon commander yelled a warning, and the platoon began to hop from row to row, avoiding the lettuce heads and stepping only in the dirt.

Stuck in the ditch, the CNN correspondent Martin Savidge yelled for his cameraman to catch up with the riflemen while he provided voice-over from the grounded Humvee. A hundred meters into the field, the platoon saw its first target, a truck with the twin barrels of a 14.5mm machine gun mounted in back. The driver's door was open, indicating the fedayeen had probably already abandoned the vehicle, but this was the first target the platoon had seen that was not already chewed up by the tanks. The left side of the platoon line let loose M-16 bursts. No reaction came from the truck.

"Let me try, Lieutenant!" the AT-4 gunner yelled. The line stopped, and the assault gunner knelt in a furrow. The platoon commander checked to ensure the back-blast area was clear, not wanting to take down his own battalion commander. Conlin was well to the right.

Blam! The AT-4 shot hit dead on, and flames from the fuel tank followed the explosion. The Marines cheered and warily trotted forward several yards to a low berm, where they flopped down to reorient. Forty rifles and two machine guns were set on a straight line; the Amtrac had not yet caught up to them. The AT-4 shot had panicked two nearby black and white cows, which galloped across the field, quite a feat for the awkward beasts. In testimony to the phrase *blind panic,* a second technical with a machine gun on the back popped out of the shrubbery near the burning truck and, like the cows, drove across the field, parallel to the platoon. The line erupted in a cacophony of fire. No shouted command could possibly be heard. The pick-up swerved to a stop, shuddered under the impacts. Flames leaped out the back, where the machine gun tilted at the sky. *[Picture 51]*

A corporal stood erect on the berm, his machine-gun squad on either side of him. "Gun one, fire!" The sharp hammer of the 7.62mm rounds sounded much more authoritative than the 5.56mm M-16s. "Gun two, fire!" More flames burst from the technical as the fuel tank exploded with a *whoosh*. More shouts, more firing, and from the over-pass to the rear came the distinct *bang* of a "friendly" tank's main gun. The infantry instinctively ducked, but the shell struck near the top of the tall tower in the distance. The platoon scoffed—the tankers had got into the act by hitting a building too far away to be a real threat to any-body. The building absorbed the shock, and the tank turned its attention elsewhere.

The .50-caliber from the tank then kicked up handfuls of dirt 70 meters to the right and slightly in front of the platoon. Anxious glances were turned toward the platoon commander, who looked for the battal-ion commander. Conlin's radio operator had the tanker on the battal-ion's tactical net frequency. The tanker claimed he was firing at a bunker. With the tank's acute optics, Conlin had no reason to doubt him. The tanker reported another bunker on the west bank of the Tigris. That was his next target.

"That's a negative," Conlin replied. "Third ID has the zone to the west. Your sector is to the south. You know that."

The tanker assured Conlin he was only doing a quick 360-degree recon.

"Then why is your main gun pointed across the river?" Conlin asked, looking at the tank through binoculars. There was radio silence as the gun traversed to the south.

The Green Machine, the Gun Club, the Green Dragon, Devil Dogs, Leathernecks—whatever the Marines called themselves, they wanted to lash out. There were prey out there, and Marines of all ages, from Conlin to private, trained taut and conditioned to respond, sensed it. The riflemen saw a third technical in the broken ground, farther to the right near the dorms. Again the line erupted with fire, the berm provid-ing rifle range comfort, chests against the earth, elbows snug in the dirt, clear sight pictures through the scraggly grass, the target a stationary vehicle a football field away.

The erect corporal redirected the machine guns, and soon three vehi-cles were blazing, one by one heating up until the flames seared the am-munition packed inside, and shells started exploding like strings of loud firecrackers. Ordered not to fire at the burning vehicles near the troops, the tank gunner pinged .50-caliber rounds into a raised mound 100 meters to the west. At first the bullets only raised clods of dirt. Then a few rounds popped off inside the mound, which was actually a bunker. Then the top of the bunker blew off and flames gushed out. In seconds heavy-caliber rounds were zinging skyward in short, brief sparkles, whizzing randomly overhead.

The television crew sensed the visual drama. In the firefight the troops simultaneously included the TV crew and ignored them. If the cameraman, Rick McKinnon, a Brit in a blue armored vest and tan jeans, wanted to film in a half-crouch above the grass line, that was his risk to run, as long as he stayed out of their line of fire. McKinnon panned back and forth between the line of Marines, who were happily shooting into four blazing fires, and the fiery red streaks of Iraqi rounds zipping by. The crackling bursts from the M-16s contrasted with the snaps of the heavier Iraqi calibers. McKinnon laughed good-naturedly when I suggested he tell the millions watching this live feed that they were viewing mostly cook-offs, ammunition ignited by the flames. To any civilian, it would look and sound like a heavy firefight. I doubted the Marines killed any more than a handful of Iraqis, but any bullet zipping downrange can kill you.

The platoon commander, First Lt. Daniel Todd, knew the cook-offs were more dangerous than the terrible marksmanship of the fedayeen. Soon the platoon was snuggled down below the berm as rounds zipped overhead at crazy angles. The explosions went on for twenty minutes, reaching a crescendo like the climax of a Fourth of July fireworks display, then subsiding for a few minutes, only to peak again.

Back at the hole in the wall in his wrecked Humvee, Martin Savidge, the CNN correspondent, got off the best line about the fight. "Since Saddam stored ammo at every grammar school," he said, "we should have known the largest dump would be at the university."

But this wasn't a made-for-TV reality show; the dead weren't props. Burned to death if not struck beforehand by the many bullets were those few fedayeen who had stayed after their comrades had run, vainly hoping to take an American with them.

The Marines didn't think of their prey as humans. They were not men who would joke with one another and write dirt-stained letters assuring their mothers or wives that they were fine. No, as far as the Marines were concerned, they were vermin—rats or weasels—sneaking onto battlefields in civilian buses, hiding behind women, wearing civilian clothes. If it weren't for them, the Marines wouldn't have shot up civilian cars. If it weren't for them, there would be no dead Americans back at Nasiriyah. The troops weren't the ones to separate out fact from fiction or rumor from truth. Truth to them was the next 200 meters, where there were three blazing technicals, an exploding bunker, and some fedayeen, still burning.

13

A Tyrant Falls

D + 19, D + 20

With battalion 1/7 in the palaces of Baghdad
9–10 April

WHILE RAY AND I WERE WATCHING Baker Company's fight at the university, Lacroix's Charlie Company had seized Saddam's family palace compound without a fight, and McCoy's 3/4 had pushed three kilometers deeper into East Baghdad. McCoy had halted at Firdos Square where a six-meter-high metal statue of Saddam loomed above the traffic with arm upraised, like a senator of ancient Rome addressing the people, or like Stalin deciding whom to kill. A tank crew looped around its neck two cables attached to an M-88 tank retriever, and after a few tries, the statue fell face first. As the head rolled loose, hundreds of Iraqis clapped, cheered, and danced, throwing flowers and kisses toward the Americans. Along with millions, President Bush and Secretary of State Powell, standing side by side in the White House, watched on television the moment that defined the fall of the Saddam Hussein regime and the capture of Baghdad.

Two days earlier, on 7 April, battalion 3/4 had assaulted across the Diyala River in a "raid" for which Colonel Hummer "forgot" to issue a withdrawal plan. An hour after McCoy seized the Baghdad side of the river, an unceasing stream of vehicles had crossed first one, then two, and finally three bridges. The first four Marine battalions to cross that day—3/4, 1/7, 3/7, and 1st Tanks—encountered no organized resistance and sensed that Saddam's army had collapsed. On 8 April RCT-7 assured the divisional command that it was time to let the battalions roll forward without even pretending to "raid." On the west side of the Tigris the 3rd ID had reached the river and sent the same message to the CFLCC. Since the CFLCC strategy—a cordon and systematic raids—did not apply to the reality of the combat, the advancing American units had tossed it aside. Asked if Saddam was still issuing orders, Major General Mattis had quipped to the press, "When you take over his country and drink his liquor, it doesn't much matter." When 3/4 pulled down the statue in Firdos Square before a worldwide television audience, it was a fitting symbolic end to his regime.

As the fighting died down at Baghdad University on the afternoon of 9 April, Lieutenant Colonel Conlin tried to radio across the river to the 3rd Infantry Division, whose tanks were visible a kilometer away. While President Bush could see what was happening in downtown Baghdad, a Marine and an Army battalion, one kilometer apart on the front lines, could not communicate electronically. The battalions waved back and forth until a Humvee crossed the bridge with some Marines who were providing air support liaison with the Army. Once they were able to talk face to face, the Marine and Army radio technicians established a common frequency path.

In the meantime, Conlin had turned to another task. The regimental command had radioed a request from the OGA, giving the coordinates for the mansion of Deputy Prime Minister Tariq Aziz. Battalion 1/7 was to raid the palace, take down anyone inside, and thoroughly search the house for documents and computer disks. If the battalion's interpreters saw any paper or passport mentioning Syria, it was to go to the regimental command right away. All other papers were to be delivered in the morning. The CIA had sources claiming Aziz had been seen in the city, and they wanted to trap him before he could reach the western border. Conlin suggested Ray and I follow him, and then he sped off in his Humvee, leaving Major Healey and Baker Company to clean up at the university.

We drove back up the wide boulevard into the shabbier section of the Snoozle, a working-class neighborhood with some wooden stools and bare benches outside raggedy coffeehouses, rows of shops behind metal grates, and billboards with brand-name logos and advertising in Arabic. It looked like the kind of street where everyone knew something about everyone else. Crowds of a dozen or so people of all ages were clustered on street corners, cheering and whistling as though we were a parade passing by. I felt like a member of a small-town baseball team that has just won the state championship. As Ray drove, I smiled and gestured benevolently as though I were used to acclaim, and every group hastily waved back, as if pleased that I had singled them out to share my aura of power and might. I was with the army that had vanquished the devil.

We turned to the right, entering a rich suburb along the Tigris. Trees and green shrubbery lined the streets, and two-story stuccoed houses with attached garages—Toyotas and Mercedes hidden away behind high walls—bespoke wealth and privilege. It was the type of neighborhood that back in the States would have a private security guard in a booth at the entrance with a clipboard to check the names of guests cleared to enter. The civilian homeowners in this Baath Party bastion had put out homemade roadblocks of rocks, palm branches, and tree stumps to ward off the looters who would soon descend like locusts. The Humvees bounced over these obstacles, and Ray easily steered around them.

Captain Lacroix's 3rd Platoon of Charlie Company arrived before we did. Conlin's Humvee pulled up at the Tariq Aziz mansion, followed by us and several embedded press—and we were greeted like honored guests at a dinner party and were granted the choicest parking spots. Corporal Ferkovich and his squad, with a proprietary air, were standing by the front door, clearly indicating that they considered the mansion of the deputy prime minister of Iraq more to their liking than the shabby oil pumping station, the Crown Jewel, that they had seized on D-Day three weeks before. When alerted to their present mission, Ferkovich's squad had led the way down the street. The coordinates they had been given weren't exact but did put them in the right neighborhood. Through the interpreter it had taken them only minutes to find a volunteer to point out the right house. Ferkovich had had to kick in the elaborate front door to gain entrance, but other than that, the mansion had come through weeks of bombing and its seizure by the Marines without a scratch.

Tariq Aziz, educated at Baghdad University, was the diplomatic face of a gang of thugs and murderers. Pudgy and soft-featured, his gifts in life were a perfect command of English, a quick intelligence, and a willingness to prostitute his values. A Chaldean Christian, he provided an urbane public face to the West, a slight gloss to deflect rays of honest journalism away from Saddam's gulag. He was the public relations front man, the person who had spoken with Secretary of State James A. Baker prior to Desert Storm in 1991 and had subsequently been trotted out on a regular basis for television interviews. With his oversize glasses, owlish features, and dumpy figure, he looked as avuncular as a Norman Rockwell doctor. Judging by the size of his mansion, the deputy prime minister in charge of furbishing Saddam's image had done quite well.

His home was smaller than a palace—it was more like one of those oversize stone mansions featured in movies about Mafia dons. Set on the banks of the Tigris with a dock, jet skis, and sailboats, the three-story yellow sandstone mansion was 70 meters long, according to Ray, who paced it off. While waiting for the engineers to arrive to blow the safe, Corporal Ferkovich showed us around. He had discovered a humidor closet with Cuban cigars, and every platoon member was puffing away, half their cigars unlit. They ignored the cases of hard liquor, and unfortunately the large refrigerator held no cold drinks or beer. The house was tastefully decorated, with bedrooms for several children; the giant his-and-hers bathrooms featured marble bathtubs and a variety of perfumes for a man as well as a woman, mostly French labels. But the magazines scattered about were American—*Time, Vanity Fair,* and *Sports Illustrated.* The dining room was formal and overstuffed, but the dark paneled library seemed well used, with two comfortable reading chairs, a large desk with a globe, and multiple shelves of books, with as many books in English as in Arabic. Aziz's taste ran to contemporary Middle Eastern politics, titles from American nonfiction best-seller lists, and memoirs by American statesmen, including former President Bush. *[Picture 53]* All the furniture was wrapped in dust covers, and not a single family photo album was left in the library. Aziz had often boasted to the press that the Iraqi leadership would fight to the death, yet all the while he was preparing to flee. To the Marines, the mansion's owner was a rich thief who was now in hiding. (A few weeks later he was arrested, still inside Baghdad.) Who Aziz had been meant nothing to Corporal Ferkovich and his squad. As Major General Mattis had said, the Marines were in charge when they were drinking the other man's liquor—or in this case, smoking his cigars. *[Pictures 52 and 55]*

When the engineers arrived, the platoon went outside. Marine engineers liked deconstruction more than construction—they blew the safe all right, and the library around the safe. The interpreters said the charred documents within the safe looked uninteresting, mostly old bank statements. So Conlin and the Marines left.

The Aziz mansion was located near the underpass of a large highway bridge, and as we walked to the vehicles, we heard a short burst of shooting near the up ramp. Conlin had left a platoon—call sign "Animal 3"—at a circle that controlled traffic on and off the bridge. After sitting for a few hours, the Marines of Animal 3 had become bored and decided to shoot up an abandoned Iraqi military truck—just as the platoon walked outside the mansion. Nighttime fireworks were nothing new—with arms caches seemingly in every school and ammo on every truck, Marines never lacked for something to blow up. But this one was a doozy. The truck had been carrying heavy artillery shells, and soon shrapnel was whizzing in all directions and pinging off the concrete pillars supporting the overpass. As the Marines scattered for cover in the darkness, a few mistook the shrapnel for incoming bullets and fired their M-16s. A CAAT joined in with their two .50-calibers, firing at the exploding truck mainly but also inadvertently into Animal 3.

With much screaming the sergeants imposed a cease-fire before the intramural firefight did any damage. Ray, who had been screaming cease-fire as loudly as anyone else, added a reprimand. "You're crazy," he yelled to the CAAT. "Don't you see that's Animal Three you're shooting at?"

There was a moment of silence, then came a response out of the dark: "Well, they shot first."

Not even the sergeant major could think of a response appropriate for that logic.

Ray and I remained with Charlie Company at the underpass, while Conlin headed back to his command post at the university. The area was dark, except for the Iraqi truck burning in the shadows of the elevated highway. There was scant noise, no aircraft overhead, no vehicles passing, no voices coming from the houses. Lacroix and his men were on foot, having left their Amtracs up the road. The captain gathered the platoon, talked to Ferkovich about checkpoints, and with one gesture had the platoon on the move back to their bivouac. Ray and I followed in our SUV with the windows down; the engine made little sound.

We were the only travelers on the narrow road, which was more like a country road with scrub pine trees reaching toward us on both sides. For once we smelled wet earth and flowers instead of dust. On either side of us behind high walls were the smug homes of the rich and formerly pampered, the civilian elite of the Saddam regime, favored by air-conditioning, marble bathrooms, high poster beds, formal dining rooms, trips to Paris, and schools in Europe and in the States. The Marines walked on either side of the road, well spaced apart, their M-16s at the ready. Not sensing any danger, they walked with easy grace, enjoying the coolness of the night. Only the occasional jingling of a piece of equipment signaled they were passing by. Gleams of light leaked out of a few houses, indicating that the electricity was still on in this part of town. Behind locked doors, families were whispering and wondering about their fate.

I thought of the Bible story about the angels with their swords passing by the doors marked by the blood of the lambs. The Marines were not reflective about a deity—they had not joined the Gun Club to find religion. But most of them believed in God and the concepts of good and evil, and they had recently seen dirt poverty in the Shiite south. The Baath Party officials here, whose wealth depended on depriving their countrymen, were lucky the Marines had not been ordered to evict them.

The Marines viewed themselves as liberators helping the oppressed, yet felt they could not trust the people they were liberating. The constant threat of a terrorist or a fedayeen fighter hiding among the population had made interaction with the people difficult at best and impossible at worst. Senior American leadership from the president on down had stressed the viciousness of the fedayeen and the suicide bombers. Even Secretary of State Powell said that as he was watching the two Marines pull down the statue of Saddam, he feared for their safety, until he saw how friendly the Iraqi crowd was. Throughout most of the campaign, unable to distinguish friendly civilians from unfriendly fighters, the troops had kept all Iraqis at a distance. They focused on the enemy, not the end political results.

Now they had come to the end of the military campaign, and we were at the end of the dark countrylike road. Ferkovich turned left and guided us down the walled driveway and into the first courtyard of Saddam's family palaces. The palace was under new management. [Picture 54] Having secured it earlier in the day, Charlie Company was spending the night in the deserted palace compound, and we were their guests. In fact, we were offered our choice of bedrooms, except for the waterbed—Lacroix had won a coin flip and was thinking of trying that one. In the end, no one went up to the bedrooms. We fired up our squad stove, had a cup of coffee, and called it a night. We would have time to look around in the morning. For weeks dust had been my bed, so I took advantage of the Bermuda grass near the flower beds overlooking the Tigris. I didn't miss the dust one bit.

When we lay down, we thought the Marines' final firefight of the campaign had been the one at the university that day, but as we were sleeping, 1/5 tore into a company of fedayeen and foreign Arabs four kilometers to our northwest. In the predawn I could hear helicopters working and tank rounds in the distance. We weren't at the scene, so we learned about it later in the day at the division's forward command post, and then from follow-up interviews with the participants.

While 1/7 had been fighting at the university, Colonel Dunford, successfully across the Diyala with RCT-5, had received a tip from the CIA that Saddam had been spotted at the Almilyah Palace on the eastern side of the Tigris. CIA and special operations forces linked up with 1/5 for a night attack. Eighteen Marines crammed into each Amtrac, where they jockeyed for the twelve open-air spots so they could see "what wanted to kill us." The losers curled up and dozed as the tracs formed up; there wasn't anything for them to do. Alpha Company was the battalion's small-boat raiding company. While the true mechanized company—Bravo—trained in the barren hills of Camp Pendleton, Alpha spent its days on exercises doing wild surf passages in rubber boats. Rubber Zodiacs were open-air, let-it-all-hang-out toboggans, sliding down the face of huge waves. Tracs were grungy, stinky, confining beasts that reduced your range of vision to the green ammo cans and green painted faces on all sides. Now Alpha Company was rolling south in those tracs through ten kilometers of dark city highway, four tanks in front, then Alpha's sixteen vehicles, followed by the entire battalion, a thousand men hunching in fifty tracs and twenty Humvees. A platoon of special forces soldiers was traveling in their own vehicles, tucked close behind the tracs.

The streets were deserted, and Capt. Blair Sokol, Alpha's commander, was sure the racket was waking every fedayeen for miles. There hadn't been time for a proper battalion order when the Almilyah Palace was targeted, and the company commanders had agreed on one rule: whatever happened, don't stop moving. Pick up anyone whose vehicle is knocked out, and keep going no matter what. Do not give the fedayeen a sitting target. Every highway overpass was infested with sandbagged bunkers that looked like hornets' nests. Every building screamed ambush. As they neared the river, the city seemed to close in on them, the buildings pressed closer together. The Marines who were standing—the officers, NCOs, and those who had won in the elimination game of Rock, Paper, Scissors—were adjusting their night-vision goggles and turning on their infrared targeting lasers, ready to snap on to steer bullets into the pitch black.

Lt. Col. Fred Padilla, the commanding officer of battalion 1/5, and his operations officer, Maj. Steve Armes, were riding in the Alpha command group Amtrac behind Alpha Company. To Armes, the route down Route 2 was a linear ambush waiting to happen. He checked with the UAV operators who had flown cameras down the entire route— "streets are pretty deserted" was what he was told. He radioed the section of Cobras riding shotgun. "We got nothing but a few civie vehicles," the pilot told him. Armes didn't buy it. In the crystalline haze of his NVGs, the route looked like it was ready to explode.

When Alpha Company drew near the Almilyah Palace, he heard dull cracks in the column behind him. It was hard to pinpoint the sound with the cranial cupping his ears. The radio was spilling a growing stream of nervous chatter from the battalion net: *"Taking fire here." "Got movement in the windows to starboard." "Contact right. Contact right." "Charlie's got incoming RPGs."*

Sokol didn't have time to worry about other companies. He was approaching the right turn to the palace gates. Ahead were three turn lanes off the highway. The lead tanks chose the first one—which soon bent back in the direction they had been coming from; in seconds Alpha Company was rumbling along an overpass back across Route 2, heading away from the palace. Sokol tried to steady his map, as the trac bounced along, so he could focus on righting the wrong. If he didn't fix it quickly, four kilometers of vehicles would be subject to the dangerous detour. *At least we aren't taking heavy fire,* he thought. A moment later a long burst from an AK-47 cracked overhead. RPGs exploded nearby, and the windows around him were lit by muzzle flashes that looked like strobe lights. The Marines of Alpha Company immediately returned fire, and in fewer than five seconds the streets were filled with red tracers. Sokol wanted to shout, *Keep moving, keep moving,* but the battalion frequency was so jammed with high-pitched orders, he would only have added to the madness. The tankers quickly discovered their error and wheeled around in a U-turn, now heading toward the oncoming column. Alpha Company followed. Sokol shouted over the radio that his men should fire only to starboard, to prevent a blue-on-blue as the friendlies passed each other in the dark.

The column straightened out, and the lead tank smashed through the gates to the Almilyah Palace. Lt. Nicholas Horton's platoon was in the lead with Alpha Company. All around him small groups of men ran forward to fire RPGs, then ducked back behind buildings and into alleyways. In the melee Gunnery Sgt. Jeff Bohr, who was riding in a Humvee, was shot and killed. The Marines had dismounted and spread out and were now hunting the fedayeen teams in the alleys. Three tanks were forward with the infantry. A fourth had been hit and was leaking oil from its transmission, which soon froze up. As dawn came up, Capt. Shawn Basco, the battalion's forward air controller, called in A-10s to make strafing runs on targets 200 meters inside the palace.

Colonel Dunford drove forward in his Humvee, bringing along Capt. Todd Sudmeyer with four tanks and infantry cover from 2/5. Ray and I had been with Sudmeyer in the 70-kilometer run-and-gun battle on 4 April. Now Colonel Dunford and Lieutenant Colonel Padilla told Sudmeyer to push his tanks forward to the Hanifah Mosque, less than a kilometer away. Along the route, contact continued to be heavy, as the fedayeen stayed to fight. The tanks moved into the intersections and waited for an RPG shot, then returned fire with the 120mm main gun. Sudmeyer said he watched the shockwaves from the main gun ripple down the alleys, knocking out windows. The impact of the shells shocked the fedayeen. When they bolted and ran, the Marine riflemen cut them down. One fire team ran around a corner and bumped into three fedayeen with their boots off, drinking water, their RPG launchers leaning against a wall. The fire team killed all three. That was the nature of the combat, hit-and-run tactics with the Marines killing one small group after another.

When the fighting ended that morning, more than a hundred fedayeen lay dead. Gunnery Sergeant Bohr was killed, and twenty-two Marines had substantial wounds. More than a dozen RPGs had struck the Amtracs but had inflicted no serious damage. Sudmeyer had to retrieve one tank with transmission damage. If Saddam had been in the palace, he had escaped before the fight.

While that fight was winding down, Ray and I had been walking through Saddam's family palace compound, four kilometers to the southeast, where we had spent the night. Discarded on the roadway was a beautiful hand-tied living-room rug, in vivid Arab patterns with dark rich reds and pale yellows and blues, easily worth fifty thousand dollars. The intrepid looter—frightened into dropping it by the sudden appearance of the Marines—had known exactly which item held the most value.

The compound held six palaces, one for each member of the dictator-murderer's family. Two were demolished—struck and imploded, as though a giant had pulled everything down and left it in a heap in the center of the floor. Windows, staircases, chandeliers, decorations, paintings, chairs, bedrooms, ceilings, and walls—all were ripped down and jumbled together. The Marines, connoisseurs of violence on a level that was more personal and human than this, marveled at what the U.S. Air Force had wrought. *[Picture 57]* The buildings left untouched were built along Greek neoclassical lines, with graceful ionic pillars, balconies overlooking the Tigris, and attention to symmetry and detail. The palace gardens were small but included a variety of flowers. There were two swimming pools, one with a slide for children.

Inside, the rooms were large, with marble floors, graceful staircases, and atrocious taste. The paintings were mostly prints and cut-outs, the furniture heavy and clunky, the bedrooms poorly laid out. It was as if Saddam had employed architects from Paris and interior decorators from a Carey brothers movie. One palace clearly was for a woman, a boy, and a girl—perhaps the widow of the son-in-law Saddam had killed. The woman had a marble bathroom with a swimming-pool-size bathtub, a large walk-in closet featuring black dresses, a dental office, a doctor's office, a beautician's office, and an exercise room with a treadmill. The girl had a marble bathroom absurd for an adolescent, a pink plastic Mickey Mouse radio, *People* magazine, and pictures of Britney Spears. The boy had several scooters and a complex water pistol that even Ray could not squirt. In the palace of Uday, Saddam's son, the Marines found a hidden room containing a collection of pistols, many of them replicas from Hollywood movies like *Dirty Harry.* The collection included dozens of tiny, shiny black .25-caliber Saturday night specials, perhaps party favors for dinner guests.

As we were talking with Lacroix, our tour of the grounds completed, the Marines were taking turns riding scooters they had found in a child's room. They cared not a whit for Saddam's vacuous wealth. Looking at how our cruise missiles had shattered the palaces like a piece of glass, I thought of the poem about the ancient king of Babylon, the pedestal of whose statue was discovered in the wind-swept desert made famous by Shelley's poem: " 'My name is Ozymandias, king of kings:/Look on my works, ye Mighty, and despair!'/Nothing beside remains."

Ray and I went up to the roof to say our good-byes to Corporal Ferkovich, who was standing guard. The campaign was over. Baghdad had fallen, and Saddam's regime had collapsed. We took a final picture of the squad. [Picture 58] Standing under the American and Marine Corps flags, Ferkovich is holding his rifle skyward. You can see that he is not aware of the rifle—it is simply part of him, an extension of his body. I tried to get the squad to smile because I thought the picture looked too serious. Then I realized that it fit. Put your hand over their bodies, covering the accoutrements of war, and look only at the faces. You will likely say that these are tough, determined young men who look like they belong together, who are a team.

They are standing on the roof of a palace they have conquered. We can substitute a nicer-sounding term than *conquered*, but to the infantryman it will still come down to the same fact: who controls the ground. To its long list of expeditions, the Blue Diamond has now added its march up to Baghdad. It was a long march, over 1,100 kilometers on our odometer. The Iraqi resistance collapsed, leaving pockets of fighters. The firefights against the Iraqi paramilitary were brief. What Shane Ferkovich most remembered about the campaign was the dirt and the dust, the lack of sleep and the claustrophobia of being packed inside an Amtrac, day after day. The squad had trained for months to seize the Crown Jewel, and they had made no mistakes. They ended their journey standing on the roof of someone else's palace and smoking his cigars. To them, Saddam was like Ozymandias, a headless statue in the dust of a Baghdad street.

As tough guys, they would not admit it, but deep inside they hope that those who do not march with them appreciate how much they sacrifice, how Spartan they are. What binds them is tradition, training, and one another. They chose to serve. Shane Ferkovich was an orphan, but now he belongs to a tribe. These men are our defenders, these descendants of Xenophon's hoplites, men with sturdy legs who eat less grass than a horse.

Epilogue

In the Footsteps of Alexander the Great

At 1st Marine Division Headquarters
10 April

On 10 April, when the palaces of Saddam Hussein came under American control, the march up to Baghdad by the Blue Diamond was complete. One final mission remained, however. In the White House, Condoleezza Rice, the national security adviser to President Bush, wanted to know what had happened to Saddam. Told no one knew, she asked when U.S. forces would seize and search the northern city of Tikrit, Saddam's hometown and the tribal base of the Baath Party. The 4th Infantry Division was due to arrive there in a week to ten days. Although Tikrit was 150 kilometers north of the Marine area, the MEF received an unofficial phone call inquiring whether a force could move immediately. The answer was yes. In September Major General Mattis had ordered a contingency plan for a quick-moving task force to assist the Kurds if Turkey did not agree to open a northern front. After Baghdad collapsed, the Kurds immediately seized Iraqi lands, and their aggressive actions were an ironic, albeit distinctly secondary, reason for securing Tikrit. Ray and I drove to the MEF command but were not able to negotiate the traffic jams in Baghdad in time to join the task

force, so the details in this chapter are based on the debriefs at the divisional command.

Intelligence indicated that about two thousand paramilitaries and elements of the Adnan Division of the Republican Guard were holding
Tikrit, while video from the UAVs was showing that military equipment
had been discarded inside the town of thirty thousand residents. Brig.
Gen. John Kelly was placed in command of three thousand personnel
and six hundred vehicles, including the 1st, 2nd, and 3rd LAR
Battalions, Golf Company from battalion 2/23, artillery battalion 5/11,
SEAL team 3, engineers, and a combat support element. The units carried four days' worth of supplies, plus a water-making capacity of
twenty thousand gallons a day. Due to their weight and their level of
fuel consumption, no Abrams tanks were included. Kelly intended to
call on the 3rd Marine Air Wing for all heavy fire support. The task force
was to seize Tikrit and cut off the escape of any organized military
units. As to the prospect of fighting dug-in troops, Kelly said, "We want
all jihad fighters to come here. That way we can kill them all before they
get bus tickets to New York City."

The task force was named Tripoli, an allusion to the refrain in the
Marine hymn "From the halls of Montezuma to the shores of Tripoli."
In 1805 Lt. Presley O'Bannon had trekked 900 kilometers across the
Sahara Desert to attack pirates along the shores of Tripoli. Now another
Marine of Irish ancestry was going on the attack, extending the Blue
Diamond over 900 kilometers from the sea in the longest expedition in
Marine Corps history. The division was following in the footsteps of
Alexander the Great. Near Tikrit in the epic Battle of Arbela in 331 B.C.,
Alexander had defeated the enormous army of Darius, king of Persia, a
victory that began the long martial ascent of the West over the Middle
East and Asia. And in 400 B.C. Xenophon, patron to all true-hearted in-
fantrymen and bane of generations of schoolboys in England and
America laboring to translate the Greek classics, had led his doughty ten
thousand past Tikrit.

Tikrit lies northwest of Baghdad on the other side of the meandering
Tigris River, while the highway network leads west through Baghdad
before turning back east across the river. Following that route would

mean making a 150-kilometer detour through the zones of two Army divisions and heavy civilian traffic, with an estimated delay of days. The SEAL team had scouted ahead along the eastern side of Baghdad and found a narrow Iraqi pontoon bridge used by local farmers, eight kilometers from a hardtop road and too obscure to be marked on any map. The approach road was a dirt trail that led through villages and along paddy dikes—the type of road that 2/5 had dubbed a "donkey path," overgrown with tree branches, shrubbery, vines, and drooping electric power lines haphazardly strung to scattered farmhouses. Golf Company 2/23 scrounged in the undergrowth, cut down tree limbs, and stood them along the path, holding up the live electric wires to allow each vehicle to pass.

Task Force Tripoli wended its way at a pace slower than a man walking. Each vehicle required a full minute to creep across the wobbly pontoon bridge. The eight-kilometer route, passing through the date-palm grove, backyards, and hinterlands, took sixteen hours. All along the way the farmers and villagers gathered to cheer, offering candied dates, tea, and water to the perspiring Marines, clutching at their sleeves, some trying to kiss the Marines on their cheeks amid much laughter and applause. This was the first time the LAV crews, who usually challenged and sometimes fired upon civilian vehicles, had the opportunity to be greeted by Iraqis as liberators. The donkey path was a nerve-wracking logistics challenge to the commanders but a satisfying experience to the troops.

Forty kilometers south of Tikrit, on the morning of 13 April, the task force dropped off 3rd LAR Battalion to guard its rear in the town of As Samarra. The townspeople greeted the Marines warmly, and the sheikhs offered bread and fruit. While the HET interpreters were chatting with them, a policeman came forward at the sheikhs' urging to say he knew where American prisoners were being held. The captors wouldn't release the prisoners, but he thought they would surrender if he told them the Marines were coming after them. He refused to go with the Marines to the house because he might be killed later as an informant. On the spot Lt. Nathan Boaz, in charge of the HET, took out his commercial GPS receiver, which fit into the palm of his hand. Pointing to a button on its face, he told the policeman to walk alone to the house with the

Americans, press the button, then meet Boaz at a nearby intersection. Fifteen minutes later Lieutenant Colonel Clardy had the GPS grid location of the house that held the American prisoners.

Clardy immediately sent a squad down an alley into a tangle of two-story cinder-block and baked-mud houses. The Marines were wondering if they had been lured into a Somalia-type ambush when a man with a light face in dingy yellow pajamas opened the door of an unmarked house and said quietly, "I'm an American." The squad burst in, ready for a firefight. The POWs had saved the lives of their demoralized captors by convincing them seconds earlier to lie on the ground. Thus were freed all the Americans still in Iraqi hands—two Apache helicopter pilots and five soldiers from the ill-fated 507th Maintenance Company, captured 700 kilometers to the south in Nasiriyah on 23 March. The American prisoners owed their freedom to the ingenuity of Lieutenant Boaz and his GPS.

While 3rd LAR was rescuing American prisoners, 2nd LAR had swung to the west and taken up blocking positions north of Tikrit, while 1st LAR pushed up from the south. For the final five kilometers into the town, the sides of the road were littered with abandoned armor, artillery, antiaircraft guns, and trucks. The LAV crews ignored the equipment, firing only at the occasional snipers and RPG teams. A kilometer outside town the fast-moving LAVs bumped into a large mound of dirt that had been bulldozed across the road. Inside two minutes traffic jammed up.

Sergeant Benson, with the lead element of 1st LAR, dismounted and moved around the dirt pile and bumped smack into a fedayeen, who promptly shot the sergeant in the stomach. The 7.62mm bullet struck a ceramic plate, a belt buckle, and a magazine, all of which protected Benson; it knocked the wind out of him but did not injure him. Luck did not similarly smile on the fedayeen when Benson fired back at his stomach. The sergeant then ran back around the berm. Other fedayeen opened fire from both sides—a poor decision, because several 25mm chain guns were only meters away from Iraqis armed only with AK-47s and RPGs, with only trees and shrubs for cover. Just as the melee began, the command vehicles drove up. The firing ranges were so close that

Brigadier General Kelly's aide, Lt. Adam Herig, and the driver, Cpl. Dave Hardin, as well as the operations officer, the intelligence officer, and the fire support coordinator for the task force, hopped out of their Humvees and opened fire with their pistols. The infantry then moved forward and dispatched the final fedayeen.

Shortly after Task Force Tripoli rolled into Tikrit, American and foreign press arrived at the Marine roadblocks, saying they wanted to stay until the Kurds, pushing rapidly toward the town from the northeast, were brought under control. Kelly told the press and the local people to spread the word that Marines intended to employ deadly force to protect the life and property of anyone who was threatened—press, Iraqi, or American military. The Kurds halted and the following day withdrew to Kirkuk.

Task Force Tripoli remained in the Tikrit area for a week. By the third day electric power and potable water were partially restored, and the Marines were patrolling on foot without flak jackets or helmets, rifles slung over their shoulders, to show they were not an occupation army. The sheikh from the town of Benji, 40 kilometers to the north, asked Kelly to meet there with the Bedouin elders. When Kelly and Arabic-speaking Capt. Ben Connable arrived, the tribal chiefs asked them to drive another 25 kilometers to "inspect" a destroyed bridge over the Tigris. They agreed, and after a feast attended by hundreds and a round of long speeches, the assembled sheikhs got down to business. They liked how things had turned out in Saddam's hometown and agreed to turn in crew-served weapons and RPGs in return for protection by the task force. Kelly assumed they were concerned about roving gangs of foreign fedayeen. No, they said, they were worried about other Americans. Tikrit was secure, but they lived outside the town. Armed helicopters were active, and they had heard that more Americans were coming. The Marines agreed to the terms of the cooperation, thereby expanding the MEF's area of operations from 250 road kilometers north of Baghdad to 315. A few days later an officer from the 4th Infantry Division flew into Tikrit to share plans for a raid on the town of Benji. Instead, Kelly suggested that he have lunch with the sheikhs and tour Benji. The raid was canceled.

On 21 April Task Force Tripoli turned over the Tikrit area to the 4th Infantry Division. As Kelly left, the sheikhs offered him three pieces of advice. First, the killings of civilians during the war were regrettable but acceptable; with the war over, however, the people would not accept further civilian casualties. Second, if the Americans acted as if they were afraid of the people, it would encourage the bad elements to shoot at them. The sheikhs approved of the Marines walking on foot without helmets, like everyone else. Everyone knew they were the best shots and would kill anyone who shot at them. Third, if the Americans stayed inside their armor, shot too randomly, and acted arrogantly, young Iraqi males, out of injured pride, would join with the fedayeen, or cheer for them. Kelly understood that the sheikhs were advising him and all other Americans not to be heavy-handed.

When Task Force Tripoli rejoined the division, Kelly passed the sheikhs' advice on to the staff. It would help in the division's new assignment. The division was in the process of leaving Baghdad to take up security posts in southern Iraq, alongside their British allies. The Blue Diamond's mission was to provide security until an Iraqi government took over. There was nothing unusual about the new assignment. The Marine Corps had trained as many constabularies in foreign lands as it had fought in major wars.

The Mayors of Summer

In April the press was praising the swift seizure of Baghdad and interviewing delighted Iraqis; by August the press was criticizing the postwar disorder and interviewing angry Iraqis. How did a victory, so stunning in early spring, turn so sour by summer?

On 1 May, President Bush appeared triumphantly on board an aircraft carrier where he declared, to a roar of applause, that the war was essentially over. The big story in May, though, was that the U.S. military had stood back while looting reached epidemic proportions, epitomized by the sack of the National Museum in Baghdad. Left unguarded, treasures dating from 1000 B.C. were carted off. Gone in a mindless stampede were the antiquities from the "cradle of civilization" between the Tigris and the Euphrates Rivers. Before our forces entered Baghdad, Ray and I had seen joyous Iraqis sacking government buildings on the outskirts. Rugs, desks, chandeliers, chairs, tables, lamps, toys, pictures, bathroom faucets, and pots and pans were hauled away in taxis, tractors, cars, pushcarts, bicycles, and wheelbarrows. In this carnival atmosphere, the revelers smiled and waved, gesturing at us to buy a broken computer screen, a flat of soiled Xerox paper, or a banged-up filing cabinet.

The bombing during the war and the looting afterward had pried loose many of the underpinnings of an infrastructure that was already crumbling after decades of neglect as Saddam and his cronies looted the country. In the searing summer heat, both the Iraqi people and the international press had to make do with episodic electricity and scant air conditioning. Tempers were short, and the news stories reflected the oppressive weather and miserable services.

Central Command had readied a task force to manage the post-hostilities and restore services. Baghdad had fallen precipitously, however, and General Franks was preparing to retire in June. CENTCOM did not move the new task force staff on scene swiftly enough. Retired U.S. Army General Jay Garner and his staff did not arrive in Baghdad until May, and even then they were not provided with adequate transportation. In the newspapers the bright victory of April quickly lost its shimmer. In less than three weeks, the genial General Garner was replaced without warning or grace as the director of the Coalition Provisional Authority (CPA).

Much worse, during the summer attacks upon American forces became commonplace in the so-called Sunni Triangle, an area inhabited by six million Sunnis that stretched 80 miles west of Baghdad and 120 miles north. Between May and September, bullets, rocket-propelled grenades, and improvised explosive devices (IEDs) claimed 176 American lives.

The attackers were a mixed lot. Some were dedicated members of the shattered Baath Party, which had prospered under Saddam. Others were former soldiers attacking to earn a few dollars, having been left jobless when the CPA abolished the Iraqi army. A few were terrorists and extremists who had infiltrated across the unguarded borders.

As the press focused upon the American casualties, the Marines in Iraq disappeared from the news, because Marine casualties were very few. In May the MEF withdrew from the Baghdad environs and assumed control over south-central Iraq, the heartland of the Shiites. The two main branches of Islam—the Shiites and the Sunnis—had feuded for twelve hundred years over religious doctrine and political power. In Iraq the Shiites were a persecuted majority terrorized by Saddam, who selected the leaders of the Baath Party and the military from the Sunni sect. When the MEF was assigned to the Shiite area, no one knew how it would be received or how it would adapt.

* * *

I went back to Iraq in August because four months after the president declared an end to major hostilities, the division was still engaged, and I wanted to see what was going on. When I returned, the MEF headquarters was outside the city of Al Hillah, operating from a moderate-sized tan palace/guest hostel atop a hill decorated by a few scruffy palm trees. From all sides the view was quite imposing because, although only fifty feet tall, it was the only hill for miles. On the plain below, an oversize statue of King Nebuchadnezzar glared at the effrontery near his stone feet of a cement-lined pool, intended for paddleboats as part of an amusement park never finished. Nearby were the ruins of his palace—the Hanging Gardens of Babylon—dating from 600 B.C., with the famed statue of a lion eating an unfortunate servant.

Division headquarters lay at the foot of the hill, alongside the slow waters of the Tigris. The last of the division's battalions were in the process of leaving, turning over the Shiite area to coalition troops from Poland, Bulgaria, and elsewhere. In April, in keeping with the division's motto—"*No better friend, No worse enemy*"—Major General Mattis had sent his tanks and artillery tubes back to the States, seeing no role for them in peacekeeping operations. At the same time he had issued a simple rule to his Marines: If anyone shoots at you, stop whatever you are doing and kill him. Since May the division had reported 189 contacts with the enemy, killing and capturing hundreds with no friendly fatalities. Mattis turned me and a fellow writer, Max Boot, over to Master Sgt. Bradley Lee, who was delighted to get away from headquartes. Mattis told us to go anywhere, talk to anyone, and draw our own conclusions.

One composite unit, called Task Force Scorpion and comprised of elements from 1st and 4th Force Recon and the 4th Light Armored Reconnaissance Battalion, had been in contact almost daily.The area just south of Baghdad was being taken over by the U.S. 82nd Airborne Division, not by coalition forces from other countries. We headed there first, ten of us riding in three Humvees.

I rode with Sgt. Anthony Stanton, a twenty-one-year-old MP with a raw scar across his forehead. In April he had been sitting at an intersection in Baghdad when a young Iraqi had run up to his Humvee, pulled a pistol from the folds of his *dishdasha*, and shot him square in the chest. Stanton felt like he had been hit with a hammer, but his ceramic armored vest stopped the bullet. He grabbed for the pistol, burning his hand on the smoking barrel, and twisted his face away as the next shot was fired. The bullet creased his forehead and Stanton tumbled out of the Humvee, wrestling with the assassin, screaming at other Marines to "Shoot! Shoot!" which they did. Stanton was rushed to a battalion aid station, where a doctor slapped a Band-Aid on the bullet crease, prescribed three aspirin, and sent him back to work. The next day Stanton learned that the deceased shooter had sworn revenge because Marines had killed his brother.

Stanton had been rapidly promoted to sergeant, and the Marine Corps wanted to pay for him to attend college. Upon graduation he would receive a commission. I encouraged him to accept.

"I don't know," he said. "I like what I'm doing now. I'd have to leave my buds."

"You mean officers don't have buds?" I asked.

"You were an officer, right, sir? You know what I mean. Being an officer is different. You didn't hang out with the guys."

"Look at Master Sergeant Lee," I said. Lee was riding in the lead vehicle. "He doesn't hang with buds. He's too senior. In a few years you'll be a platoon sergeant, and then all the buddy stuff stops."

"I'll think about it, sir."

I hadn't made a dent. Stanton had his tight-knit group right there with him—Lance Corporal McColl on the .50-cal and Corporal Sutkowski riding shotgun in the front seat. Seven Marines in three Humvees were under Sergeant Stanton's command. They had been together for six months and two thousand miles. They had choked in sandstorms, shivered through nights in March, and sweated in July, driven on night-vision goggles through muddy rain, shot up a group of fedayeen firing rocket-propelled grenades at a supply convoy, unsnarled massive traffic jams of Amtracs and tanks, killed an assassin, manned civilian checkpoints to search for hidden weapons, visited the ruins of Alexander the Great's palace on the banks of the Tigris, and wandered warily through the souks in a half-dozen run-down towns. Not many twenty-one-year-olds had the chance to lead and to live as Stanton was doing. He didn't want to give it up.

Thirty miles northwest of Al Hillah we pulled into Task Force Scorpion's small encampment. The S-2 Intelligence officer, Maj. Steve Manber, explained that the primary mission in North Babil province was to protect the highway leading to Baghdad. The tactics were patrols, working with the police and conducting raids based on single-source intelligence. The textbooks advised waiting for multiple corroborating sources of intelligence, but Manber said they were averaging about a 50 percent success rate—arresting men with weapons or explosives—based on immediately responding to the walk-ins, Iraqis who literally walked up to a barbed-wire guard post and offered information.

In fact, Manber said, Force Recon had a raid going the next morning. He pointed to Maj. Joe Cabell, a reserve captain in 1st Force. Cabell, who had just come in from patrol, looked disheveled and in need of sleep after weeks of daily raids and patrols. But he was already planning the next day's raid.

"We're going to raid a house up north," Cabell told us. "It's our second visit. We have documents and prisoners confirming the owner is running a terrorist cell involved in two bombings. A couple of weeks ago we had word he was at home, a big place with thick doors and a high cement wall, right on the Tigris. Lots of bulrushes and vines along the bank. We surrounded the house at night, then banged on the door, our translator yelling to open up or we blast our way in. Well, the door opens, women and children come screaming out, and this guy in his skivvies runs out and leaps into the bushes.

"With kids screaming and running all over the place, we don't shoot. We run after him, and our gear gets us all tangled in those damn vines. It's a swamp, like the Everglades. Two Marines strip down and go after him with their K-bars. He leaps into the river, and they dive in but can't find him. Two days later he's reported in Baghdad, all scratched up.

"So we're going back. Maybe he's stupid enough to go back home. I really want that bastard. Want to come along?"

I looked at Max Boot, who is an intellectual's intellectual with a quiet, reflective personality, a serious academic expression, and an international reputation as a geopolitical writer. In short, he fits his job title: Senior Fellow at the Council on Foreign Relations in New York City. Only now Max's mild eyes behind his tortoiseshell glasses were glowing, and he was leaning forward, nudging me to say yes.

Max and I had arrived at an exceptional time. Ordinarily there is no room for journalists on such missions. Raids by special operations forces like Force Recon normally follow prescribed, strict procedures. Prisoners, captured documents, informants, electronic intercepts, and airborne video supply data, analyzed and fused together to target a terrorist cell. Senior staff then set priorities and designate tasks for the operational units, which in turn carefully plan and rehearse each step in the conduct of a raid. This process usually takes days and involves dozens of experts from all services to include the CIA, involving sensitive sources and methods and so restricting access to all outsiders.

At Task Force Scorpion the MEF had adapted its procedures to reinforce success. During the march to Baghdad, Cabell had sat at the back table in a side wing of the division's operations tent, serving as the Force Recon liaison from the MEF. Though frustrated not to be part of the action, he had watched how frequently Mattis and Kelly had improvised on the spot. After Baghdad fell, Cabell was sent to Task Force Scorpion to help plan operations to keep the highways clear. Soon he was suggesting raids combining Force Recon, skilled at forcible entry and close-quarters shooting, and the LAVs, which provided speedy transit, firepower, and a dismounted infantry to cordon off the raid area. The MEF provided UAVs and helicopters for overhead surveillance, and Cabell worked out the procedures on the ground.

So an hour after arriving at Scorpion, we were sitting in on the by-the-numbers brief. Cabell, the mission commander, laid out intelligence pictures of the target area, shown in PowerPoint via a laptop hooked to a TV screen. (The joke in the Pentagon was that without PowerPoint the military couldn't go to war.) Max and I would travel in two separate LAVs as part of the cordon element commanded by Captain Taylor of Alpha Company, 4th LAR. The recon Marines would move by Humvee and enter the house as the raid element.

To catch a few hours' sleep, we were given cots with the recon platoon in a wrecked building. Before settling down, Sergeant Stanton and his MPs exercised by holding a push-up contest. Stanton won with 185. Max and I were impressed; the recon Marines did not look up from cleaning their weapons. At three in the morning we assembled for an intel update, gear inspection, final review of immediate action drills, and vehicle assignment. Before first light we were on the road in five ve-hicles, spaced about fifty meters apart.

That spacing saved us. We drove out of the compound in the early dawn. About ten minutes later we were emerging from a bend in a two-lane road, with open farmland and irrigation ditches on either side, when explosions went off. My LAV wobbled like it had been struck by a giant hammer, and the vehicle commander, Staff Sgt. Chris Barry, shouted "Stop! IED! IED!" The improvised explosive devices sounded like artillery shells, a loud and sudden *bang!* We were bounced around but unscathed, and the Marine sitting next to me, Lance Cpl. Jeremiah Horton, grinned in amazement and said, "I don't believe those fuckers really did that."

For Horton, the near-miss didn't signal danger; instead, it meant he was free to attack the enemy. The hunt was on. The hatches were un-latched, and a dozen Marines swarmed off the road, forming into a loose skirmish line, running across the fields, looking left and right, shouting back and forth in the dim early light. Majors Reese Rogers, Mike Fahey, and Mark Hashimoto took command of three small units and spread out in different directions. Cabell remained in a Humvee to monitor the radios.

An LAV crew reported over the radio net: "We've got three on IR [infa red] running bent over behind that farmhouse. Request permis-sion to fire."

"Negative on lethal fire," Captain Taylor replied. "Fire a burst high to stop them."

Taylor's instinct proved correct. The runners in the farm field were a woman and two children, who immediately told a Marine translator that a blue van parked on the other side of the canal had driven away after the explosions went off. The pilots of two Huey helicopters, listening in on the radio talk among the raid force, circled the area and reported a van headed west. Cabell told Taylor to send an LAV to check it out.

The LAV, with Max in it, charged off across the fields. The rest of us moved off the road when a Marine shouted that there were three artillery shells wired together that hadn't gone off. We waited in the fields until some engineers arrived and blew the shells. By that time the LAV was returning with a prisoner. We watched as the Iraqi, blindfolded and handcuffed, was dragged out and led away for pick-up by the MPs. Max and the LAV crew followed, joking among themselves and rehashing the capture. Directed by the Hueys, the LAV had forced the van to stop. The driver, dressed in a track suit, defiantly denied doing anything. The Marines broke out a police gunpowder residue kit and sprinkled powder on the suspect's hands, which promptly turned blue. The man tried to flee, but a Marine tackled him. The Iraqi kicked back hard, frantic to escape. As the two fell wrestling to the ground, the Marine thrust his pistol to Max so the Iraqi couldn't grab it.

"Cover him for me," the Marine shouted.

It took a few minutes to flex-cuff the thrashing Iraqi, with Max later saying he was prepared to shoot the man if he had to, an attitude that won him instant acceptance among the LAV crew. We then proceeded to the house of the terrorist who had swum the Tigris, but he wasn't home. When we returned to base after the twelve-hour mission, Max and the LAV crew, having taken a prisoner, held the bragging rights over recon. Considering us good luck, Cabell invited us on the next day's raid, but Master Sergeant Lee said we would miss Lieutenant Colonel Conlin's change of command in Najaf if we didn't get moving.

On the outskirts of Najaf, two hours south of division headquarters, the traffic thickened, and we proceeded at a crawl in the midst of hundreds of economy-size cars with bad mufflers. Choking in the exhaust, we were surrounded by Iraqi drivers who scarcely gave us a glance. We were all fellow commuters, bonded by boredom and irritation.

Pedestrians dodged among the cars, and men in white or tan *dishdashas* and women in black *burkas* crammed the shops on both sides of the road, wandering among umbrella-covered pushcarts and stalls offering tomatoes, corn, wheat, potatoes, fly-covered meats, picture cards, TV antennas, soda, ice, and cigarettes. Sergeant Stanton held a shotgun in his lap, muzzle outward. Eyes constantly scanning, every Marine had a weapon pointed outboard. This was what Major General Mattis termed a "deterrent effect." I asked Stanton if we could wander through the souk on our return trip. Since he had been shot once, I could understand if he said no.

"Easy do," he said. "We're in here all the time. It's a soft cover zone."

The MEF rule was that everyone in a vehicle wore a helmet and an armored vest in case of an explosion. Once afoot, though, the division left it to each company commander to decide the rules for local security. In Najaf the local Marine rules for foot patrols were a soft cover and no armored vest.

Lt. Col. Chris Conlin, whom I had last seen smoking a Cuban cigar at Tariq Aziz's palace, had commanded the 1st Battalion of the 7th Marines for a year, leading them from the Crown Jewel in the Rumaylah oil fields to the final firefight at Baghdad University. After the fall of Baghdad, Major General Mattis had assigned each of nine battalions to a city and its outlying areas. Conlin drew the Najaf region and its million people. Mattis refused to negotiate with any local official or sheikh, who habitually appealed to ever higher authority to get what they wanted. With Mattis, the final authority in any city was the American lieutenant colonel, period.

Najaf was home to the Grand Ayatollah Ali al-Sistani, the most prominent Shiite cleric in Iraq. The city was famous for its mosque shrine to Ali, son-in-law of the prophet Muhammad and revered by all Shiites. Najaf was both a cherished destination for pilgrims reflecting their piety by making a hajj and for thousands more the desired burial ground near the sacred bones of Ali, who was murdered while praying in a mosque in A.D. 661.

On the march up to Baghdad, Chris Conlin had made sure his staff and commanders knew what the mission was each day. Then he stood back and let them do their jobs, letting the problems bubble up and come to him when the staff could not resolve them. In Najaf, Conlin soon learned the problems were not with security; his company commanders handled those. What reached him were the demands for reestablishing local government and basic services. Electric power-generating plants, water pumps, sewage filtration, and fuel stations were operating erratically; the hospitals and police and fire departments had to be staffed and reopened, bridges repaired, and rubble cleared. Reflecting a management focus typical of most U.S. Army and Marine battalion commanders, Conlin spent most of his time in Najaf acting as the city manager.

Technically, providing services and political advice was the province of the Coalition Provisional Authority. But the CPA was so lacking in presence outside Baghdad that the military commanders said the acronym CPA stood for Cannot Provide Anything. The U.S. government simply had not been prepared to send in the number of civilian advisers and technicians needed to set up a government from scratch and repair the infrastructure of a country ruined by three decades of neglect. Because the CPA lacked the manpower and expertise to restore governance, the job fell by default to the military, especially to the Army and Marine battalion commanders overseeing the cities and provinces.

To Chris Conlin, the summer had been satisfying. The major setback had been the assassination of the imam Abdel Majid Khoei in April at the sacred mosque of Ali. Khoei, recently returned from years of exile, had counseled his followers to work with the coalition. He was murdered by followers of the Muslim cleric Moqtada al-Sadr, a twenty-six-year-old radical suspected of inciting several killings. Najaf's leading mullahs, fearing an uprising, had urged Conlin not to arrest Sadr. Having only circumstantial evidence and wary of a trial that was certain to be a circus, Conlin had agreed.

Over the next several months Sadr gained a modest following among the poorest Shiites in Baghdad and organized a militia gang of toughs. His rallying cry was vehement rhetorical opposition to the presence of the coalition. In late July, seeking to gain power in the Shiite center in Najaf, Sadr bused in about four thousand of his followers, declaiming that all Marines had to leave the city. Screaming threats, the mob marched to the government encampment at a local college. Among the women and children were rough-looking men brandishing machetes, gesturing that they would cut off the heads of the Marines. Knowing Sadr wanted to provoke a bloody clash, Conlin told his men no one was to fire unless the situation appeared life-threatening.

The mob had no shade from the baking sun, and the temperature was over one hundred and five degrees. After the battalion chaplain murmured a suggestion to Conlin, Marines in fighting gear waded into the demonstrators, handing out bottles of ice-cold water. The mob organizers continued to scream invective and brandish clubs and machetes, pressing the mob to attack the Marines. Conlin had less than 120 Marines facing four thousand screaming Iraqis. He ordered his Marines to form a line and fix bayonets. The mob stopped, wavered, and fell back. Marines offering water was one thing; Marines offering steel was another. It was the last mob Sadr could muster in Najaf while the Marines were there.

Over the course of the summer Conlin had outmaneuvered his most potent political enemy—Sadr—and ousted a corrupt mayor, previously appointed by Americans. When the battalion had first arrived, there were threats of violence if the Marines dared to patrol the streets. Part of the city had been badly damaged in the fighting in early April, and resentment ran high. When Max and I arrived in August, with a few Marines we could walk anywhere—if we could stand the scorching heat. Such was Conlin's deportment in Najaf that on the day of his departure, the mullahs invited him to tea at a mosque, a gesture without parallel in a city where the Ayatollah Sistani, as a show of independence, had refused to meet with any American.

After wishing Chris Conlin good luck in his new assignment, we left Najaf—deciding not to wander about the souk in the sweltering noonday sun—and swung north to Karbala to visit Lt. Col. Matt Lopez, who had succeeded Lt. Col. Mike Belcher as the commander of 3/7.

Lopez was on his way to his final city council meeting and invited us along. We hopped into a SUV piled high with soccer balls, a gift from a sporting goods chain in the States. We bumped down a dozen side streets to the town dump, where the SUV twisted among mounds of trash and the rusted hulks of cars, each packed with scrawny women and children, who peered out like timid fish, set to dart back into the dark crevices if we glared at them. Lopez rolled down his window and tossed out a soccer ball, then another, and another. Children came pouring out of holes in the mounds, sprinting barefoot in the dust, their excited shrieks in the still air sounding thin, matching their bodies.

"They're at the bottom of the heap. Rats in New York City live better than they do," Lopez said. "We drop off what we can, MREs, bottled water, basic stuff like that. I think a soccer ball counts as a basic for a kid."

As we drove toward the city hall, I saw a small transformer station with a hundred wires leading to nearby houses. Lopez laughed.

"Electric power is free," he said. "Whenever the power comes on, it goes to anyone who's plugged in. So everyone tries to tap in. Probably keeps the population down."

At the city hall the town council, nineteen men and one woman, sat in straight-backed chairs along the walls. Karbala's mayor (in a wrinkled shirt and tie) and a few sheikhs (in traditional Arab robes) stood in front of an imposing desk at the far end of the room. When Lopez, a big grin on his face, burst in with his Marine interpreter, everyone rushed forward and began talking to him at once. Like a practiced politician, Lopez raised his arms in supplication, genially asking for order, then slowly circling the room, talking for a few minutes to each council member. Lopez then introduced his replacement, a Bulgarian colonel who smiled uncertainly. The Iraqis nodded politely and immediately turned back to Lopez, besieging him with a dozen requests. The mayor stepped out and returned with a stout man in tow, who thrust himself in front of Lopez and began talking volubly. Lopez shook his head at his interpreter.

"The answer is still no. He was supposed to deliver sixty men for work. I gave him two chances and he failed both times. He gets no contract. And make sure the Bulgarian colonel understands why."

It was an hour before Lopez could get out the door with his final, final good-byes. As he left, the council members were still acting as if they expected him to return the next week, flying back from California. The Bulgarian colonel looked discomfited. (I heard a few months later that the colonel refused to attend the next council meeting, sending word that his mission was security, not local governance. And technically he was correct.)

From Karbala the next day we pushed south to drop in on Lt. Col. Pat Malay and Battalion 3/5 in Diwaniyah. From inside the city I could see the palm grove where I had joined Lieutenant Colonel McCoy and Sergeant Major Howell in April as the infantry of 3/4 had assaulted over the berms and shot the Iraqis in the trenches. In my meanderings around the country, the only Kawasaki motorcycles I had seen were the ones McCoy had seized that day and had refused to let his Marines ride. Amid the traffic and bustle of the city, it was strange to look out at a normal highway overpass, where a few months earlier so many men had died. The scene seemed dull and unmemorable. I wondered what the Iraqi officer in his white underwear, the last one to die that March day, had been thinking when he had first seen our tanks, dropped his breakfast cup of tea, and ran to the trench line, shouting to rally his men.

Lt. Col. Pat Malay had heard vaguely about 3/4's fight at Diwaniyah. Now that he controlled the city, he was too busy with his own problems to spend time on old battles. He was an energetic, stocky man with prematurely white hair, black eyebrows, and a ruddy complexion suggesting his Irish heritage. He drove Max and me to the scene of his persistent headache—a huge, abandoned warehouse complex. There the parking lot was crammed with thousands of Iraqi men, former soldiers seeking the final mustering-out payments offered by the CPA. On both sides of the parking lot, barbed wire was stretched like the sides of a funnel, forcing the men as they moved forward to form a single-file line under a long awning. After each veteran's papers were examined, he shuffled forward to a series of pay windows fronting a row of plywood offices. Behind each window an Iraqi woman doled out dinars. Over the course of three weeks the Marines organized and supervised a severance pay system for eighty thousand former members of the Iraqi military, pumping six million U.S. dollars into the local economy.

Not one armed Marine could be seen. When I commented on the patience and orderliness of the Iraqis, Malay burst out laughing, saying all was not as it seemed. He brought me to an office where a heavily armed Marine squad sat on alert, hidden. Then we climbed a ladder to the roof, where two teams of snipers were covering the pay windows and the crowd. In the past three days, the snipers had succeeded in directing the Iraqi police to shoot one man firing a rifle and another trying to pull the pin on a grenade. The gunman turned out to be a robber, and the would-be grenade-thrower had been turned away from the pay line for presenting forged papers.

Malay's major headache had begun two weeks earlier, when a mob rioted in the middle of the city, throwing rocks and trash. After the Marines restored order, the rioters complained that they had worked for weeks without the pay promised by the Americans. It seemed the Coalition Provisional Authority, in order to decrease the huge ranks of the unemployed, had offered a few dollars a day to all who would clear the irrigation ditches of weeds that grew as tall and thick as hedges. Thousands of men slogged barefoot through mud, hacking their way through hundreds of kilometers of undergrowth. It was hard, stinking work, and when payday came, the Iraqi paymasters began handing out twenty-dollar U.S. bills, one per every two men, telling them to find a local money-changer. In the course of an hour, the value of the dollar in Diwaniyah plummeted, and the paymasters fled for their lives, leaving behind a huge mob of furious laborers with rough manners and sharp machetes. The shopkeepers slammed down their metal grates, traffic thinned to a trickle, and the city council begged Malay to step in with his Marines and set things right.

Malay was furious with the CPA. The job-creation scheme was sensible, but no one had informed the Marines, who were the only security force capable of handling mobs. To clean up the mess and prevent chaos in the city, Malay set up shop in the abandoned warehouse, stringing barbed wire to create corridors, slapping up plywood offices, and deploying one company for crowd control and another as paymasters. Working fourteen hours a day, in four days the Marines paid seventeen thousand Iraqi workers, with no loss of life and no injuries save a few bloody noses to those who tried to jump ahead in line. Once the day laborers were paid, the Marines returned to paying the thousands of former Iraqi military.

When Max and I arrived, things were normal and orderly. We toured the line of young men who were happily lined up, as if buying tickets for the Super Bowl. The men waved at Malay and joked as he passed by. He explained to us that as long as the line moved, no matter how slowly, there wasn't a problem. But when it stopped, the mood of the crowd quickly soured.

For our last stop, a few days later we visited with Lt. Col. John Mayer and battalion 1/4 in Al Hillah, a few kilometers from the division headquarters. I had last seen Mayer on Route 7 north of Nasiriyah, where he had refused to allow a tank to fire into a mud village in response to a rocket-propelled grenade. He had shown the same forbearance ever since. Confronted in Hillah by a restive mob shouting for jobs and electricity, Mayer had tried to reason with them, to no avail. The mob started throwing stones, and Mayer was struck in the forehead. He removed his helmet so the mob could see the blood trickling down his face.

Through an interpreter he shouted, "Why do you throw rocks at me? Is this how you treat a guest?"

Grumbling but more subdued, the mob gradually dispersed.

In June and July battalion 1/4 had to cope with occasional RPG attacks along the highways. By midsummer these incidents had subsided, and Mayer turned his attention to restoring government and basic services. When I visited, he was preparing to turn the city over to a Polish brigade. Battalion 1/4 had provided a modicum of training to four thousand Iraqi police, a modest start toward normalcy in a province of one million people.

That was all the MEF had intended to do. Like their U.S. Army and British counterparts, the Marines had not planned to become heavily involved in municipal government. But as Brig. Gen. John Kelly put it, "We'll do windows. It doesn't change our pay rate." The battalion commanders were the mayors of summer, that brief interlude that offered a glimpse of a turbulent but hopeful future and illustrated the fundamental contradiction: Iraqis wanted the Americans to leave, yet didn't want them to leave. But it was time for the Blue Diamond to return to California. As an expeditionary force, the Marines came from and returned to the sea.

Within six months the MEF would be ordered back to take control of Fallujah and other rebellious cities in the Sunni Triangle where ambushes were frequent. The city of Fallujah continued to be the heart of the insurgency, a place of daily skirmishes, heavy casualties and rabid extremists, who dragged American corpses through the streets. The MEF would return with many of the same commanders, including Conway, Mattis, Dunford, Lopez, and McCoy. In 2003, the Marines had attacked swiftly from Kuwait to Baghdad, as Saddam's army crumbled before it. In 2004, they would battle determined insurgents west of Baghdad in a province the size of North Carolina.

The march up was over.

Organization for Combat

1st Marine Division
The Blue Diamond

Commanding General: Maj. Gen. James N. Mattis
Assistant Division Commander: Brig. Gen. John Kelly

**Augmented by Marines from throughout the Marine Corps
to total over 20,000 Marines and over 8,000 vehicles.**

REGIMENTAL COMBAT TEAM 1
Commanding Officer: Col. Joe Dowdy; later, Col. John Toolan

Comprised of:
Three infantry battalions:
3rd Battalion, 1st Marines, commanded by Lt. Col. Lew Craparotta
1st Battalion, 4th Marines, commanded by Lt. Col. John Mayer
2nd Battalion, 23rd Marines, commanded by Lt. Col. Geffrey Cooper

Reinforced by:
2nd Light Armored Reconnaissance Battalion, commanded by
  Lt. Col. Eddie Ray
1st Battalion, 11th Marines (Artillery), commanded by
  Lt. Col. Jim Seaton
Alpha Company, 1st Tank Battalion
Charlie Company, 2nd Engineer Battalion
AAVs from both 2nd and 4th Assault Amphibian Battalions

REGIMENTAL COMBAT TEAM 5
Commanding Officer: Col. Joe Dunford

Comprised of:

Three infantry battalions:
1st Battalion, 5th Marines, commanded by Lt. Col. Fred Padilla
2nd Battalion, 5th Marines, commanded by Lt. Col. Pete Donohue
3rd Battalion, 5th Marines, commanded by Lt. Col. Sam Mundy

Reinforced by:
1st Light Armored Reconnaissance Battalion, commanded by
    Lt. Col. Duffy White
2nd Tank Battalion, commanded by Lt. Col. Mike Oehl
2nd Battalion, 11th Marines (Artillery), commanded by
    Lt. Col. Paul O'Leary
Bravo Company, 1st Engineer Battalion
Bravo Company, 4th Engineer Battalion
AAVs from both 2nd and 3rd Assault Amphibian Battalions

REGIMENTAL COMBAT TEAM 7
Commanding Officer: Col. Steve Hummer

Comprised of:

Three infantry battalions:
1st Battalion, 7th Marines, commanded by Lt. Col. Chris Conlin
3rd Battalion, 7th Marines, commanded by Lt. Col. Mike Belcher
3rd Battalion, 4th Marines, commanded by Lt. Col. Brian McCoy

Reinforced by:
3rd Light Armored Reconnaissance Battalion, commanded by
    Lt. Col. Stacy Clardy
1st Tank Battalion, commanded by Lt. Col. Jim Chartier

3rd Battalion, 11th Marines (Artillery), commanded by Lt. Col.
   Kirk Hymes
Charlie Company, 1st Engineer Battalion
AAVs from both 2nd and 3rd Assault Amphibian Battalions

And all magnificently supported by the Marines and Sailors of
Col. J.J. Pomfret's CSSG-11
and
the Cannoneers of the 11th Marine Artillery Regiment

Notes

PROLOGUE

page 2 *Xenophon, a disciple of Socrates* . . . Geoffrey Household, *The Exploits of Xenophon* (Eau Claire, Wis.: E.M. Hale, 1955).

CHAPTER 1: THE CROWN JEWEL

page 7 *knew where Saddam was hiding* . . . Bob Woodward, "The War Plan," *Washington Post,* 23 March 2003, p. A1.

page 8 *strike U.S. troops sooner or later* . . . Juan Tamayo et al., "U.S. Forces Buzzing with Preparations for Conflict," *Miami Herald,* 18 March 2003, p. 1.

page 18 *Mattis didn't want to destroy the Iraqi observation post* . . . Staged in Kuwait were the 1st Marine Division and elements of the 2nd Marine Division called Task Force Tarawa. These units, along with the First U.K. Division, which included a brigade of British Royal Marines, the 3rd Marine Air Wing, and First Force Service Support Group, comprised the 1st Marine Expeditionary Force, or I MEF, commanded by Lt. Gen. James Conway. The MEF oversaw the general conduct of maneuver of the forces and provided additional intelligence sources, fire, and air support. The MEF had planned to support Mattis's division with 250 air strikes on D-Day.

page 19 *Central Command agreed the 1st Marine Division* . . . Rick Atkinson et al., *Washington Post*, 31 March 2003.

page 19 *Conlin's 1st Battalion had passed through the berms* . . . A few days earlier the Kuwaiti military had obligingly sent a Filipino construction crew to cut lanes in the berm, each a bit wider than a tank. UN observers, followed by the press, had hastened up to the party as it was bulldozing the paths, complaining that this clearly violated the UN cease-fire rules. Caught off guard, a Marine officer hastily picked up a shovel and pretended to be a laborer, saying he didn't speak English, while an angry UN officer pointed at the Marine emblem on his uniform. Coming as it did before President Bush's twenty-four-hour ultimatum to Saddam, cutting the breach was briefly front-page news.

page 27 *accomplished much more than they gave themselves credit for* . . . Jonathan Finer, "Marines Lay Their Hands on a Jewel," *Washington Post*, 22 March 2003, p. A1; see also Finer's "War? Nothing to It for Young Troops, *Washington Post*, 23 March 2003.

page 28 *had abandoned the tanks* . . . If the Iraqis were not going to fight in their armor, how were they going to fight?
    A four-man crew from Britain's Independent Television News, unaffiliated with the 1st Marine Division, found out when it sneaked across the Kuwaiti border into Iraq, driving in two SUVs with TV written on the hood. Apparently an Iraqi "technical," a pick-up truck with a machine gun mounted in back, intercepted them, seized control of one SUV, and chased after the other. The three vehicles raced toward an interpass guarded by the 1st Tank Battalion. Believing they were being charged by three suicide bombers, the tankers fired. One European reporter was killed, and two were missing and presumed dead. The tragedy, but not any details, was promptly reported to the division.

Major General Mattis immediately dispatched his top lawyer, or staff judge advocate, Lt. Col. John Ewers, to investigate. Ewers rode in the lead Humvee; the division public affairs officer, Capt. Joe Plenzler, came in a second. They waved as they passed the British roadblock where CAAT Red had been and drove on a kilometer to the small town of Az Zubayr. As they approached, an RPG whizzed across the road in front of them. It zipped by quickly, a dark blob, gone in a blink. Seconds later a man stood up in the grass to their left. This time they saw the flash of flame and heard the *whoosh* as the RPG streaked by them.

Staff Sgt. Jamison, driving the lead vehicle, sped through the kill zone, followed by Sergeant Goff, driving the second Humvee. The road led deeper into Az Zubayr, with mud and adobe huts on both sides, set back about 40 meters. Straight ahead about 300 meters, Ewers saw people running to get away from the road.

There were four Marines in Ewers's Humvee and two in Plenzler's, and all six had their weapons out as they turned to the right, where the people had scattered. Goff saw men in doorways, dressed in brown robes with military belts, jump up and run inside. In seconds they were back on the street firing AK-47s. Every Marine now was firing, the Humvees bouncing over potholes. Ewers fired his 9mm, and when he went to change clips, he saw blood on his left forearm. He had been shot through both arms. He changed clips and fired several more rounds. As they rounded a corner, Lt. Col. Peter Zarcone, the division's civil affairs liaison officer sitting behind Jamison, shot an Iraqi who was raising an RPG. Between six and twelve RPGs whizzed by the vehicles as they raced through the small town.

Goff followed Jamison. A bullet hit the stock of his rifle, stinging him. Plenzler, having fired all dozen shells from his twelve-gauge shotgun, drew his 9mm pistol and blazed away. Sitting behind Ewers, Lance Cpl. Henry Lopez was shot in the back while trying to clear a jam in his M-16. Bullets sounding like insects were whizzing through the canvas of both Humvees. Jamison and Goff never slowed down. After a series of sharp right turns, they drove back out where the first RPG had been fired. Someone had dragged large rocks and tires onto the road. Goff and Jamison sped around them without slowing. A few more RPGs arced by at crazy angles, and then they were out of it.

Ahead Goff saw the British roadblock and skidded to a halt. The British looked at them with mild curiosity; the road behind them was empty. Captain Plenzler took out his iridium cell phone—a perk of his job as press officer for the division—and called the division staff, 70 kilometers away, for a medevac. Jamison tried to contact 1st Tank Battalion to come forward and deliver some immediate payback into the town, but—like Conlin, Ferkovich, and his men—the tanks had headed west, toward An Nasiriyah.

In a quirk of fate, a few days before the war the division public affairs chief, Staff Sergeant Jamison, had asked Ray to talk with his staff section about combat. They had one burning question: What should they do if they were shot at? Ray said they would know when bullets were personally addressed to them and that immediate return fire was key. If they didn't put out as much or more fire than they were taking in, the enemy would sense weakness and pour it on them. You need to keep the enemy busier ducking your fire than you are ducking his.

Ewers and Jamison and the others had done that and survived.

CHAPTER 2: AMBUSH ALLEY

page 41 *at first light the next day, 24 March* . . . As Ray and I learned later by talking with Marines up and down the chain of command, the other two Marine regiments, RCT-5 and RCT-7, had pushed equally hard, then been hit by the same dust storm that slammed into us on Route 7. While RCT-1 had been moving up Route 7, RCT-5 and RCT-7 had swung 60 kilometers west to drive up Route 1, a wide four-lane highway. They had found the going easier than did RCT-1, but with their own adventures beginning on 23 March.

On schedule that evening the 3rd LAR Battalion screening in front of RCT-5 had crossed the Euphrates River 15 kilometers northwest of the embattled city of Nasiriyah. As dusk fell, the LAV drivers, proceeding at a slow pace, noticed gear and food in the trenches by the side of the road—a helmet, a few shovels, a teapot, a few plates with food. Then a sergeant saw a technical—a Nissan pickup with a machine gun mounted in the back. A quick burst from the LAV's chain gun set the truck ablaze and initiated a larger battle.

The fedayeen and other Iraqi soldiers had been eating supper and were caught out of position. Perpendicular to the highway, bulldozers had scooped out a line of holes to conceal the technical pickups with their machine guns facing south. This would have provided a good field of fire if the LAVs had approached in a wide wedge formation. But they were in a single column that had split the Iraqi line, able to concentrate their fire, while the Iraqis couldn't swing around their dug-in vehicles. The Iraqis got off a few mortar rounds with no effect against the fast-moving vehicles. The fedayeen were firing RPGs with their usual poor aim, and the green tracers from their machine guns were going high, signaling the Marine gunners where to fire. Lt. Col. Stacy Clardy, the commanding officer of 3rd LAR, watched through a thermal sight as about thirty Iraqis stood and ran toward the highway. The chain guns cut most of them down. The remaining few jumped up after a few seconds and completed their hari-kari.

Clardy drove past the enemy positions, then ordered a re-attack down the highway. Most of the shooting was done by the gunners on the 25mms looking through the thermals, while the two riflemen scouts in each LAV fired their M-16s out the back hatches. During the fight an excited radio operator yelled the code word *"Slingshot,"* meaning "a friendly unit is being overrun." The MEF sent dozens of fixed-wing aircraft to the general location, but in the dark, only Cobra attack helicopters fired near the LAVs. There were no friendly casualties. The two RCTs continued up the highway without incident—until the dust storm swept in on 25 March.

When it did, 3rd Battalion, 5th Marine Regiment (3/5), commanded by Lt. Col. Sam Mundy, was leading RCT-5, 90 kilometers north of the Euphrates crossing, when India and Lima Companies, together with Mundy's command group, were hit on their western flank by an Iraqi company hiding behind a large berm, not 40 meters from the highway. Reacting with immediate action drills, the companies counterattacked, climbed over the berm, and shot Iraqis at distances of five meters. Almost immediately the Abrams tanks farther in front received some desultory mortar and RPG fire. One rocket hit a Humvee, killing a corpsman and injuring a Marine. Mundy, wishing he had some Cobra helicopters overhead to provide him with a sense of the battlefield, sent Kilo Company forward while a CAAT with a .50-caliber turned off the highway and killed more than twenty Iraqis who were running down a deep ditch.

As the Marines closed in by fire and maneuver, the Iraqis tried to run. But the desert offered no cover, and more than fifty were killed. With the dust storm upon them, Mundy pulled his companies back into a circular defense. There were reports of soldiers coming down the highway in a minibus, and a few vehicles were hit. In the blinding dust and raging wind, the thermals wouldn't work, and tragically a father and two children were killed in a car. Lima Company radioed that armor could be heard approaching from the direction of Diwaniyah, about 12 kilometers north. Artillery was called on the suspected coordinates, and Lima heard no more noises of engines or track treads.

As the weather that night deteriorated from bad to terrible, Lieutenant Colonel Conlin and battalion 1/7 were near the rear of the two-regiment line of march. Told that an Army convoy behind him was stuck and with rumors swirling of fedayeen closing in, Conlin sent back Bravo (Maj. Dan Healey) and Charlie (Capt. Tom Lacroix) Companies to help out.

Healey found the fuel convoy first. Stepping out of the dark in the wind and dust, he said he was a Marine rifle company commander and asked if anyone needed a hand. A group of fuel truck drivers engulfed him. They were all alone in the middle of fedayeen country, they said. Several of their trucks were mired in soft muck, dogs around them were barking like hyenas, the dust made driving impossible, the rain had turned the roadside into mud, hailstones were pelting them, it was freezing, and the fedayeen were closing in—the drivers were sure of it. With a row of bulk fuelers parked near one another, the first RPG would cause an inferno. A young woman grabbed Healey's arm and wouldn't let go, convinced that the Iraqis would carry her off as they had Pfc. Jessica Lynch. She didn't care what anyone said; she was staying with the major. The others agreed—they would leave the fuel trucks and stay with the Marines. Then Captain Lacroix came up, and the two company commanders offered to have Marines drive the fuel trucks. The Army drivers were horrified. Marines couldn't drive scooters! They would crash into one another, with the same results as fedayeen rockets.

Eventually they settled on a mix of Army and Marine drivers, who before dawn had most of the fuel trucks returned. Three, though, were still stuck in the muck. The Army did not want to hold up the huge convoy another day. Captain Lacroix offered to take care of it. Twelve hours later Col. Steven Hummer, commanding RCT-7, had a slightly longer convoy, with more fuel.

Both RCTs, delayed by the storm, were Oscar Mike, on the move, on 26 March and picking up speed.

page 47 *a white cloth over the burned body* . . . Darrin Mortenson, "Marines Honor Casualties of War," *San Diego North County Times,* 25 March 2003, p.1.

page 48 *Nasiriyah had exhibited the same lack of coherent information . . .* Accounts of Nasiriyah vary widely. See Nicholas Kulish (with Michael Phillips), "Street Fighting," 25 March 2003, and Dexter Filkins and Michael Wilson, "Marines Battling in Nasiriya," both *New York Times,* 25 March 2003, p. 1; Anders Gerlin, "U.S. Tightens Grip on Nassiriyah," *Miami Herald,* 30 March 2003, p. 1; Alessandra Stanley, "In Hoopla over a POW, a Mirror of U.S. Society," *New York Times,* 18 March 2003, p. B9; Robert Schlesinger, "U.S. Forces Brace for More Tricks," *Boston Globe,* 25 March 2003, p. A17; Mark Franchetti, "U.S. Marines Turn Fire on Civilians," *Sunday Times,* 30 March 2003, p. 1; "Marines Describe Harrowing Gantlet of Iraqi Defenders," *Washington Post,* 28 March 2003, p. A32; Susan Glasser and Rajiv Chandrasekaran, "Clashes at Key River Crossing Bring Heaviest Day of American Casualties," *Washington*

Post, 24 March 2003, p. 1; James Meek, "Marines Losing Battle for Hearts and Minds," *Guardian*, 25 March 2003, p. 1.

CHAPTER 3: A LAND THE COLOR OF DUST

page 52 *RCT-1, which had been put together only recently, consisted* . . . The 2nd Battalion, 23rd Marines was comprised of reservists from Arizona, New Mexico, and California. Activated soon after 11 September, they had been on active duty just over a year. The 3rd Battalion, 1st Marines had been deployed in the Persian Gulf region on board ships for six months, returning to California just in time to turn around and come back to the Gulf with RCT-1. The 1st Battalion, 4th Marines had trained at Camp Pendleton, California. The Amtracs and the 2nd Light Armored Reconnaissance Battalion were from North Carolina. The artillery battalion, 1st Battalion, 11th Marines, was from Camp Pendleton, while the attached tank company, Bravo Company, 1st Tank Battalion, was from 29 Palms, California.

page 61 *yelling at his Marines* . . . See Jim Landers, "Marines Wrestle Attacks, Weather," *Dallas Morning News*, 27 March 2003, p. 1; "Panning the Dust, Biding Our Time," 27 March 2003; and "Marines Overpower Iraqi Group," 28 March 2003. See also Darrin Mortenson, "Marines Run Gantlet of Sniper Alley," 25 March 2003. On Frei, see lcannon@californian.com, 29 March 2003. See also Robert Schlesinger and Thanassis Cambanis, "Supply Line Traversing Iraq Faces Guerrillas," *Boston Globe*, 26 March 2003, p. 23; Scott Nelson, "Sandstorms to Snipers," *Boston Globe*, 20 April 2003, p. A23.

page 67 *"This is lousy"* . . . For a good summary, see David Zucchnino and Tony Perry, "Allied Forces May Be Quicker to Fire," *Los Angeles Times*, 29 March 2003, p. 1.

CHAPTER 4: SCREECHING TO A HALT

page 81 *having hungry soldiers, had paused for resupply* . . . Peter Baker and Rajiv Chandrasekaran, "Sandstorm Delays Army's Advance," *Washington Post*, 26 March 2003, p. A1.

page 81 *"bizarre" behavior of Iraqi fighters* . . . Robert Burns, "Army Commander Says Iraqis Found Creative Ways to Defend Against U.S. Invaders," Associated Press, 8 May 2003, and John Broder, "Views of War: On the Ground and at the Top," *New York Times*, 29 March 2003, p. 1.

page 81 *likely lead to a longer war* . . . Rick Atkinson, "General: A Longer War Likely," *Washington Post*, 28 March 2003, p. 1, and Carla Anne Robbins and Greg Jaffe, "U.S. Considers Options in Event of a Longer War," *Wall Street Journal*, 26 March 2003, p. 1.

page 82 *commander in the Iraqi theater was General Franks* . . . Susan Baer, "War Chief's Four Stars on a Blue Collar," *Baltimore Sun*, 25 March 2003, p. 1.

page 82 *stop for fuel, ammunition* . . . After the war, Lt. Gen. McKiernan said, "And I would refute any notion that there was any kind of operational pause in this campaign. There never was a day, there was never a moment when there was not continuous pressure on the regime of Saddam by one of those components—air, ground, maritime, Special Forces and so on." By selecting words carefully, the obvious became obscure. Lt. Gen. McKiernan, Briefing to reporters on April 23, *Defense Link*, *Department of Defense News*, Washington, D.C., April 26, 2003, p.2.

page 83 *Halting the ground attack to the north made sense for V Corps* . . . Rick Atkinson, Peter Baker, and Thomas E. Ricks, "Confused Start, Decisive End," *Washington Post*, 13 April 2003, p. A1. The story reports that on the morning of 25 March the "three top commanders of U.S. ground forces"—McKiernan, Wallace, and Conway—"convened a grim video teleconference." According to a Marine, "one Army general expressed doubt that U.S. forces were ready for the push to Baghdad." Conway said, "[W]e are now ready for the push to Baghdad."

page 83 *rooting for the 3rd Infantry Division* . . . V Corps was organized around the 3rd Infantry Division, supplemented by the 101st Airborne Division and a brigade from the 82nd Airborne Division. Units from the 82nd and 101st were reassigned to route security. See Max Boot, "The New American Way of War," New York: *Foreign Affairs Magazine*, July/August 2003; Rick Atkinson, "As Battle Escalates, Holy Site Is Turned Into a Stronghold," *Washington Post*, April 1, 2003, p.1; Vernon Loeb, "U.S. Acts to Shore Up Supply Lines," *Washington Post*, March 26, 2003, p. A25.

page 83 *did not need to halt* . . . The embedded press reported what Ray and I were hearing: Marines had been ordered to stop. There was an "operational delay" of several days in the advance toward Baghdad. "I hate to see it," Staff Sergeant Douglas Patton of the 11th Marines told Mr. Scott Nelson of the *Boston Globe*. "But we do what the President tells us to do. He said to stop, so we stop." Scott Bernard Nelson, "As March Slows, Marines Pass Time," *Boston Globe*, March 30, 2003, p. A27.

page 83 *the path to Baghdad might be long* . . . Greg Jaffe and Michael M. Phillips, "U.S. Is Opening a Second Front in the Iraq War," *Wall Street Journal*, 27 March 2003, p. 1.

CHAPTER 6: THE NON-PAUSE PAUSE

page 102 *"both products of the same institution"* . . . Rick Atkinson and Thomas Ricks, "War's Military, Political Goals Begin to Diverge," *Washington Post*, 30 March 2003, p. 28.

page 105 *ambushed and riddled with bullets* . . . Mary Beth Sheridan, "Ground Fire Repels Copter Assault," *Washington Post*, 25 March 2003, p. 1.

page 105 *Gen. Barry R. McCaffrey who had commanded* . . . Thomas Ricks, "War Could Last Months, Officers Say," *Washington Post,* 27 March 2003, p. 1.

page 105 *protect an ever-lengthening supply line* . . . "The Vulnerable Supply Lines," editorial, *New York Times,* 28 March 2003.

page 105 *"having distracted significant parts"* . . . Steven Lee Myers, "A City Is Encircled in a 36-Hour Battle," *New York Times,* 27 March 2003, p. 1.

page 105 *alarmingly low on water, and in danger of running short of food* . . . Peter Baker and Rajiv Chandrasekaran, "Republican Guard Units Move South," *Washington Post,* 27 March 2003, p. 1, and Thomas E. Ricks, "War Could Last for Months," *Washington Post,* 27 March 2003, p. 1.

page 105 *Asked if the war was likely to last much longer* . . . Rick Atkinson, "General: A Longer War Likely," *Washington Post,* 28 March 2003, p. 1.

page 106 *Conway was quoted as saying I MEF* . . . Oliver North, "From the Frontlines," Fox News, 28 March 2003.

page 106 *Instead, the* Washington Post *cited "top Army officers"* . . . Rick Atkinson and Thomas Ricks, "War's Military, Political Goals Begin to Diverge," *Washington Post,* 30 March 2003, p. 1.

page 106 *principals still agreed with the strategy* . . . Vernon Loeb, "Rumsfeld Assails War Critics," *Washington Post,* 29 April 2003, p. 1. According to the article, Air Force Col. Steven Pennington, chief of current operations at CENTCOM, said that when fedayeen started hitting the supply lines in the south, Franks was "very, very direct with his commanders" that they must focus on pushing ahead to Baghdad, not become overly concerned about a tactical problem.

page 106 *After the Camp David meeting*... Appearing on 30 March on ABC, Secretary Rumsfeld said, "We have no plans for pauses." Bryan Barnard, "U.S. Defends War Plan as Troops Inch Toward Baghdad," *Boston Globe*, 31 March 2003, p. A22.

page 107 *"There is no pause," an administration official said*... David Von Drehle and Mike Allen, "Push Toward Baghdad Is Reaffirmed," *Washington Post*, 30 March 2003, p. 1.

page 107 *The Camp David meeting reversed*... Rick Atkinson, Peter Baker, and Thomas E. Ricks, "Confused Start, Swift Conclusion," *Washington Post*, 13 April 2003, p. 1.

CHAPTER 8: ACROSS THE TIGRIS

page 138 *resistance there had been scant*... Jonathan Finer, "For Marines, a Fight with a Foe That Never Arrived," *Washington Post*, 4 April 2003, p. 23; Michael Phillips, "U.S. Troops Meet Friendlier Faces in Iraq," *Wall Street Journal*, 4 April 2003, p. A10; Michael Phillips, "In An Numaniyah, a Warm Welcome for U.S. Cools Fast," *Wall Street Journal*, 7 April 2003, p. A1; Michael Phillips, "As Marines Search Door to Door, Tears and Tense Moments," *Wall Street Journal*, 31 March 2003, p. A1; Jonathan Finer, "Marines Within Striking Distance of Baghdad," *Washington Post*, 2 April 2003, p. A1.

page 149 *were slamming into it earlier that day*... Bryan Bender, "U.S. Says Two Divisions No Longer a Threat," *Boston Globe*, 3 April 2003, p. A33; CNN report, Martin Savidge, 3 April 2003.

page 149 *change commanders in RCT-1*... Thomas E. Ricks, "Marines Relieve Commander," *Washington Post*, 5 April 2003; Tony Perry, "In Rare Move, Commander Loses Post," *Los Angeles Times*, 5 April 2003.

page 149 *Saddam was "in full control of the army and the country"*... Dan Morse and Michael M. Phillips, "Troops Find Little Resistance,"

Wall Street Journal, 3 April 2003, p. A6.

page 149 *saying reports of U.S. advances on Baghdad were "illusions"* . . . Matt Murray, "U.S. Armed Forces Advance Quickly Toward Baghdad," *Wall Street Journal,* 3 April 2003, p. A3.

page 151 *sandbags he had placed around his turret hatch* . . . Jim Landers, *Dallas Morning News,* 18 May 2003, p.A14.

CHAPTER 9: RUN AND GUN

page 153 *"I'm going to have to put a bit on Iron Horse"* . . . Jim Landers, *Dallas Morning News,* 18 May 2003.

page 155 *"we all go home in one piece"* . . . Diary #3, page 19, dinner with Johnson & Smith, F/2/5.

page 160 *same high school, Boston College High* . . . Douglas Belkin, "Pembroke Marine Is Killed," *Boston Globe,* 6 April 2003, p. A14.

page 161 *killed in the last half-hour* . . . see Jim Landers's complete reports on 2nd Tank Battalion: "Alone and Unafraid," *Dallas Morning News,* 3 April 2003; "New Life for the Tank," 20 March 2003; "In the Trenches, Forged Respect," 14 April 2003; "Ambush Costly for Marine Battalion," 9 April 2003.

page 161 *hostiles who wanted to take his life* . . . Jim Landers, "Ambush Costly for Marine Battalion," *Dallas Morning News,* 9 April 2003, p. 1.

page 162 *destroying the Al Nida Division regulars as they went* . . . Rajiv Chandrasekaran and Peter Baker, "U.S Forces Probing Inside Baghdad," *Washington Post,* 5 April 2003, p. 1.

page 166 *struck in the head and killed* . . . Elliot Spagat, "Edward Smith Is Honored at Camp Pendleton," Associated Press, 24 May 2003.

CHAPTER 10: RING AROUND BAGHDAD

page 185 *then driving back out again* . . . Alan Sipress and Rajiv Chandrasekaran, "Tanks Move Through City," *Washington Post*, 6 April 2003, p. A23: "3rd Infantry Division Armored Column Entered Baghdad . . . did not seize any territory during the mission, which appeared to be more psychological muscle-flexing than an advancement on Hussein's nucleus of power."

page 185 *Army had favored raids to attrit* . . . Rajiv Chandrasekaran and Peter Baker, "U.S. Forces Probing Inside Baghdad," *Washington Post*, 5 April 2003, p. 1.

page 185 *did not constitute a plan for taking control* . . . Karen DeYoung, "U.S. Wants Better Odds on Baghdad," *Washington Post*, 31 March 2003, p. A15. Joint Chiefs chairman Richard Myers "acknowledged that US positions outside Baghdad are now stationary, saying that 'it may be an operational pause in the macro sense,' but not a siege." Vernon Loeb and Bradley Graham, "U.S. Military to Impose a Light Cordon on Baghdad," *Washington Post*, 5 April 2003, p. 19: "The US military plans to establish a loose 'cordon' around Baghdad . . . The cordon would differ from a siege, officials explained, in that people who wanted to leave the city would be permitted to go."

page 186 *they were still unresolved* . . . Thomas Ricks, "New Strategy Slower and More Methodical," *Washington Post*, 31 March 2003, p. A24: "Under this approach, the two Army divisions engaged in Iraq probably will resupply and consolidate their position for days or weeks . . . some Army commanders think it could be a month or more before the battle for Baghdad is joined . . . The wild card in all this is the Marine Corps . . . Marines could break through their opponents before the Army does."

page 187 *faced the question of what to do next* . . . Vernon Loeb and Bradley Graham, "U.S. Seeks to Avoid Siege of Baghdad," *Washington*

Post, 5 April 2003, p. A22: "We'll be very, very deliberate about the work that we do," said Brig. Gen. Vincent Brooks, CENTCOM spokesperson. On the other hand, see Vernon Loeb, "Rumsfeld Assails War Critics," *Washington Post,* 29 April 2003, p. A11: "[General] Franks directed them to head downtown quickly instead of sitting 'out on the periphery forever.'"

CHAPTER 11: ASSAULT INTO BAGHDAD

page 206 *winding concrete driveways* . . . See Jonathan Finer, "Marines Find Chemical Suits, Labs at Atomic Energy Site," *Washington Post,* 7 April 2003, p. A23.

CHAPTER 12: SEIZING THE SNOOZLE

page 225 *"That's OBE—overtaken by events," Conway said* . . . Peter Baker, "Marines' Orders; Ready, Set, Switch," *Washington Post,* 10 April 2003, p. A35.

CHAPTER 13: A TYRANT FALLS

page 232 *"When you take over his country and drink his liquor"* . . . William Branigin and Anthony Shadid, "U.S. Makes Gains in a Collapsing Baghdad," *Washington Post,* 9 April 2003, p. A27.

page 234 *the deputy prime minister in charge of furbishing Saddam's image* . . . Jonathan Finer, "An Iraqi Official's Better Home and Garden," *Washington Post,* 11 April 2003, p. A1.

page 235 *(A few weeks later he was arrested, still inside Baghdad)* . . . John F. Burns, "Tariq Aziz Finally Emerges from the Elusive Shadows," *New York Times,* 23 April 2003, p. A13.

page 240 *more than a hundred fedayeen lay dead* . . . Gordon Dillow, "Marines Get Their Wish, and More," *Orange County Register,* 11 April

2003, p. 1; Mark Landler, "The Fighting Dies Down, and Yet the Scars Are Fresh," *New York Times,* 17 April 2003, p. A18; Peter Baker, "Marines Take Casualties from Firefight," *Washington Post,* 11 April 2003, p. A29.

EPILOGUE

page 245 *The 4th Infantry Division was due to arrive . . .* Jonathan Weisman, *Washington Post,* 11 April 2003, p. 36.

page 246 *"We want all jihad fighters to come here" . . .* Kelly quoted in *USA Today,* 7 April 2003.

page 248 *freed all the Americans still in Iraqi hands . . .* Peter Baker, "Rescuers Nearly Called Mission Off," *Washington Post,* 16 April 2003, p. A1.

THE MAYORS OF SUMMER

page 261 *Conlin . . . ordered his Marines to . . . fix bayonets . . .* Pamela Hess, "Marines Walk Tightrope In Najaf", United Press International, July 29, 2003.

page 261 *a corrupt mayor, previously appointed by Americans . . .* Shaila K. Dewan, "Iraqi Citizens Claim Victory With Ouster of U.S.-Chosen Mayor", *New York Times,* July 1, 2003, and William Booth, "In Najaf, New Mayor Is Outsider Viewed with Suspicion" *Washington Post,* May 14, 2003.

Glossary

AAV (assault amphibious vehicle)—a tracked vehicle capable of swimming ashore from Navy shipping and then performing as a troop carrier on land. Since World War II the Marine Corps has fielded a unique series of these vehicles. The current vehicle series is the LVT-P7 (troop carrier) and LVT-C7 (command and control variant). Marines refer to these vehicles by a variety of names: tracs, Amtracs, P-7s, and C-7s, occasionally even pigs or hogs. Regardless of name, the AAV is the main mechanized troop carrier in the Marine Corps inventory: a large aluminum-hulled vehicle that carries twenty combat Marines, on sea or ashore. The P-7 also carries two weapons in a turret: a .50-caliber machine gun and a 40mm automatic grenade launcher. The turret was adapted to the current vehicle in the 1980s in an effort to "up gun" the firepower of the AAV—hence most Marines refer to it as the "up gun." The C-7, the command and control variant, contains work spaces along each side of the compartment with map boards and a variety of racks for radios. The top of the vehicle is covered with a number of antennae of various types, connected to the interior racks. Normally, when an infantry battalion is "mech-ed up," two C-7s provide the battalion with its mobile command and control capability.

AAV battalion—a separate battalion that is responsible for maintaining and housing AAVs and for training their crews. The vehicles, with crews, are then normally attached to an infantry regiment and battalion for operations.

Abrams tank—*see* M1A1 Abrams tank.

AK-47—a short automatic or semiautomatic assault weapon, built originally by the Soviet Union but copied by the Chinese and nearly all of the former Soviet satellites. Designed by a Russian weapons designer named Kalashnikov (AK stands for "assault Kalashnikov"), it is the most widely copied and widely carried assault weapon in the world. There have been many versions and copies. The AK-47 is a 7.62mm weapon; the AKM version is 5.54mm. There are folding stock versions, versions with bayonets and without, and so on, but the AK-47 is the most numerous. It is also often called the Kalashnikov. The U.S. equivalent weapon is the M-16.

Alpha Command Group—a group that contains half of a unit's command element. Marine Corps infantry units—battalions, regiments, and divisions—normally split their command elements into two groups. The Alpha Command Group (also often referred to as the TAC) normally consists of the commander and the principal staff officers of the command: intelligence, operations, fire support coordination, and logistics. *See also* Bravo Command Group.

Amtrac—*see* AAV.

Base plate—a component of an infantry mortar. An infantry mortar, either 60mm or 81mm, consists of a bipod, a mortar tube, and a base plate, into which the mortar tube is fastened to hold it down when firing. The base plate is a large, heavy metal disk that has a socket in the center into which the ball—much like a trailer hitch ball—on the base end of the mortar tube is fitted. When infantrymen carry mortars on their backs—which they do often—the mortars are broken down into the three main parts. The base plate is the heaviest and the most awkward to carry.

BMP—a Soviet (Russian)-made infantry fighting vehicle that is armed with a 72mm smoothbore cannon. Its Marine Corps equivalent is the LAV; *see* LAV.

Bravo Command Group—a group that contains half of a unit's command element, consisting of its executive officer and the staff assistants for intelligence, operations, fire support coordination, and logistics. (*See also* Alpha Command Group.)

C-7—*see* AAV.

CAAT (combined anti-armor team)—a team of several Humvees from within the weapons company of an infantry battalion. Its weaponry includes TOWs, .50-caliber machine guns, and Mk-19 automatic grenade launchers. The infantry battalion uses them, especially in mechanized operations, as scouts and guides as well as "ambush" teams to block and destroy enemy vehicular movement, both armored and soft-skinned vehicles.

CENTCOM (Central Command)—a unified command that reports directly to the National Command Authority through the chairman of the Joint Chiefs of Staff. Based in Tampa, Florida, CENTCOM is responsible for planning and conducting military operations in North Africa, the Middle East, South Central Europe, and Southwest Asia. A joint command staffed with members of all the armed forces, CENT-COM is commanded by a four-star general. The commander may come from any of the services but has traditionally been either an Army or a Marine four-star.

CH-46—the Marine Corps' primary troop lift helicopter. The CH-46 Sea Knight is a twin-rotor aircraft designed to carry twenty-four Marines. Fielded in the early 1970s, the CH-46s flown in Operation Iraqi Freedom are older than their pilots and certainly older than most of the Marines they carry. As a result, although designed to carry twenty-four, they rarely carry more than fifteen.

Civil affairs—a military occupational specialty that provides essential civil tasks, with and through the local civil administration, in a military theater of operations. Civil affairs officers learn, for example, who runs the sewer plant, and they ensure that the function is performed even during combat operations.

Coil—to circle vehicles into a defensive position. Used by tankers and other mechanized forces, the term is a metaphor based on the coil of a snake.

CP (command post)—the place where a commander maintains his command; also, the staff of such a command. Thus a Marine may refer to the CP when talking about where the commander "hangs his hat" or about the people who make up the commander's staff.

DASC (Direct Air Support Center)—a group that provides the direct link between a Marine ground unit, or division, and the Marine air unit, or wing. Part of the Marine Wing Air Command and Control System, the DASC performs both a communications function, linking the division communications back to the wing's air base or bases, and an air traffic control function, tracking and routing airplanes and handing them off to terminal controllers on the ground.

Defilade—protection by terrain or buildings from direct-fire weapons.

81mm mortar—a battalion commander's organic "artillery." The weapons company of a Marine infantry battalion contains a platoon of eight of these mortars, which have a range of 4,500 meters and a killing radius of 35 meters.

Enfilade—fire that hits along the long axis of a target; also known as enfilade fire.

EPW (enemy prisoner of war)—a term that replaced POW several years ago. Under the Geneva Conventions, an enemy prisoner of war has a number of protected rights. The capturing force is required to protect EPWs, feed them, and provide them with medical care in the same way that it provides protection, food, and care to its own forces.

E-tool (entrenching tool)—a small folding shovel carried as part of the personal equipment of all Marines. Designed primarily for digging individual fighting positions, it is used for myriad functions in the field, including, in extreme cases, as a close-in fighting weapon.

G-2 Intelligence—the section of a commander's staff responsible for intelligence. Marine (and Army) commanders' staffs are divided, at a minimum, into four staff sections: the 1, 2, 3, and 4. A unit commanded by a general officer is called a "G" section: G-1, G-2, and so on. A unit that is not commanded by a general is called an "S" section: S-1, S-2, and so on. Typically, a G-1 is responsible for administrative and personnel functions; G-2 for intelligence collection, analysis, and dissemination; G-3 for planning, operations, and fire support; and G-4 for logistics and maintenance.

GOSP (gas-oil separator plant)—a plant that separates natural gas from oil. Iraqi oil fields are "artesian," in that the combination of gas and oil underground there exists under natural pressure. When tapped, the combined pressure brings the gas and oil to the surface at (currently) approximately four hundred pounds per square inch. The pressure is, of course, in the gas, which must be separated from the oil and handled differently. GOSPs not only separate the gas from the oil but reduce the pressure on the oil so that it can be handled more effectively. Both the natural gas and the oil are very valuable.

Herringbone—a parking technique in which alternating vehicles pull in off an angle on either side of a road, forming a herringbone pattern.

H-Hour—in military operations, the hour when an operation is to commence. The day it commences is designated D-Day; 6 June 1944 was D-Day at Normandy. The time of attack is H-hour, as in "H-hour is

scheduled for 0515." Interestingly, although the attack time is called H-
Hour, the time is really set to the minute.

Humvee—the replacement vehicle developed in the 1980s for the ubiquitous Jeep. The Hummer is now sold as a high-end civilian SUV, so
nearly everyone is somewhat familiar with it. The Marine Corps uses
several versions of the Humvee. One is the four-door, soft-top vehicle,
with zip-in plastic windows. This variant is used as a communications
vehicle, called the Mark vehicle (for MRC, mobile radio communications), or as a general all-around utility vehicle. It carries a driver and
three passengers. Another variant is the two-door model with a bed,
much like a full-size pick-up bed. It normally has a high canvas cover
over the bed, which gives it its common name, the high-back Hummer.
The high-back can carry two people in the front and as many as eight in
the back. It is used extensively to carry supplies as well as personnel. The
third variant has four doors too, but also has a sloping hard cover that
has a hole in the top that is used to mount a ring mount for a weapons
platform. This variant, also called the hard-back Hummer or sometimes—because of the sloped back—the lobsterback, is used by a CAAT
as its primary weapons carrier. The ring mount through the hole in the
top allows a gunner to swivel his machine gun 360 degrees.

Joint Forces Command—based in Norfolk, Virginia, the command responsible for developing and refining joint doctrine and training joint
command elements.

JSTARS (Joint Surveillance and Targeting Aperture Radar System)—
a very high-tech surveillance suite, carried over a battlefield in a Boeing
707–type aircraft. The sensors in the airplane feed to a staff that is on
board and provide highly accurate wide-area coverage of any moving
vehicle on the ground. The sensors not only "see" moving vehicles but
track them accurately enough to target them precisely if needed. The
data can be fed back live to a commander and his staff either on the
ground or airborne in another aircraft.

LAR battalion (light armored reconnaissance battalion)—a Marine division's primary mobile ground reconnaissance unit. The LAR battalion is used for reconnaissance, screening, and delay missions. It is fully mounted in the several versions of the LAV.

LAV (light armored vehicle)—an eight-wheeled lightly armored fighting vehicle that is capable of "swimming" if necessary for crossing rivers and other water barriers. A unique Marine Corps vehicle, it has several variants:

LAV-25—the most common variant, which features a turret-mounted 25mm chain gun, capable of firing high-explosive and armor-piercing-incendiary rounds at a high rate of fire. The thermal and optical sights in the turret make the system extremely accurate and lethal at ranges up to 2,500 meters, day or night. In addition to its driver, gunner, and vehicle commander, the LAV-25 can carry four infantry scouts in its rear compartment.

LAV-AT (antitank, most often referred to simply as AT)—an LAV that mounts four TOW missile launchers. *See* TOW.

LAV-R (recovery)—a maintenance vehicle that includes a hoist. It is used for recovering, towing, and repairing other LAVs. It also carries a pintel-mounted 7.62mm machine gun.

LAV-C2 (command and control, or C-squared)—a vehicle that mounts a number of radios and whose internal compartment can carry a battalion's principal staff officers. It too carries a pintel-mounted 7.62mm machine gun.

Line of Departure—in military operations, that position where advancing military formations should move out of march formation and into attack formation. It is normally designated along the FLOT, or forward line of troops.

M1A1 Abrams tank—the United States' main battle tank, named for re-tired U.S. Army Gen. Creighton Abrams. Called either "the M1" or "the Abrams," it is without doubt the most efficient and effective tank ever built. Armed with a 120mm smoothbore main gun, a 7.62 coaxial ma-chine gun, and a .50-caliber pintel-mounted machine gun and pro-tected by a laminated armor plate that will stop most of the world's antitank weapons, the M1 has highly sophisticated thermal and optical sights that allow the crew to see and engage targets as much as five kilo-meters away with better than 95 percent first-round hits. The main gun and coaxial machine gun are gyro-stabilized so that they can achieve tremendous accuracy whether the tank is moving or sitting. The sight computer calculates the target speed, wind velocity, and other variables so that the guns can achieve the same accuracy against a moving target.

M-16A2—a lightweight infantry weapon that can be fired either semi-automatically or in automatic three-round bursts. It is the Marine Corps' basic infantry weapon, carried by the vast majority of all Marines, whether infantry or not. The M-16 fires a 5.56mm round ac-curately enough to hit a man-size target at over 500 meters.

M-203—an M-16 with a 40mm grenade launcher attached under the rifle barrel. The single-shot launcher can fire the 40mm grenade 500 meters. Each fire team of a Marine infantry squad has one, totaling three per squad.

M-240G (called the 240 Golf by Marines)—a 7.62mm machine gun that fires five hundred rounds per minute out to 1,000 meters. The weapons platoon of a Marine infantry company contains a section of six of these machine guns. It is also mounted on pintel mounts on some Humvees and some LAV variants. It is a superb light machine gun, probably the best in the world.

Mk-19 (called Mark 19 by Marines)—a 40mm automatic grenade launcher that fires grenades up to 2,300 meters. With a lethal bursting radius of five meters, the 40mm is a fine suppression weapon against personnel and will destroy soft-skinned vehicles such as trucks and some personnel carriers. The heavy machine gun platoon in the weapons company of each infantry battalion carries six of these weapons, which are normally mounted on hard-back Humvees as part of a CAAT.

M2 .50-caliber machine gun—an old stand-by heavy machine gun. Six of them are in the weapons company heavy machine gun platoon, normally mounted on hard-back Humvees as part of a CAAT.

MAW (Marine air wing)—a Marine Corps aviation combat element. Each wing contains several aircraft groups, normally at least five; each group is roughly the equivalent of an Air Force wing in numbers of aircraft. A MAW normally contains about 350 aircraft, both fixed-wing and rotary-wing, for example: one or two groups of F/A-18 Hornets (72 fighter/attack jets), one or two groups of AV-8B Harriers (72 attack jets), two groups of troop lift helicopters, both CH-53E and CH-46 (72 of each type), and one group of mixed AH-1 Cobras (48) and UH-1N Hueys (36).

MEF (Marine expeditionary force)—a Marine Corps unit responsible for planning combat operations and integrating the firepower of a wing in support of a division. All Marine Corps units are organized for combat in a Marine air ground task force, or MAGTF; a MEF is the largest MAGTF. It consists of at least one division, a wing, and a force service support group. The force service support group, roughly the equivalent of an Army Corps support command, provides logistical and maintenance support to the MEF.

MSR (main supply route)—the route along which a military commander plans to deliver the bulk of the needed supplies. In the vernacular Marines often use the term for any good road or highway.

NVG (night-vision goggles)—any of a fairly wide variety of night-viewing devices that are widely fielded in U.S. forces. These goggles gather and intensify ambient light so that the wearer can see, almost like daylight, on all but the very darkest of nights. No moon is necessary for them to work, but at least a few stars must be showing.

OGA (other government agency)—shorthand within the Department of Defense for the Central Intelligence Agency.

PRC–119—The basic tactical radio used by Marines for voice communication at all levels below the division. It is a VHF (very high frequency) radio that used a frequency hopping technology. It is not set on a single frequency, rather it "hops" between a range of frequencies in micro-second intervals. The range of frequencies for a given network is refered to as the 'load'; all radios set to that load then frequency hop at the same micro-second. This makes intercepting the broadcast near impossible unless using the same radio and on the same load. The radio is a line-of-sight radio with a fairly limited range (15 miles). Rarely is the line of sight 15 miles, however, so the range is really limited even more.

Public affairs—a military occupational specialty that serves as a liaison between a unit commander and the public media or press. All major military commands—those commanded by a general officer—have a public affairs officer, whose primary task is to provide the link and coordination between the public's right to know and the need for operational security. He normally also functions as the command's official spokesperson.

RPG (rocket-propelled grenade)—any of a number of antitank weapons dating back to the German *Panzerfaust* in World War II. The most common is the RPG-7, a Soviet (now Russian)-built weapon that has been widely copied by many nations, including China and the former Soviet satellites. It can be fired accurately out to about 300 meters but can be elevated and lobbed like a mortar almost a mile. The warhead is capable of penetrating much of the world's armor, but it cannot penetrate the armor of the M1A1 Abrams tank. While designed to be an antitank weapon, it can also be used effectively against personnel, other vehicles, and "hard targets" such as bunkers or buildings. The U.S. equivalent weapon is the AT-4.

SAW (squad automatic weapon)—a lightweight automatic weapon carried by one member of each Marine infantry fire team, totaling three per squad. It fires the same 5.56mm round as the M-16 but at a rate of six hundred rounds per minute.

60mm mortar (called "60 mike mike" by Marines)—an indirect fire weapon that can fire a 60mm mortar round 2,700 meters. With a lethal bursting radius of 25 meters, the 60 mike mike is an excellent light mortar used primarily to suppress enemy fighting positions, to "keep their heads down" while infantry squads maneuver into killing range. The weapons platoon of an infantry company contains a section of three 60mm mortars.

T-54, T-55—a 1960s-era Soviet tank armed with a 100mm cannon and rudimentary optics. The T-54 and its Chinese-made copy, designated the T-55, are the most commonly fielded tanks in the developing world. Although it is a good, solid, easy-to-maintain tank, it is no match for the Abrams on the battlefield.

T-72—a Russian-made tank, armed with a 115mm cannon and a 1970s-era optics system. It was believed to be a near-match tank for the M1A1 Abrams until Operation Desert Storm, when the world learned that it was far from a match. The T-72 is, however, a very good tank, especially in the hands of well-trained and determined soldiers.

TOW (tracked optically wire-guided) missile—a heavy antitank missile that can penetrate the armor of most of the world's tanks and destroy them at ranges in excess of 4,500 meters. The missile launcher includes an optical sight system. The current version of the TOW's optical sight is a fourteen-power telescope with a computer "brain." When fired, the missile "spools" a fine wire behind it that connects the computer in the missile to the optical sight. A gunner can send corrections to the flight of the missile down this fine wire as he tracks the target in the sight. The missile is very accurate and lethal, but the gunner has to hold the cross-hairs in his sight on the target during the entire flight, especially when the missile reaches the target. On a modern armored battlefield, after a battle, the ground may be completely crisscrossed with these fine tracking wires.

Trac—*see* AAV.

UAV (unmanned aerial vehicle)—any of a number of drones used by U.S. military forces, primarily as reconnaissance vehicles. These unmanned airplanes are programmed to fly over a target area taking video or infrared pictures and feeding the information back to a terminal on the ground.

Up gun—*see* AAV.

Acknowledgments

Throughout the campaign we talked to hundreds of Marines. Often it was inappropriate to stop the action to gather names. We regret the absence of many of those who contributed, but wish to acknowledge them anonymously, along with the following:

Capt. Michael Ackerson, Staff Sgt. Chris Barry, Lance Cpl. Belfezar Alvarez, Cpl. J. Alex Alvirez, Sgt. Ericson Ariaga, Pfc. Alfonso "Mighty Mouse" Arroyo, Cpl. Robert Arroyo, Major Arsenault, Sgt. Nieves Avida, Maj. Brian Baker, Captain Banning, Lt. Richard S. Barclay, Capt. David Bardorf, Lt. Josh Bates, Lance Cpl. Jonathon "Outcast" Battle, Lance Cpl. Kevin Baynes, Lt. Gen. Emil "Buck" Bedard, Lt. Col. Mike Belcher, Lance Cpl. Tomas Bennett, Sgt. Maj. Henry Bergeron, Maj. Andy Bianca, Lt. Jimmy Birchfield, Capt. Ethan Bishop, Capt. G. Russell Boyce, Lt. Col. J.J. Broadmeadow, First Lt. Casey Brock, Cpl. Jarryl "Dutch" Brown, Maj. Benjamin Busch, Maj. Joseph Cabell, Lance Cpl. David Canto, Cpl. Juan "Preacher" Carachure, Lt. Col. and Mrs. Bill Card, Lt. Michael J. Cerroni, Gunnery Sgt. Michael Cheramie, Cpl. Jesus Chichil, Lt. Col. Stacy Clardy, Lt. Kevin Cleary, HM3 Antonio Clement, Gunnery Sgt. Chuck Colleton, Lt. Darrel Commanders, Lt. Col. Christopher Conlin, Lt. Gen. James T. Conway, Maj. Pete Copeland, CWO Glenn Coughlin, Staff Sergeant Coughlin, Lance Cpl. Michael Cowles, Cpl. Dennis Crossen,

Lt. Mathew Custance, UK Captain Dalton, Pfc. Justin Davis, Maj. Richard DaVore, Capt. Chris "Dino" DeAntoni, Pfc. Matthew R. Deaton, Captain Delpitro, Maj. Richard DeVore, Staff Sgt. Jim Disbro, Col. Joseph Dowdy, Col. Joseph Dunford, UK Captain Eastonough, Staff Sgt. Eldridge, Maj. Kyle B. Ellison, Cpl. Timothy "Homer" Erickson, Lt. Brett Eubanks, Cpl. Mark Evnin, Lt. Col. John Ewers, Maj. Michael Fahey, Cpl. Shane R. Ferkovich, Lt. Col. Steve Ferrando, Capt. Steven Fiscus, Cpl. Alejandro Garcia, Cpl. Michael Glowacki, Sgt. James Goff, Gunnery Sgt. Jerald Goncalo, Cpl. Desmond Gosier, Pfc. Kyle Green, Sgt. Ken Griffin, Capt. Taylor Lee Grimes, Lance Cpl. Christopher Guardiola, Col. Chris Gunther, Sgt. Lee Hahn, Lt. Gen. Edward Hanlon, Maj. Dan Healey, Lance Cpl. Moses Hernandez, Lance Cpl. Jeremiah Horton, Capt. Jeffrey Houston, Colonel Howcroft, Sgt. Maj. David C. Howell, Col. Steven Hummer, Mr. Avda Ilimghashghash, Mr. R. Campbell James, Warrant Officer Craig James, Lance Cpl. Young Jameson, Staff Sgt. John Jamison, Staff Sgt. P.J. Jerka, Sgt. Miles Johnson, HN Brunel Joseph, Capt. Henry June Jr., Lance Cpl. Timothy Kelley, Brig. Gen. John Kelly, Cmdr. Ken Kelly, M.D., Warrant Officer Mark Kissinger, HM3 Q'wame Kleckley, Sgt. Aaron Knizely, Maj. Paul Konopka, Brig. Gen. Mary Ann Krusa-Dossin, Capt. Thomas G. Lacroix, Lt. Joseph Landgraf, Cpl. Demond Lashley, Sgt. P.C. Laurie, Cpl. Joshua "Swampthing" Leahy, Master Sgt. Bradley Lee, Sgt. Maj. Jimmie Lee, Lieutenant Leeks, Major Legowski, Lt. Col. Clark Lethin, Capt. Brian R. Lewis, Pfc. Joshua Lewko, Capt. Devin Licklider, Lt. Col. Patrick G. Looney, Lance Cpl. Henry Lopez, Lt. Col. Matthew Lopez, Pfc. Joseph Losinski IV, Hospitalman "Doc" Lowry, Lt. Adam Macaluso, Cpl. Chris Madia, Capt. Brian Magnet, Lt. Col. Pat Malay, Maj. Steve Manber, Captain Manning, Lance Cpl. David Marsee, Captain Martinez, Cpl. Daniel Mata, Lance Cpl. Michel Matt, Maj. Gen. James Mattis, Pfc. E.J. Mayer, Lt. Col. John L. Mayer, Lance Cpl. Flint W. McColl, Lt. Col. Brian P. McCoy, Maj. John A. McDonough, Staff Sergeant McDuffy, Lt. Tim McLaughlin, Lance Cpl. Garua Mendoza, Pfc. Jose Mendoza, Lance Cpl. T.J. Mikolas, Maj. Michael Miner, HA Kurt Monington, Lt. Keith Montgomery, First Lt. Ty Moore, Cpl. Mitch Moorehead, Staff Sergeant Moreno, Maj. Jason Morris, Lt. Col. Sam

Mundy, Mr. Arthur Murphy, Warrant Officer Mike Musselman, Lieutenant Navarre, Lance Cpl. B.M. Neu, Sgt. Eric Nordwig, Capt. Kevin Norton, Major Nugent, Sgt. Christopher Obanek, Cpl. Ryan O'Mara, Lieutenant Colonel O'Rourke, Gunner Pauliton, Gunnery Sgt. Roy Pena, Sgt. Jason Perez, Lance Cpl. Raul Perez, Sgt. Tony Perolio, Private Perry, Colonel Petronzio, Lance Cpl. Roberto Pickering, Major Piddock, Sgt. Jesse Pineba, Capt. Joseph Plenzler, Col. J. J. Pomfret, Staff Sergeant Popovich, Lance Cpl. Scott Price, Corporal Ramiro, Mr. Nafi "Nick" Rayus, Ms. Elizabeth Regan, Lt. Ben Reid, Cpl. Robert Rench, Maj. Reese Rogers, Sergeant Romeo, Capt. Brian Ross, Lance Cpl. Joslia Ruby, Maj. Michael V. Samarov, Lance Corporal Sandridye, Pfc. J.M. Sawyer, Maj. John Schaar, Capt. George Schaeffler, Capt. Douglas G. Schaffer, Sergeant Schott, Maj. John Shafer, Sgt. Stewart Shine, Mr. N. P. Shull, Cpl. Joseph Smarro, Mrs. Colleen Smith, First Sgt. Edward Smith, Lance Corporal Smoke, Pfc. Tyler P. Speck, Gunnery Sgt. Scott Stalker, Sgt. Anthony W. Stanton Jr., Cpl. Garret Stone, Capt. Todd Sudmeyer, Sgt. David Sutherland, Cpl. Garrett B. Sutkowski, Lance Cpl. Mohsen Taheri, Pfc. Scott Tate, Cpl. Shawn Taylor, Lance Cpl. Peter Tenenika, Lance Corporal Trigo, Sgt. Anthony R. Truijillo, Capt. Shaun Tull, Sgt. Seth VanBuren, Sgt. Joseph Vasquez, Lance Cpl. Richard S. Wagemaker, Capt. Tim Walker, Lt. Bruce Webb, M.D., Cpl. Daniel Weighe, Capt. Owen O. West, Mr. Patrick West, First Lt. Waylon White, Corporal Wick, Lance Cpl. Daniel Wilson, Lt. Col. Chris Woodbridge, Cpl. James Woolford, Staff Sgt. Eric Zamora, Lt. Col. Peter Zarcone

We would like to thank our skillful agent, Dan Mandel, for putting this work together. As for our editor, John Flicker, he showed that as a scout team leader in the 82nd Airborne Division, he had learned how to endure, persist, and lead by example. He was with us every day of the writing.

Index

Ad Diwaniya, Iraq, 109–10, 113–26, 263–65

Afak, Iraq, 90–93

Afak Drill, 92–93, 97, 110, 113, 118, 119

Afghanistan, 79, 106, 127

Air-Land Doctrine, U.S. Army, 219

Al'Azizyah, Iraq, 140, 143–52, 162, 163, 172, 194

Al Budayr, Iraq, 76–77, 93–96, 100

Alexander the Great, 246, 254

Al Hillah, Iraq, 253, 265

Ali, sacred mosque of, 259, 260

Al Karradah, Baghdad, 217–30

Al Kut, Iraq, 80, 137, 149, 194–95

Almilyah Palace, Baghdad, 237–42

Alvarez, Belfezar, 223–24

Alvirez, J. Alex, 54, 55

American POWs, 210, 247–48

Amos, Jim, 127

Anabasis (Xenophon), 2

An Nasiriya, Iraq, 33–48
  defense of, 35–36, 48, 49–50
  507th Maintenance at, 36–37, 248
  news stories about, 81, 105
  post-war, 265
  rumors and fog of war in, 37, 40–41, 42, 44, 45, 47, 54
  traffic jams in, 46–47, 151

An Nu'maniyah, Iraq, 133–40, 142, 148, 223

Answitz, Lance Corporal, 10

Apache helicopter, downing of, 105

Arbela, Battle of (331 B.C.), 246

Armes, Steve, 238–39

Army, U.S.
  Air-Land Doctrine of, 219
  Blue Force Tracker of, 77
  cooperation with, 13, 277
  dual-purpose improved
    conventional munitions
    (DPICMs) of, 226–27
  4th Infantry Division, 245, 249, 250
  fuel convoy of, 276–77

infantry of, 186, 221
Operational Detachment Alpha
    (ODA), 197
in post-war Iraq, 260, 266
in Somalia, 35, 45
3rd Infantry Division, 36, 81, 83,
    105, 185, 186, 232
V Corps, *see* V Corps
in war games, 185–86
Ar Rumaylah oil fields, 13–17, 32,
    33
Aspin, Les, 103
As Samarra, Iraq, 247–48
Atomic Energy Commission,
    Baghdad, 205, 206
Avida, Nieves, 172
Aviles, Andrew, 200–201, 207
Aziz, Tariq, 149, 232–36, 259
Az Subayr oil pumping station
    capacity of, 15, 23
    civilian workers in, 22, 23–25, 27
    as Crown Jewel, 15–17, 18
    sabotage of, 24
    seizure of, 8, 11–13, 16–17, 18,
        19–29, 33, 85, 242
Az Zubayr, Iraq, 273–74

Baath Party, xiii, 21, 35, 36, 42, 71,
    93, 97, 139–40, 245, 252
Baghdad
    American POWs in, 210, 247–48
    assault into, 189–207
    Aziz mansion in, 232–36
    as central objective, 31, 83, 106–7,
        147, 148, 149, 155, 168,
        184–87, 207
    clearing the streets in, 202–6,
        210–13, 214–15

defense of, 79, 147, 190–92, 194,
    197, 199–201, 202, 203, 213
East Baghdad, 205, 209–30,
    231–32
embassies in, 225
fall of, 251, 259
first armored raid into, 184
looters in, 192, 206–7, 215, 241
Marine control of, 242, 245
as Marines' longest march, 3, 242
MEF withdrawal from, 252
missile attacks on, 7, 9, 19, 31, 67,
    180
palaces in, 231, 237–42
post-war, 252
Red Zone of, 79, 102
Saddam City in, 171, 184–85, 187
Snoozle in, 216–30
statue of Saddam in, 231, 232,
    237, 242
strategies for attack on, 205–6
target sites in, 205, 210, 240
traffic leaving, 180–81, 185
in war games, 185–86
Baghdad Bridge, 187, 189, 191,
    197–98, 201–2, 204, 206–7, 209
Baghdad International Airport, 185
Baghdad University, 205, 225–30,
    231, 232, 237, 259
Bailey, Colonel, 44–45
Baker, James A., 234
Bardorf, David, 138, 155–56,
    159–62
Barrow, Robert, 207, 218
Barry, Christopher, 257
Basco, Shawn, 240
Bates, Joshua, 21–22, 27–28
Baynes, Kevin, 111

BBC, 64, 71, 100, 101

Belcher, Michael, 138, 197, 206, 210, 256, 261–62, 268

Benson, Sergeant, 248

Bergeron, Henry, 214, 221, 222, 226

Bishop, Ethan, 163

Black Hawk Down (film), 48, 94

Blair, Tony, xiii

Blount, Buford C. III, 83

Blue Diamond, symbol of, 3

Boaz, Nathan, 247–48

Bohr, Jeff, 240

Boot, Max, 253, 255–57, 261, 263

Boyd, John, 11, 12

British military
  Air Assault Brigade, 73
  at Az Subayr, 24, 25
  in I MEF, 31, 82, 83, 259, 271
  Military Works Force, 16
  mission of, xi, 186
  in post-war Iraq, 266
  in southern Iraq, 250

British Petroleum, 16

Broadmeadow, Chuck, 78–79

Brock, Casey, 163, 164, 165

Buesing, Pfc., 39

Bulgarian troops, 253, 262, 263

Bush, George H. W., 35, 235

Bush, George W., 82, 83–84, 106–7, 180, 231, 232, 251, 253

Cabell, Joseph, 255, 256, 257, 258

casualties, U.S., 252, 254

Cederburg, Russell, 89

Central Command (CENTCOM), U.S., 13, 82, 252

Chartier, Jim, 141, 142, 256, 268

Cheney, Dick, 82

Cheramie, Michael, 161

CIA (Central Intelligence Agency)
  agent recruitment by, 15–16
  at Az Subayr, 25
  intelligence reports from, 7, 64, 70–71, 185, 226, 232, 237–38
  liaisons with, 18, 28
  in post-war Iraq, 256

Clardy, Stacy, 248, 268, 275

CNN, 28, 221–22, 224, 227, 229

Coalition Forces Air Component Commander (CFACC), 182

Coalition Forces Land Component Commander (CFLCC), 80, 82–84, 100–103, 106–8, 184–85, 186–87, 205, 232

Coalition Provisional Authority (CPA), 252, 260, 263, 264

Cobra attack helicopters, 20, 26, 182

Colleton, Chuck, 161

Combined Anti-Armor Team Red (CAAT Red), 21, 22, 27, 88, 114

Conlin, Christopher, 31, 268
  advancing to Baghdad, 148, 206, 217, 276
  at Az Subayr, 15–16, 17, 24, 25, 26, 27, 85
  in Baghdad, 220–24, 225–28, 232, 233, 236
  departure of, 261
  entry into Iraq, 19, 20
  and Maneuver Warfare, 220–21
  in post-war Iraq, 258, 259–60, 261

Connable, Ben, 249

Conway, James T., 100, 271–72
  at An Nasiriyah, 44, 45
  in Baghdad, 224–25

in Kuwait, 7
return to Iraq of, 266
strategies of, 78, 83–84, 106, 147
Cook, Warren, 150
Cooper, Geffrey, 267
Craparotta, Lew, 46, 267
Crossen, Dennis, 63
Crown Jewel, *see* Az Subayr oil
    pumping station

Darius, king of Persia, 246
Defense Department, U.S.
  Central Command, 13, 82
  civilians vs. military powers in,
      104–8
  Pentagon budget of, 12, 105, 186
Delpitro, Captain, 92
Desert Storm, *see* Operation Desert
    Storm
Direct Air Support Center (DASC),
    20, 78
Diyala River, crossing of, 134,
    170–80, 181, 183–84, 189,
    197–98, 201–2, 204, 209–10,
    231–32
Donohue, Pete, 128, 129–30,
    133–34, 268
Dowdy, Joseph W., 267
  advance of, 49, 53, 56, 73, 99
  at Al Kut, 137
  at An Nasiriyah, 34, 41, 42, 43, 44,
      45–46, 47
  at Ash Shatrah, 58–59
  as senior officer airborne, 149
Dragon Eye, 171, 172
Dunford, Joseph, 135, 140, 213, 268
  advance of, 127–28, 142, 153, 155,
      161, 167, 168, 183–84, 186

at Al'Azizyah, 145, 147, 148–49,
    151
in Baghdad, 237, 240
mobile command center of, 170,
    181
return to Iraq of, 266
strategies of, 127–28, 145, 147–49,
    151, 153, 155–56, 171, 184–85,
    187

82nd Airborne Division, 253
Eisenhower, Dwight D., 104
11th Marines, 114, 169, 269
Elliott, Corporal, 39, 40
Evnin, Mark, 111, 193, 194–95,
    207
Ewers, John, 273–74
Exxon Corporation, 16

Fahey, Michael, 257
Falcon View software, 16
Fallujah, Iraq, 266
fedayeen
  at Ad Diwaniyah, 109–10
  at An Nasiriyah, 35–36, 43, 54
  Baghdad HQ of, 205
  functions of, 36, 71, 114, 125
  hiding, 99, 117, 164
  intelligence reports of, 64, 84, 88,
      110
  killing of, 92, 96, 109, 121–24,
      126, 165, 214, 240, 248–49
  as poor shots, 93, 114, 120, 144,
      164–65, 169, 222, 229
  reinforcements of, 48, 54, 82, 125,
      163–65, 250
  running away, 116–17, 121–22,
      172, 212, 214, 227, 240

skirmishes with, 56, 71, 74, 76,
110, 125–26, 161, 226, 229,
237, 240, 248, 275–76
see also Iraqis
weapons caches in schools, 96,
139
Ferkovich, Shane R.
and Az Subayr, 12, 15–17, 19–24,
26–28
background of, 9–10
in Baghdad, 233–36, 237, 242
in Kuwait, 8–9, 17–19
and Marine infantry, 10, 12, 13,
243
and OODA loop, 11
Ferrando, Steve, 68
Finn, Douglas, 156, 157, 158–59,
161
First Force Service Support Group,
31, 271
First Marine Expeditionary Force
(I MEF)
advance toward Baghdad, 79, 82,
205
and An Nasiriya, 35, 44
and Ar Rumaylah oil fields, 15
equipment destruction stats of,
182
mission of, 17, 31, 271–72
pause ordered for, 82–83, 100,
102–3
in post-war Iraq, 253, 255, 266
and Task Force Tarawa, 31, 271
First U.K. Division, 31
1st Battalion, 2nd Regiment (1/2),
35, 37, 41, 45
1st Battalion, 4th Regiment (1/4),
46, 52, 63, 68, 88, 265–66, 267

1st Battalion, 5th Regiment (1/5),
237, 238, 268
1st Battalion, 7th Regiment (1/7),
268
advancing to Baghdad, 204, 206
at Al Kut, 194–95
at An Nu'maniyah, 137, 142
and Army fuel convoy, 276–77
and Az Aubayr pumping station,
11–12, 15–17, 19–29, 85
in Baghdad palaces, 231–43
crossing the Diyala, 232
crossing the Tigris, 148, 149
entry into Iraq, 19–20
in Kuwait "assembly area," 7–13,
17–19
in post-war Iraq, 259
in the Snoozle, 216–30, 237
training of, 15, 16
1st Battalion, 11th Regiment
(1/11), 267, 278
1st Light Armored Reconnaissance
Battalion (1st LAR), 170–80,
184, 246, 248, 268
1st Marine Division (REIN)
advance of, xii, xiii, 5, 31, 32, 49,
100–101
American prisoners released by,
247–48
at An Nasiriya, 36–48
at Az Subayr, 19–29
Baghdad attack plans of, 185–86
command center of, 77–80
deaths in, 250
equipment destruction charts of,
182
first aid in, 61–62, 144–45, 161–62
in Kuwait "assembly area," 7–13

LAVs of, 171–72, 256, 257, 258
mission of, xvi, 5, 14–15, 17, 23,
   31–32, 171, 250
nightly ritual of, 109–12
organization of, 18–19, 267–69
pause ordered for, 80, 82–84,
   99–103, 106–8
as Supporting Effort, 83, 100
1st Tank Battalion, 19, 113, 141,
   198, 204, 232, 268, 272
507th Maintenance Company,
   36–37, 248
Ford, Gerald R., 105
4th Infantry Division, U.S. Army,
   245, 249, 250
4th Light Armored Reconnaissance
   Battalion (4th LAR), 253
Franks, Tommy, 19, 82, 100, 103–4,
   106, 107, 148, 180, 252
Frei, Jason, 56, 58

Garcia, Alejandro, 11, 23, 24
Garner, Jay, 252
Glossen, Buster, 19
Goff, James, 273–74
Gray, Al, 220
Greek hoplites, 2, 5, 243
Grenada, 221
Gulf War (1991), see Operation
   Desert Storm
Gulf War (2003), see Operation
   Iraqi Freedom

Halleck, Gunner, 111
Hanging Gardens of Babylon, 253
Hanifah Mosque, Baghdad, 240
Hantush airstrip, 108–9
Hardin, Dave, 249

Hashimoto, Mark, 257
Hassan al-Majid "Chemical Ali,"
   42
Healey, Dan, 223, 225, 226, 232,
   276–77
Herig, Adam, 249
Holden, Corporal, 162
hoplites, 2, 5, 243
Horton, Jeremiah, 257
Horton, Nicholas, 239–40
Houston, Jeffrey, 159, 161–62, 168
Howell, David C., 90, 95, 96, 111,
   115–18, 120, 125, 190–95, 197,
   199–200, 201, 263
Hudspeth, Captain, 172, 173,
   174–76
human exploitation teams (HET),
   70, 91, 114, 116, 139, 163
Hummer, Steven, 84–85, 277
advance of, 33, 148–49
at Baghdad Bridge, 197, 199, 204,
   207
strategies of, 85, 87, 88, 109, 110,
   113, 126, 137, 148, 187, 205–6,
   231
Hussein, Saddam
control held by, 5, 13, 42, 74–75,
   102, 149
disappearance of, xiii, 31
as enemy, 35, 180
hometown of, 245–50
looting by, 251–52
missile attacks against, 67
oil fields destroyed by, 14
palaces of, 217, 231, 237–42
and regime change, 106, 242
Shiite persecution by, 252
statue of, 231, 232, 237, 242

survival of, 13, 35, 42, 74, 97,
  237–38, 240
Hymes, Kirk, 269

Ilimghashghash, Avda, 42–43
Iraq
  Baghdad in, *see* Baghdad
  chemical weapons expected in,
    79, 102–3, 136, 196
  dust in, 8, 33–34, 49, 51, 58–61,
    71, 81, 112, 276
  establishment of new government
    in, 250
  extremists in, 252
  Hussein's looting of, 251–52
  as Mesopotamia, 2
  Ministry of Defense, 205
  oil in, 13–17
  post–war, 251–66
  Shiites in, 69–71, 171, 252, 253,
    259, 260–61
  simultaneous wars in, xiii
  Sunnis in, 252, 266
  terrorists/snipers in, 252, 255, 264
  see also Operation Desert Storm;
    Operation Iraqi Freedom
Iraqi Americans
  language service provided by, 19,
    42, 96, 114, 163
  views about Americans of, 266
Iraqi police, 264, 265
Iraqis
  at An Nasiriyah, 36–48, 213
  battle styles of, 213, 272–74
  Bedouin elders, 249–50
  casualties, 62, 123–24
  civilians, xiii, 20–21, 47, 50, 62,
    64–68, 91, 97, 142–43, 169–70,

  171, 173, 176, 178–79, 204,
    247, 250, 264–65, 276
  defenses of, 32, 109, 128, 136,
    143–44, 150, 157–60, 168–69,
    199–200, 201, 232
  disinclination to fight, 26, 28,
    32–33, 36, 52, 74, 97, 99,
    116–17, 146, 148, 151–52, 153,
    163, 164, 172, 213, 217
  11th Infantry Division, 35, 36, 213
  as enemy, xii–xiii, 10, 32, 120–21
  intelligence networks, 79
  lack of military discipline, 74,
    120–21, 136, 151, 213
  looters, 27, 28, 95, 170, 173,
    206–7, 251
  as POWs, 258
  prisoners, 62, 65, 122, 141, 155,
    163, 164, 172, 223
  rumors about, 63–65, 90–91
  suicide bombers, 67, 204
  vehicles abandoned by, 184–85,
    213, 227
  see also fedayeen; Republican
    Guard

Jamieson, John, 273–74
job-creation scheme, 264–65
Johnson, Captain, 154
Johnson, Lyndon B., 218
Johnson, Miles, 57–58, 60–61
Joint Chiefs of Staff, 103–4
Jones, Corporal, 161
Jordan, Phillip, 39

Karbala, Iraq, 261–63
Kelly, Doctor, 65, 66
Kelly, John, 44, 45–46, 58, 59,

66–67, 73, 75, 80, 93, 148, 246, 249–50, 256, 266, 267

Kelly, Ken, 58, 62

Khoei, Abdel Majid, 260

Kissinger, Henry A., 104

Kleckley, Q'wame, 172

Koopman, John, 192–93, 196

Korean War, 3, 50, 212, 218, 219

Kurds, 245, 249

Kuwait
  "assembly area" in, 7–13, 17–19
  CFLCC HQ in, 185
  in Operation Desert Storm, 180–81, 213

Lacroix, Thomas G., 22–23, 26, 231, 233, 236, 237, 241, 276–77

Lebanon, 5, 45

Lee, Bradley, 253, 254, 258

Leeks, Lieutenant, 203

Leventhal, Rick, 224–25

Lewis, Brian R., 114, 118–19, 120, 125, 191

Lopez, Henry, 273

Lopez, Matthew, 261–63, 266

Luder, Jon, 150–51

Lynch, Jessica, 81, 277

Madia, Chris, 54, 55

Malay, Patrick, 263–65

Manber, Steve, 255

Maneuver Warfare, 217–21

Marine Corps, U.S.
  Army cooperation with, 277
  barebones expeditions of, 102
  bridging companies of, 135, 171, 191, 204, 209

cleaning up, 65

Congress and, 219

enlistment in, 10, 218

equipment accountability system in, 144–45

"families" in, xii, 110–11, 154, 195, 207, 243

gear carried by, 195–96

human exploitation teams (HET) of, 70, 91, 114, 116, 139, 163

infantry of, 10–11, 12–13, 111–12, 146, 148, 154–55, 186–87, 221

as liberators, 237, 247

maintenance crews of, 36–37, 141–42

Maneuver Warfare of, 217–21

military machine of, 2–3, 17, 124, 218, 219, 223, 228, 230, 242–43

in post-war Iraq, 252, 260, 265

public affairs efforts of, 8, 28, 43, 139

reputation of, xi–xii, 218–19

sniper, 222, 223–24

symbols of, 3, 218, 228

tradition of, xi, 3, 5, 67, 218, 243

training of, 10, 243

in Vietnam, 217–18, 219, 220

in war games, 185–86

see also specific units

Mattis, James N., 267, 273
  at Baghdad Bridge, 197–98, 199, 216

Marine family of, 111, 150

message to all hands from, xvi, 5, 67

military career of, 18, 78

movement of, 140, 150

order to kill issued by, 253

in post-war Iraq, 253, 256, 259
on Saddam's regime, 74, 232, 235
strategies of, 18, 19, 32, 44, 45, 54,
    73, 75, 78–79, 84, 93, 102, 106,
    109, 111, 127–28, 137, 147–49,
    150, 155, 247, 253
Mayaguez, seizure of, 105
Mayer, John, 63, 68–70, 277–78
McCaffrey, Barry R., 105
McColl, Lance Corporal, 254
McCoy, Brian P., 85, 111, 268
  at Ad Diwaniyah, 109–10, 113–15,
    117–21, 125–26
  advancing to Baghdad, 148, 187,
    192, 195, 197, 199, 200, 202,
    204, 231
  and civilian killings, 204, 211
  and East Baghdad, 210–11,
    213–14, 216, 231–32
  and pause, 100, 107–8
  and Route 17 advance, 87–97,
    99–100
  and Saddam statue, 231, 232
McDonough, John A., 217, 220
McDuffy, Staff Sergeant, 194
McKiernan, David, 100, 102, 279
McKinnon, Rick, 229
McNamara, Robert S., 218
McPhillips, Brian, 159–60, 207
Medellin, Martin, 200–201, 207
media
  embedded reporters, 28–29, 48,
    67, 81–82, 101, 192–93, 198,
    203, 217, 221, 224–25, 229,
    233, 249
  Iraqi use of, 234
  leaks to, 104

negative stories in, 48, 81, 105–6
  in post-war Iraq, 251, 252
  unembedded, 196, 272
  White House views on, 231,
    232
Mesopotamia, 2
Meyers, General, 103–4
Mikolas, T. J., 154
Mogadishu, Somalia, 35, 42, 45, 213
Monge, Corporal, 111
Moore, Harold G., 48
Moorehead, Mitch, 161
Moorer, Thomas, 104
Moore, Ty, 53–54, 55, 56, 57, 60, 61,
    62, 64, 65, 66, 67
Moreno, Staff Sergeant, 116, 193,
    194
Morris, Jason, 143, 144
mullahs, 261
Mundy, Sam, 145, 147, 151, 155,
    161, 162, 163, 165, 268, 275–76
Musselman, Mike, 171–72, 173

Najaf, Iraq, 258–61
National Imagery and Mapping
    Agency, 16, 221
National Museum (Baghdad), 251
Natonski, Rich, 34, 44
Nave, Kevin G., 89
Nebuchadnezzar, king of Babylon,
    253
Newman, Yaniv, 150
Norton, Kevin, 197, 200, 201, 202

O'Bannon, Presley, 3, 246
Oehl, Mike, 154, 156, 168, 268
O'Leary, Paul, 268

O'Mara, Ryan, 172
OODA loop, theory of, 11–12
Operation Desert Storm, 5
  battle style in, 213
  comparisons with, 19, 100,
    180–81, 182
  Marines in, xi, 3
  oil fields destroyed in, 14
  power centers in, 103
  Saddam's survival in, 13, 35, 42
Operation Iraqi Freedom
  Main and Supporting efforts in,
    83, 100–101
  Marines in, see Marine Corps,
    U.S.
  speed of advance in, 5, 48, 101
Owen, Pete, 53
Ozymandias, king of Babylon, 242

Padilla, Fred, 238, 240, 268
Peixotto, Lance Corporal, 161
Peking, Marines in, 3
Pentagon, 12, 105, 106, 186, 221,
    256
Perolio, Tony, 222, 223–24
Pickering, Roberto, 152
Plenzler, Joseph, 273, 274
Pokorney, Fred, 39
Polish troops, 253, 265
Pontford, J. J., 269
Powell, Colin, 103, 231, 237
Price, Scott, 21–22

Qual'at Sukkar airfield, 68, 79

Ray, Eddie, 50, 56, 59, 267
Regimental Combat Team 1
  (RCT-1)

  advance of, 32, 33, 34, 49, 51–57,
    62–71, 73–74, 78, 148, 149,
    204–5, 213
  at Al Kut, 137, 149
  at An Nasiriya, 33–48
  in Baghdad, 205, 216
  organization of, 18, 52–53, 267,
    279
  pause ordered for, 99–103
  picket technique of, 87–89
Regimental Combat Team 5
  (RCT-5)
  advance of, 33, 48, 73–74, 78,
    79, 80, 108–10, 126, 127–31,
    137, 140, 141, 148, 150–52,
    156–66, 183–84, 186,
    275–76
  at Al'Aziziyah, 150–52
  in Baghdad, 205, 216
  at Diyala River, 170–80, 181,
    183–84, 237
  entry into Iraq, 19
  at Hantush, 108–9
  at oil fields, 32
  organization of, 18, 268
  pause ordered for, 100–103, 108–9
  and Saddam City, 171, 184–85
  at Tigris River, 83
Regimental Combat Team 7
  (RCT-7)
  advance of, 33, 48, 73–74, 78, 80,
    85, 126, 141, 149, 165, 217, 232
  at An Nu'Maniyah, 136–40
  in Baghdad, 205, 216
  and Baghdad Bridge, 187, 189,
    197
  Crown Jewel as objective of, 18
  at oil fields, 32

organization of, 18, 141, 268–69
pause ordered for, 100–103
Regimental Combat Teams,
   organization of, 18, 267–69,
   279–80
Reid, Ben, 39, 40
Republican Guard, Iraqi, xiii, 32,
   74, 79–80, 81, 137, 143, 147,
   148, 149, 157–58, 213, 246,
   252, 264, 265, 266
Rice, Condoleezza, 245
Robinson, Simon, 193, 196
Rogers, Reese, 257
Rolls-Royce turbines, 16
Roman centurions, 2
Rumaylah oil fields, 259
Rumsfeld, Donald, 12, 104, 105
Russell, Larry, 163–64, 165

Sadr, Moqtada al-, 260–61
Saturday Night Live (TV), 74–75,
   149
Savidge, Martin, 227, 229
Schwarzkopf, Norman, 100, 103
SEALs, U.S. Navy, 246, 247
Seaton, Jim, 56, 267
2nd Battalion, 5th Regiment (2/5),
   126–31, 133–36, 142, 240,
   268
2nd Battalion, 11th Regiment
   (Artillery) (2/11), 268
2nd Battalion, 23rd Regiment
   (2/23), 267, 278
2nd Light Armored
   Reconnaissance Battalion (2nd
   LAR), 44, 45, 47, 49–50, 52,
   246, 267, 278
2nd Marine Division, 31

2nd Marine Expeditionary Force,
   34
2nd Marine Regiment, 34, 36, 37,
   41, 42, 44–45
2nd Tank Battalion, 141, 147, 148,
   153–66, 268
Seely, Mike "Moose," 39
September 11 attacks, 106
Shealy, Lance Corporal, 111, 120
Shelley, Percy Bysshe, 242
Sipernet, 101
Sistani, Grand Ayatollah Ali al-,
   259, 261
Smarro, Joseph, 63
Smith, Colleen, 3
Smith, Edward "Horsehead,"
   154–55, 160, 166, 167, 180,
   189, 207
Smith, Ray, 3, 180
  with 1st Marine Division, 1, 59,
   190, 197, 274
  in Grenada, 221
  in Vietnam, 1, 9, 181, 197, 207
Snoozle, Baghdad, 216–30
Sokol, Blair, 238–39
Somalia, 35, 42, 45, 48, 103, 212–13
Southern Cross, symbol of, 3
Special Operations Command,
   18–19
Stalker, Scott, 88
Stanton, Anthony, 253–55, 257,
   259
Stokes, Lieutenant, 195
Stone, Garret, 54, 55, 68
Sudmeyer, Todd, 150, 156, 157, 160,
   240
Sutherland, David, 92
Sutkowski, Corporal, 254

Tactical Air Operations Center, 182

Task Force Scorpion, 253, 255, 256

Task Force Tarawa, 31–32, 33, 34–36, 41, 44, 45, 46, 83, 271

Task Force Tripoli, 246–50

Tate, Scott, 1–2, 5

Taylor, Captain, 256, 257, 258

3rd Battalion, 1st Regiment (3/1), 46, 89, 204–5, 267, 278

3rd Battalion, 4th Regiment (3/4), 141, 268, 278
  at Ad Diwaniya, 109–10, 113–26
  at Al Kut, 137, 149, 194–95
  assault on Baghdad, 190–207, 224
  crossing the Diyala, 232
  crossing the Tigris, 148
  in East Baghdad, 210–16, 231–32
  pause ordered for, 100, 101, 103, 107–8
  in post-war Iraq, 263
  on Route, 17, 85, 89–97, 108–9

3rd Battalion, 5th Regiment (3/5), 268
  advance of, 155, 275–76
  at Al'Azizyah, 140, 143–52, 194
  at An Nu'maniyah, 138
  mopping-up operation of, 162–65
  in post-war Iraq, 263–65

3rd Battalion, 7th Regiment (3/7), 268
  advancing to Baghdad, 204, 232
  at An Nu'Maniyah, 137–40
  entry into Iraq, 19
  night raids of, 197, 206, 210
  in post-war Iraq, 261

3rd Battalion, 11th Regiment (3/11), 269

3rd Infantry Division, U.S. Army, 36, 81, 83, 105, 185, 186, 232

3rd Light Armored Reconnaissance Battalion (3rd LAR), 246, 247–48, 268

3rd Marine Air Wing, 31, 101–2, 127, 182, 246, 271

Thompson, Harry, 47

Tigris River
  advance to, 126–31
  crossing of, 79–80, 128, 133–36, 140, 148, 149
  MEF headquarters near, 253
  pontoon bridge site on, 129–30, 134–36, 148
  seizure of bridge across, 145, 148
  terrorist swimming of, 258

Tikrit, Iraq, 245–50

Todd, Daniel, 229

Toolan, John, 149, 204, 267

Tripoli, Marines in, 3, 246

V Corps, U.S. Army
  advance on Baghdad, 17, 31, 32, 79
  as Main Effort, 83, 100, 186
  organization of, 280
  pause ordered for, 100–102
  strategy of, 17, 81, 82–84, 107

Vietnam War
  author in, 1, 4, 207
  battle style in, 212
  body counts in, 218
  comparisons with, 1, 81–82, 92, 119–20, 145, 177, 178, 181, 185, 207
  fog of war in, 48
  Marines in, 217–18, 219, 220

Ray Smith in, 1, 9, 181, 197, 207
transformation in military since,
12, 217–18

Wallace, William S., 81, 100, 102,
106
war
battle styles in, 212–13
chain of command in, 103,
175–76, 182, 191, 221
civilians in, 47, 64–68, 91, 104–8,
204, 211, 250
coup d'oeil in, 147
death and, 89, 179–80, 201, 207,
229–30
fire capping in, 56
fog of, 4, 40–41, 45, 48, 82, 200
friendly fire in, 39–40, 45, 56–58,
178, 182, 199, 200, 235–36
helmet fires in, 119
infantry in, 186
kill boxes in, 182–83
power centers in, 103–8, 218
rumors in, 37, 42, 64, 67, 90, 101
suicide bombers in, 67, 204
on terrorism, 106
in urban centers, 196–97
war games, 185–86
warriors
hoplites, 2, 5, 243
Roman centurions, 2
see also Marine Corps, U.S.
Washington, power center in,
103–8, 218, 219
Webb, Bruce, 161–62
Weighe, Daniel, 170
West family, 4
West, Owen O., 4, 154

White, Duffy "Highlander," 170,
171, 172, 182, 183, 268
White, William, 89
Wilson, Lewis, 218
Wittnam, Dan, 38, 40, 41, 45
Woolwort, Ryan, 150
World War II, 3, 12, 48, 50, 74, 196,
219

Xenophon, 2, 5, 243, 246

Zamora, Eric, 154
Zarcone, Peter, 273

About the Authors

F. J. "BING" WEST served as Assistant Secretary of Defense for International Security Affairs in the Reagan administration. He was a Marine infantry officer in Vietnam, where he wrote *Small Unit Action*, a firsthand description of the combat. He is also the author of *The Village*, a Vietnam classic, and the bestselling war novel *The Pepperdogs*. Visit his website at www.west-write.com.

MAJ. GEN. RAY L. SMITH, USMC (Ret.), is one of the most decorated Marines since World War II and served as a rifle company commander in the battle for Hue City in 1968. He commanded the Marines in Grenada in 1983 and in Beirut. He later commanded the 3rd Marine Division. He is a national expert on infantry and urban warfare.